C000138547

AMATEUR
GUNNERS

AMATEUR GUNNERS

*The Great War Adventures,
Letters and Observations of
Alexander Douglas Thorburn*

Edited by

Ian Ronayne

Pen & Sword
MILITARY

First published in Great Britain in 2014
By Pen and Sword Military
an imprint of
Pen and Sword Books Ltd
47 Church Street
Barnsley
South Yorkshire S70 2AS

Copyright © Ian Ronayne, 2014

ISBN 978 1 78383 201 9

The right of Ian Ronayne to be identified
as the author of this work has been asserted by him in accordance
with the Copyright, Designs and Patents Act 1988.

A CIP record for this book is available from the British Library.

All rights reserved. No part of this book may be reproduced or transmitted
in any form or by any means, electronic or mechanical including photocopying,
recording or by any information storage and retrieval
system, without permission from the Publisher in writing.

Printed and bound in England by
CPI Group (UK) Ltd, Croydon, CR0 4YY

Typeset in Times New Roman by
Chic Graphics

Pen & Sword Books Ltd incorporates the imprints of
Pen & Sword Archaeology, Atlas, Aviation, Battleground, Discovery,
Family History, History, Maritime, Military, Naval, Politics, Railways,
Select, Social History, Transport, True Crime, and Claymore Press,
Frontline Books, Leo Cooper, Praetorian Press, Remember When,
Seaforth Publishing and Wharncliffe

For a complete list of Pen and Sword titles please contact
Pen and Sword Books Limited
47 Church Street, Barnsley, South Yorkshire, S70 2AS, England
E-mail: enquiries@pen-and-sword.co.uk
Website: www.pen-and-sword.co.uk

Contents

Part 3: Observations

Foreword

Brigadier C.W. Tadier, CBE,
former Director of Royal Artillery, 2007–2009

There are many books that cover the First World War, but this one is very different. It is a first-hand account of an 'amateur' gunner officer who between 1916 and 1918 fought in France and Belgium, and also in Greece, Egypt and Palestine. Alexander Douglas Thorburn's articulate account of his battery's experience, throughout three years of war, is both telling and compelling. It is filled with amusing anecdotes and vignettes, as well as stories that will horrify. You will come away knowing the true meaning of the words stoic and heroic.

You follow Thorburn from mobilisation training in the UK, to victory in 1918. At that point, in his words: 'we were no more amateur gunners, but actually experienced hard-bitten soldiers with more experience of war as it is, among our little party, than was to be found in the entire British Army of pre-war days.' This is an absorbing read which will allow you to see war through the eyes of a junior officer, both in his account as well as in his letters home. The book is one of extremes. One moment you will be reading about artillery bombardments, and then you will read how he was 'acquiring' equipment from other units to improve their life on the front. And for those particularly interested in gunnery matters, read his 'Tips for Gunners' in Part Three, some of which are relevant today.

Although Thorburn has written much about artillery life and gunnery, this book also highlights the importance of the animals which, amongst other things, pulled the guns and carried stores and rations, often under enemy fire. Not only the 'war horses', but also the many camels and mules that were used in the various campaigns. Throughout the book, you can see how reliant the men were on their animals – a deep affection was formed. He even gives advice on the 'use and habits of camels' and considers mules to be 'hard working hybrids', which he could not have done without!

If you have a desire to learn more about 'life in the trenches' from an artillery perspective, discover how soldiers survived extraordinary hardships on a daily basis, and how an 'amateur' soldier very soon became highly 'professional' in the middle of a war, I would commend that you read this absorbing book – you will not want to put it down.

Introduction

One of the fascinating aspects of the British Army that fought and eventually won the First World War is its diverse origins. In contrast to both allies and enemies that entered the conflict with huge trained armies, most of Britain's soldiers were civilians when the war started in August 1914. As volunteers or conscripts, they joined the army with which Britain had gone to war: a small core of professional 'regular' soldiers and a part-time home defence force, contemptuously nicknamed 'Saturday night soldiers'. Yet together, these three groups formed the largest and arguably most successful army Britain ever fielded. It remains a remarkable fact, however, that the majority were purely amateurs – there to do a job and to return home once it was finished.

Alexander Douglas Thorburn was firmly in the amateur camp, and evidentially proud to be there. To him, longstanding army practice and tradition meant little; what mattered was a sense of duty, willingness to work hard and the invaluable experience that comes from actually fighting a modern day war. He and millions of other men clearly brought these qualities to the British Army between 1914 and 1918, helping to shape it into a war-winning weapon. At the end of the fighting, however, most had returned quietly to civilian lives, proud of their achievements but determined to move on. Thorburn decided to do something different. He had also brought to the army a keen eye for detail, a lucid writing talent and an acerbic detachment from the professional soldiers with whom he served. These were put to good use in 1933 when publishing his wartime experiences and observations in the book *Amateur Gunners*. From it, and a recently discovered collection of his letters, we gain a remarkable and edifying personal account of one 'amateur' soldier's First World War.

Thorburn had arrived in the world on 27 July 1882, the second and final child of Alexander Thorburn, a Scottish-born cotton broker, and Catherine Thorburn, an American from the then quiet Chicago suburb of

Naperville, Illinois. At the time, the family lived in Kensington, London. By the start of the twentieth century, however, young Thorburn had moved with his parents and sister Nellie to Bebington on the Wirral. His father's business appears to have thrived well enough to allow the family to employ two servants and send their son to public school. Thorburn followed up Charterhouse boarding school in Surrey with further education at Victoria University, Liverpool where he gained a second-class honours Classics degree in 1901. A language course at the University of Marburg completed his studies and also appear to have given him a zest for travel and language.

Thorburn started his working life as a schoolmaster, teaching French and classical history. By 1911, however, the family business had beckoned and he was working as a clerk at cotton brokers Thomas Thorburn & Co in Liverpool. The outbreak of war in August 1914 interrupted this career and he volunteered, along with more than two million others, to join the British Army.

Travel and language were clearly not the only interests held by Thorburn before the war. From his writings, we find a great passion for horses and horsemanship. This passion may have been instrumental in his decision to join a branch of the army in which horses and horsemanship played a pivotal role.

Throughout the war, the Royal Artillery remained enormously reliant on four-legged horsepower. In France and Belgium, where trench warfare limited mobility, hundreds of thousands of animals still laboured behind the lines moving men and guns and bringing up supplies. In more remote theatres of war, such as Salonica and Palestine, animals moved armies and their guns across thousands of miles of terrain often lacking roads, rivers and railways. This must have been greatly appreciated by Thorburn who clearly relished the opportunity to work with horses as well as less glamorous mules, donkeys and camels. What he did not know at the time – or at least fully realise – was the extent to which this centuries-old relationship between army and animal was coming to an end.

Artillery had played a leading role in armies since its emergence in the Middle Ages. By the start of the First World War, it was one of the army's three principal subdivisions, along with infantry and cavalry. It didn't take long for the longstanding roles of each to change, however, as the reality of a modern industrialised conflict swept away established tradition and tactics.

Exposed in the war's opening battles, cavalry swiftly diminished in importance as the futility of men on horseback charging an enemy armed with rifles and machine guns was realised. The infantry too soon found its traditional role – advancing in formation against an enemy battle line – proved mostly impossible. Military technology had developed before 1914 to give defenders a considerable advantage over attackers. The answer, realised in the closing months of 1914, was to get soldiers out of sight of each other. And with the emergence of trench warfare, the artillery soon assumed a new role as master of the battlefield.

By 1916, a British infantry division, which was the main tactical formation of armies, controlled three brigades of Royal Field Artillery (RFA), each of which had four batteries. Three of the batteries, designated A to C, were equipped with the 18-pounder gun, while the fourth, or D Battery, had 4.5-inch howitzers to provide high-trajectory 'plunging' fire. The three RFA brigades of the 60th Division that Thorburn joined in July 1916 were 301st, 302nd and the 303rd. Between them, they possessed seventy-two guns of both varieties. Thorburn was posted to a howitzer battery, and remained serving with that type of gun until the end of the war.

The 60th Division, or 2/2nd London Division as it was also known, was formed in 1914. Designated as second line, its role was originally as a recruiting and training unit for first-line divisions that went overseas on active service. It was part of the Territorial Force (later renamed Territorial Army), which was Britain's part-time army created in the years leading up to the First World War primarily for home defence duties. Territorial soldiers were civilians who volunteered for military training at the weekends and in the evenings, and during a two-week army camp in the summer months.

On the outbreak of war, the Territorial Force mobilised to release the regular army – that is the full time soldiers – for service on the Continent with the British Expeditionary Force, or BEF. But heavy losses in 1914, along with a realisation that Britain needed more soldiers at the front, led to first line Territorial Force divisions deploying overseas for active service at the start of 1915. By 1916, the need for troops had become so high that even second line divisions joined them. In June 1916, the 60th Division left Britain after an extensive period of training, and crossed the Channel for service on at the front.

The Western Front had formed at the end of 1914 as the war of movement in the opening months lapsed into positional warfare. All along the front line, both sides created increasingly sophisticated and formidable trench systems to prevent a breakthrough by the other side. Among the strongest positions were those on the German-held Vimy Ridge.

Lying a few miles north of the French city of Arras, Vimy Ridge commanded the countryside all around. There had been heavy fighting there in 1915 as the French Army tried and failed twice to take the ridge. By 1916, when the 60th Division and Thorburn arrived, it had become a 'quiet' sector of the front, with both sides heavily engaged elsewhere, fighting the Battle of Somme and Battle of Verdun. This made Vimy Ridge an ideal location for newly arrived divisions to gain trench warfare experience before moving to a more active sector. Thorburn's writing and letters clearly reflect this, with only limited action taking place and low casualty rates as a result. It was a time for building skills and experience for future use on the battlefield – which for most new British divisions in 1916 meant the Somme, with all its attendant horrors.

The 60th Division was an exception however. As a second line unit, it was labelled – clearly undeservedly according to Thorburn – as a 'lesser' division, and therefore better suited to secondary theatre of war. One such theatre was Salonica, far off across the Mediterranean Sea. At the end of 1916, he and the 60th Division left France for service there.

The origins of the Salonica front are complex. Britain and France had promised to send military aid to Serbia, which had been attacked at the start of the war by its far larger neighbour, Austria-Hungary. Distracted by the 1915 Gallipoli Campaign, however, nothing serious was done to aid the Serbs before October that year, and even then the Allies only landed a small force in the Greek port city of Salonica (today Thessaloniki). The intervention of Bulgaria, which entered the war on Germany's side, together with uncertainty over Greek intentions brought the wisdom of Allied strategy into question. It was pursued, nevertheless, with the Salonica front eventually attracting hundreds of thousands of soldiers from Britain, France, Russia, Italy, Serbia and Greece.

INTRODUCTION

The 60th Division arrived to find a stalemate. The British Salonica Force, or BSF, had advanced north as far as the Struma River, where it faced a determined and dug-in Bulgarian Army. As Thorburn discovered, the intensity of fighting was sporadic compared to the Western Front in France, the opportunity to engage the enemy more fleeting. Conditions did not help. The British Army had advanced into sparsely populated mountainous country crossed by few roads but with no lack of lakes, rivers and bogs. Unable to move forward and uncertain of security behind them, the Allied armies sat largely where they were for 1917 and much of 1918, earning the nickname, 'the Gardeners of Salonica'. Thorburn and the 60th Division would not stay long enough for the depreciating label to stick however. In June 1917, they were transferred once more. And once more, their destination was one of the First World War's 'secondary' fronts.

Soon after arriving in Palestine, the 60th Division gave up some of its artillery to a new British infantry division that also had the misfortune to attract a second line label. The 74th (Yeomanry) Division had formed in Egypt in January 1917 from a number of dismounted cavalry units protecting the Suez Canal from Turkish attack. Prior to the First World War, Territorial Force cavalry regiments were known as the Yeomanry, a historic title dating back to the Napoleonic Wars. In 1917, the British Egyptian Expeditionary Force, or EEF, had plans that required infantry, however, meaning the Yeomanry were not to regain their horses.

Egypt had become a theatre of war in November 1914 when Britain declared war on German's ally in the region, the Ottoman Empire. At the start of 1915, the Ottoman Army had attacked towards the Suez Canal, which lay in British controlled Egypt, but failed to achieve a decisive breakthrough. A stalemate followed, as both sides battled not only each other but also the harsh conditions. In March 1917, however, the British commenced an offensive into Palestine. It was an enormously challenging undertaking, as Thorburn meticulously explains, with a great reliance placed on the animals needed to move the army across the desert. Eventually, in December that year, Jerusalem fell to the British, with the 74th (Yeomanry) Division performing commendably in its first battles.

For the Allies, the capture of Jerusalem was a welcome highlight in a year that generally failed to produce any real success. And there were worrying signs ahead for 1918. An armistice with Russia had freed Germany from the need to fight a two-front war, and released large numbers of soldiers for an attack in the west. In March 1918, the German Army smashed through the British lines near the French town of St Quentin and threatened to split the Allied forces in two. After three years of trench warfare, a war of movement had returned to the Western Front. Reinforcements were required, which for Thorburn meant a return to where his war had started.

In April and May 1918, the 74th (Yeomanry) Division left the Middle East for Marseilles – the same port Thorburn had left from seventeen months earlier. By then the German offensive had expanded north to attack towards the French Channel ports. A further attack was about to strike the French armies to the north-west of Paris. It was a time for everyone to fight 'with their backs to wall,' in the words of the British commander-in-chief, Douglas Haig.

By the time Thorburn and his battery re-entered the fighting in Belgium, however, the crisis was passing. Allied counter-attacks inflicted heavy defeats on the German Army, both materially and psychologically. And it now faced an Allied force growing in strength with the arrival of thousands of American soldiers. In September 1918, they, along with British, French and Belgian armies, began an offensive later called the 'Advance to Victory'.

The 74th (Yeomanry) Division was part of the Allied forces that relentlessly pressed forward in the closing months of 1918. The strategy, which aimed to prevent the Germans having time to rest and regroup, resulted in some of the most intense and exhausting fighting of the war, as Thorburn records. The breaking of the formidable 'Hindenburg Line' defences along with a growing restlessness at home, left the Germans with little choice other than to sue for peace. With the signing of the Armistice on 11 November 1918, the First World War finally comes to an end for Thorburn and millions of other amateur soldiers.

After the Armistice, Thorburn remained in uniform for a while, serving as an education officer with 44th Brigade, RFA, and commanding a battery in Belgium. He also helped with the demobilisation of 74th (Yeomanry) Division's horses, which must have been a painful time for him as most were sold off locally for work or slaughter. But a return to civilian life was inevitable, and he left the army in 1919 to resume a career in teaching.

He returned to live in Cheshire, settling in Oxton near Chester, not far from the family home on the Wirral. During the inter-war years he married Catherine in 1924, and they had a daughter, Dorothy, in 1928. Thorburn lived to see the world at war once more, and fighting in many of the same locations he had served. He did not see it end however. While undergoing surgery in March 1942, Alexander Douglas Thorburn died aged just fifty-nine.

I Ronayne, 2014

Part 1: Adventures

CHAPTER 1

Training

A civilian in uniform

The general excellence of the training undergone in England by a candidate for a commission in the Royal Field Artillery during the Great War was beyond question. The material was remarkably uneven in character, in previous occupation, and in age.

I started my training in No.14 Barrack Room in the regular Royal Horse Artillery (RHA) barracks at St John's Wood in London, where my colleagues were, probably, the most varied group of men ever assembled in one place together.

In one room were to be found a famous Australian barrister, a surgeon-captain of the Chilean Navy of Irish origin, an elephant hunter from East Africa, a Cambridge professor, a South African, three English ranchers from the Argentine, a missionary from China, a planter from Jamaica, an Australian sheep-farm manager, two boys about 19-years-old, a New Zealand barrister, who used to talk Maori with a New Zealand acquaintance, a Welsh farmer, a middle-aged dog-breeder, and others, like myself, Englishmen of ordinary occupation in this country.

The system, or lack of system, by which it was hoped to convert this collection of men of ages from nineteen to forty-five into competent officers of the artillery and first class fighting men, was utterly incredible.

The first two tasks set me, in company with 'C' (the Cambridge Professor) were washing our barrack room floor with mops and buckets, cleaning the windows, apparently for the first time for many years, whitewashing the inside of large iron tanks used as coal scuttles, and blackleading the lower halves of the iron posts in the stables and the old round cannon balls which decorated the barrack square. After a few days,

1

I was promoted to the duty of burnishing the steel and brass mountings of the funeral gun carriage, an ancient 13-pounder used as a hearse whenever a general's funeral procession takes place in London.

The rest of our daily life consisted of 'physical jerks' in the dark before breakfast, stables – cleaning out filthy stalls with our hands, no tools being provided – very elementary gun drill, grooming and feeding horses, riding school and lectures on field artillery training, delivered mostly to classes seated on the tan in the riding school by regular non-commissioned officers (NCOs) whose knowledge of the matters on which they lectured was pitifully inadequate.

The only officer-instructor, while I was at St John's Wood Barracks, was the riding master, a captain who as a riding-master was far inferior to Sergeant 'L' as a horseman, and to Corporal 'R' as an instructor.

There was also some semaphore drill, endless polishing of spurs, boots, and buttons (we even had to black the part of the sole on the underside of our boots beneath the instep). In fact hours every day were wasted in the modern equivalents of the pipeclay fetich of the British Army of Wellington's period.

The food was ample, but so abominably cooked in the perfectly equipped kitchens, that most of it was uneatable and wasted. Had our cooks on active service, cooking over damp wood with a hole in the ground for a kitchen, produced from rations far inferior both in quality and quantity, such uneatable food for the men, they would have been severely punished by the battery commander, half-murdered by the men, and treated by everyone as contemptible scoundrels.

Taking it all round a more inefficient school of instruction and a worse organised unit than St John's Wood Barracks RHA I never saw in the whole of my army career. Of course, with our total lack of military experience, we did not realise how badly the whole show was run, or how a brigade which never saw an officer (except the orderly officer of the day) could ever be anything but a 'comic unit', as we later learned to call such dud affairs.

We learned naturally very little and it was only through the keenness of all the students that we learned anything whatever except terms of abuse. The instruction given in this department of military proficiency was incomparable and eventually most valuable

TRAINING

In every circumstance of life a lively sense of humour serves to make anything tolerable and the ability to see the funny side of St John's Wood was always an asset.

In that region these incidents are worth recording. The Australian sheep farmer had originally been a trooper in a Queensland cavalry regiment, and possessed a very smart tunic evidently made by a first class tailor. The tunics issued to us were of all shapes and sizes, and had to be fitted at a cost of three shillings and sixpence paid by the individual to the regimental tailor, who also sold the globular RHA buttons without which a man was punished for being improperly dressed. One morning the Australian appeared on parade in his Australian tunic, which had a single collar instead of the regulation turnover collar, and black fiat buttons. Immediately every NCO on parade fired at him, and the sergeant major yelled at him to know what he thought he was wearing. After explanation, he was ordered to appear wearing his other issue tunic. He then remarked 'You won't like it sergeant-major.' In the afternoon the Queenslander appeared in a green, woolly tunic (as issued) at least twenty inches too big round the waist, and so large in the neck that his shirt was visible. The buttons were flat, and made of bone. As soon as we fell in, all the NCOs again rushed at him, and the sergeant-major bellowed, 'What the – have you got on now?' The reply of 'my maternity tunic, sir', was so apt and unexpected that the entire party of critics turned their backs, and doubled up with uncontrollable laughter, and a soft answer had once more turned away wrath.

The China missionary had evidently not been warned, as I had, to conceal the fact that he was not a novice in the riding school. As well as the indoor riding school there was an outdoor manège floored with cinders, which had a small lake at one end, where the rain had collected, through which the horses plodded, and which had gradually reached a depth of two and a half or three feet of black cinder and water soup, about the consistency of whipped cream. On the first morning that we paraded for riding in the manège, the sergeant-instructor who was taking the riding school asked each man if he had ridden before. Obviously some, like two Canadians, had to admit it. Others, like myself, who had been warned what to say replied 'Not for a long time' or something inoffensive of that kind. The missionary, however, imprudently said 'All my life'. The

3

sergeant then uncoiling a long stock-whip, which he habitually carried, waited until the missionary's horse was just about to plod into the black porridge; then, giving the sour-tempered animal a vicious cut across the hocks, he called out, 'That man, that's ridden all his life, he's coming off now,' and he did, head over heels, up to the ankles, head down, into the black slime, whence he forthwith extricated himself, dripping with what appeared to be liquid tar from every inch of his person.

The riding school itself was an arena of terror to the many beginners at riding. Our ride, 'K-ride', went in at 6.45 am to the light of one poor gas jet. The season of the year was midwinter. Many of the students were over forty, and, of these, some had never 'forked' a horse. The experience of riding a horse, that had had full corn and no exercise over the weekend, on a Monday morning, without reins or stirrups over a log jump in semi darkness under orders from a sergeant armed with an active stock-whip and suffering from a weekend of beer not yet worked off, was an experience not calculated to calm the nerves of an equestrian novice, especially when he had sat on Sunday through the service at St John's Wood Church staring at a memorial slab in the wall inscribed, 'Sacred to the memory of Driver 'X', killed in St John's Wood riding school.'

Enough however, of the Wood as we called it. Eventually orders arrived for two dozen of us to go down to Topsham Barracks, Exeter, to start a new Royal Artillery (RA) cadet school. By the kindness of the regimental sergeant major (RSM) I was allowed to take the place of one man who had been detailed for Exeter without his brother, whom he did not want to leave, they being colonials.

So we transferred to Exeter, and it was just like being transferred from a lunatic asylum to a well-run public school.

So far, I have refrained from giving any names but now I must thank, by name Colonel King who was officer commanding (OC) RA Cadet School at Topsham Barracks, Exeter, Major Trussler, the Riding Master, Major Thornton, the chief instructor of gunnery, Lieutenant Moore, horsemastership and driving Lieutenant Uncle and Sergeant Finch and all the other instructors, both officers and sergeants, for their extraordinarily fine performance of tedious and trying duties.

If any body of men contributed more than the staff at the Exeter Cadet School towards the winning of the Great War on land – I shall be surprised.

4

If any gunners of wartime training, in any army, knew more of their duties than the Exeter cadets, I never met them, although I worked with all varieties of gunners, professional Englishmen from Woolwich, French, Portuguese, Greek, Italian, French Naval, British Naval Colonial including New Zealand, Australian, South African, Hong Kong and Shanghai Mountain, garrison, and other varieties too numerous to mention in detail.

When we left Exeter to go to Larkhill, I think we had learned all the practical gunner needed to know of horsemanship, horsemastership, discipline, shooting and observation, director-work, gun-drill, parts of guns, and casualties to equipment, and general military methods. Instead of one orderly officer for a brigade, we had an officer instructor and three NCOs for each squad, in place of one NCO per squad. The work was hard, but interesting, the food was eatable, the discipline was stricter, but reasonable, gunnery was intelligibly taught by intelligent instructors, and one could be proud of being an Exeter cadet.

Humour, while valuable at Exeter, was not essential to existence, as it had been at St John's Wood, so I will only relate two examples.

The first was in a lecture on 'Minor ailments of the horse', by the incomparable Lieutenant Moore, ex-Sergeant Moore. Arrayed in overalls, we were sitting on heaps of manure in the stables under instruction by Mr Moore. The veterinary knowledge imparted was first class, and the manner of it unforgettable.

'Now we comes to worms. 'Orses 'as worms, most of 'em. You might get into a battery where the commanding officer was crazy on worms, and 'ad all the bombardiers collecting 'em in empty match boxes. On the other 'and, you might get into a battery like this 'ere, where worms is treated reasonable. Wot I ses is, if a thin 'orse passes a worm, make a note of it. It's probably why 'e's thin. If a fat 'orse passes a worm, damned 'ard luck on the worm I calls it, 'e's lost a comfortable 'ome.' Ask any vet if that's not the correct attitude to worms.

The other amusing incident I want to remember relates to the same Queensland sheep farmer as produced the tunic episode.

Church parade was a dreadful affair at Exeter. RA marching pace is about fifty per cent faster than infantry, and so the slow march behind the Salvation Army band to the cathedral at Exeter was most annoying after the eyewash parade inspection before church parade.

After we had been at Exeter for about six weeks somebody discovered that the Queenslander had never attended any church parade of any denomination. So, next Sunday, a search of the whole brigade camp took place, and the Queensland cadet was discovered in his usual Sunday morning refuge, smoking a pipe in his shirt sleeves with the sergeants' bath man, while the rest of us were shining ourselves up like advertisements for popular brands of metal polish.

About this time, a senior officer from the War Office came to Exeter and, all the cadets being paraded in a hollow square, delivered a most serious address to all undergoing training. By that time, the original squad of about thirty had grown into a school of over four hundred, who, on occasion, were accustomed to describe themselves as 'a fine body of men'. The substance of the excellently delivered appeal was that all of us should do our utmost to qualify ourselves as rapidly as possible for service in France, as the casualty lists kept growing so fast in the artillery that the speaker was at his wit's end to find enough officers to replace casualties.

With so keen and enthusiastic a body as the cadets at Exeter, an appeal of this nature could not fail of its purpose, although such was already the spirit of enthusiasm that only the slightest evidence of increased keenness was possible to be noticed.

Physically we were already as fit as prizefighters, and we were working from about six in the morning until ten o'clock every night. Every bit of spare time, such as the half hour after dinner, and most of Saturday and Sunday afternoons, was being used for a little extra and much needed sleep, but we had all, by then, learned the lesson, so often driven home on service abroad, that a willing man, who is already doing his utmost, can, from somewhere or other, find resources to achieve even a little bit more. And, at Exeter, this was easier, as we were no longer treated as half-witted shirkers, but rather as what 99.9 per cent of us were, keen, well-educated, intelligent men of varied ages and previous occupations, who were prepared to devote every possession of body and mind to help our country through the greatest trial that ever confronted her.

After a test examination, the top five of us, of whom I had the honour to be one, were sent to Larkhill to show what Exeter could produce in the way of budding artillery officers.

6

TRAINING

The squad we formed – for the chief instructor, at my request, allowed us Exeter cadets to keep together – was completed to the necessary nine of a gun detachment, by the addition of a New Zealand sergeant major, a New Zealand sergeant, and two officers undergoing further training.

I think our performances at gun drill and gun parts caused some little astonishment, both to the instructor and the others undergoing instruction. Some of these feats were examples of genuine smartness, but others were low cunning carefully thought-out. Of the latter, the most successful was our scheme for 'numbering-off' the detachment. In battery gun drill, the order is shouted from a great distance, 'detachments, tell off'. The front row is Nos. 1, 3, 5, 7 and 9, and the rear rank 2, 4, 6 and 8. The smartest gun team will, of course, number off the quickest, and ours was always numbered off before any of the other teams had half finished. The method, which I think was never spotted, was that we numbered 1 – ha – 9, ha being shouted in chorus by 2, 3, 4, 5, 6, 7, and 8. As we always occupied the same positions it went like clockwork.

Here I may interpolate what I believe to have been the two most useful exercises at Larkhill for gunners. First, the guessing of distances, most useful afterwards to me in country where map details were non-existent, and second, the miniature range, where the gun, an old 18-pounder, had the breech fitted with a block of wood with the business end of a morris-tube rifle sighted through it, the target a toy landscape, and the aiming points blocks of wood on a bench. I think the experiments we tried there were largely responsible for my later successfully passing the shooting test through which I was put by the eagle-eyed commander of D/303, the first battery I served with in France.

From Larkhill (where, to our surprise, we found the larks sing in chorus all day long) we went in a body to do actual firing with live rounds at Okehampton, in Devonshire, taking with us our excellent Larkhill instructor. I doubt if any RA amateur officer enjoyed any part of his service more than the Okehampton target practice.

After Okehampton, we went to our various homes for eight days' leave to get our uniforms and other equipment, before proceeding (army people always 'proceed', when not with their unit) abroad, being warned that we must never be more than two hours away from the telegraph. In spite of all the urgency for officer reinforcements RA, the five of us were

7

forgotten for over a month, until we wrote, and reminded the War Office of our continued existence. We then were commanded by telegraph to report at Topsham Barracks, Exeter, for orders to proceed to France.

We arrived next day, feeling extremely smart and self-conscious in our new uniforms, and, having spent two days in a good hotel in Exeter, about twenty of us proceeded to Southampton, and crossed the Channel together, and having landed in Le Havre, marched to the terribly uncomfortable base camp near Harfleur, where we spread out our new valises on wooden boxes in tents.

Then next day we had our first experience of troop-trains. We left Havre about 11.00 pm and arrived at Rouen at 7.00 am, less than forty miles in eight hours.

At Rouen, we were sorted out by various coloured signposts and tickets, and three of us were allotted brown signposts and tickets, having become, by magic, officers RA for reinforcements to, I think, the Third Army.

After some hours wait – by that time we had learned that, in the army, everybody below the rank of general always waits hours and hours on every possible occasion – the train started, and proceeded at about three miles an hour, apparently in a northward direction. Having, by this time, got used to expecting the worst, 'T', my sole remaining companion, and I, imagined we were bound for the Salient. But no, eventually the train stopped with the usual sudden jerk at a station marked Aubigny which, naturally, we had never heard of. An officer, with RTO (Railway Transport Officer) on his arm, came along, checked our names, and told us to decant ourselves, as a general service (GS) wagon was outside for us.

So far everything was as secret as possible. It is difficult to see in what way the chances of victory for the Allies would have been jeopardised if we had been told – two, more or less, meek one-pip wallahs (second lieutenants) where, and to what division we were being sent. But never until the Armistice was I permitted to know my destination beforehand, even when second-in-command of a battery. Which probably explains why almost everyone in the entire British Army lost himself on so very many occasions.

'T' and I then sat on the floor of the Army Service Corps GS wagon, which delivered us in a village (of which I never knew the name) to an infantry drummer-sergeant, who found us a billet in a farm, and bestowed upon us bacon, and about 2lbs of tea, and some bread and other rations.

Being able to talk French, I had little difficulty with madame, who made us a meal, including some of the tea. Naturally, as thereby she acquired at least $1^{15}/_{16}$lbs of some excellent tea for her own private use. Later on I learned much about army cooking, but madame's method of tea making was one that I have never met with before or since. She boiled a saucepan of milk, and then put in a small handful of tea and sugar, and boiled the lot together.

You may believe it or not, but the resultant jug of hot fluid was extraordinarily good.

Nobody having given us any orders of any kind, 'T' and I decided next morning to go for a walk, and have a look round. On our way we saw over the door of a house a drawing of a wasp very well executed in colours, and underneath it, in large black print, the letters RA HQ. As this was the first symptom of artillery we had seen, we were interested, and went in. We found a sergeant-clerk, then a brigade-major RA, who gave our names to a brigadier general RA. After five minutes conversation, the general informed us we were attached to particular batteries, I to D Battery 303rd Brigade (D/303), and 'T' to, I think, C Battery 301st Brigade. I never saw 'T' again until we met by chance in the summer of 1929, when I was motoring through Haverfordwest in south Wales.

That afternoon the GS wagon appeared, and carted me and my valise to the wagon lines of D/303, bearing a note addressed to Lieutenant Colonel 'B', officer commanding D/303. Arriving at the wagon lines, where, being so lately risen from the rank of gunner, I had the greatest difficulty in refraining from addressing the sergeant major as 'sir', I was given a first class dark chestnut mare, belonging to one of the subalterns, and, guided by his groom, rode to Maroeuil, the farthest point a horse could be taken in daylight, decided that gas masks and first aid dressings might be left where they were. I endeavoured to find my way along the first communication trench I had ever seen, at the village end of which was a farm with a dozen large shell holes in it, in front of which was a barrier across the road with a sentry, whose obvious duty was to see that nobody removed the barrier for fuel or building purposes.

I enquired of him if the communication trench was called 'Territorial'. He thought it was, but had no knowledge of, or interest in, any other part of the geography of the entire sector. As, however, the groom had told me to go along Territorial Trench until I struck the battery, I started trudging along the duckboards. After a mile or two it became evident that, (1) I had too many clothes, belts, map cases and water bottles on; that (2) that spurs were a quite unnecessary adornment in trenches; that (3) the art of walking on duckboards with comfort was one I had yet to learn; and that (4) the bangs I could hear, and the black bursts I could see, were hostile 5.9s.

Eventually I reached my battery located in a bend in the very same trench, presented my note to a little lame, very sharp-eyed colonel, was allotted a dugout, a most respectful servant called Buggins, and had tea, and met two or three of the battery officers.

Such was the casual method of arrival of an officer RA reinforcement in France in those days. The note, as I learned long afterwards, contained only these words: 'Dear 'B', herewith a subaltern, you won't find him any good. HAD S-B.'

Considering that the general had only had five minutes' conversation with me, the letter was scarcely what a fair-minded man would call a kindly introduction. However, I knew nothing about it until the general had made handsome amends by promoting me from second lieutenant to captain six months later. Of course, the general knew Colonel 'B', and Colonel 'B' knew the general, and both were magnificent soldiers with no use or consideration for the inefficient.

After about five weeks, the colonel, by asking the general to post me permanently to his battery, undoubtedly raised the value of my stock with the general to an extremely high figure, because, as I soon discovered, D/303 was easily the first howitzer battery in the 60th Division, and Colonel 'B' regarded rightly as the best battery commander any general could desire to have in his command.

CHAPTER 2

BEF Vimy Ridge, Roclincourt Sector

Novices

A subaltern officer in the army is a kind of half-trained apprentice.

When a battery is in the undivided state, that is, either out of the line or engaged in 'moving warfare', I am of the opinion that a subaltern, with one star, has the finest job that any young man can ever be set to do. Each section commander is in charge of a section consisting of two sub-sections, each of a gun, its detachments of eight or nine gunners, with drivers and horses for two guns and four wagons, and to assist him his two sergeants, two corporals and several bombardiers. He has also to help him the services of the sergeant major – who keeps his wide-open eye on the battery as a whole, especially as regards discipline – and what are known as the employed men, wheeler, saddlers, fitter, veterinary sergeant (attached from the Army Veterinary Corps), the farrier, and the various shoeing smiths.

The section commander is entirely responsible for everything included in his section, and it is a fine and inspiring feeling for a subaltern, mounted upon a well-groomed and well-schooled charger, to lead into action even on a field day with no shell bursts overhead or round about, a section of a battery of the Royal Field Artillery knowing, as he should know, that every one of the forty-odd horses and thirty-five NCOs and men under his command is as fit and perfectly trained as all his care and attention can make them.

In a battery in action in trench warfare, the position of section commander was almost nominal. The battery commander and the four sergeants were with the guns; at the wagon lines, usually several miles away, were to be found the sergeant major and the four corporals, with an officer in command who was having a fortnight's holiday from the gun line. To assist the battery commander at the guns were three subalterns, who generally took in turn the duties of, (1) officer in charge of the guns (or battery officer); (2) a forward observation officer (FOO), who lived as a guest of the company commander of one of the infantry companies of the battalion in the line; and (3) odd job officer, who was likely to be detailed for anything that had to be done, such as gas-proofing dugouts, repairing roofs or floors of gun pits, improving telephone arrangements, etc., etc.

With this explanatory preface, I will try to set down intelligibly how my first experience of real war came about.

After breakfast in a most comfortably planned battery mess, the colonel informed me – it being my first morning in the line – that for two days I would have no other duties than to learn all about the position, and the sector of the enemy lines opposite, which was, in fact, the southern end of the famous Vimy Ridge. I was handed the necessary squared map, and found that the gun position was Roclincourt K, 27, B. a. 20, 50'. These mystic letters and numbers indicated, to anyone instructed in the use of squared military maps, the exact position of the line of guns true to a very few yards. (When inviting an acquaintance to pay a call one always added this 'Roclincourt K, 27. A. a. 20, 50' as an address whereat the battery could be found. Any competent gunner could find the place from that, and the other kind were not invited. They were usually to be found living with ammunition columns, so we did not run across them. Infantry guests were usually given fuller particulars, as they were not particularly efficient in the use of maps.)

My whole daylight was spent in the private observation post (OP) of D/303, a hole in the ground in a field some 400yds to the left front of the battery position, well arranged, having a small dugout with a bunk for the telephonist, a seat for the officer, so arranged as to leave only his head above ground. To assist identification in the enemy lines, the colonel had sent home for a small, but powerful, Davon telescope, which revolved on a graduated plate. By noting on the dial the bearing of any object observed, the telescope could be brought to bear at once for a further inspection, by placing the indicator in the position noted.

I spent all day for two days identifying various objects on Vimy Ridge with points on my map, those on our side of no-man's-land being obliterated, so that I could see nothing whatever of villages and townships marked in the map by such high sounding names as Neuville St Vaast and La Targette. In the evenings I poked about the four gun pits, made the acquaintance of the 'No. 1s' (sergeants), the gunners, signallers, cooks, and so on. I copied out the night-line targets (special defensive barrages to be fired in case of an SOS call from the infantry at night). In the case of howitzer batteries, such as D/303 (I served entirely with 4.5-inch howitzer batteries until the Armistice) each gun had a different night-line, and the line was checked in each gun pit by the battery officer every evening.

On the morning of my third day, soon after breakfast, the colonel told me he was coming along to the OP with me to see what I had learned about our bit of German line, and to see what I knew about shooting.

On arrival at the OP with a telephonist, my CO directed the telescope on to an object half way up Vimy Ridge that looked, for all the world, like a heap of grey cement. He said, 'That's a target called Dugout House. See how many rounds you need to hit it.'

Referring to various notes in my notebook, and after consulting my contoured 1/20,000 artillery map, I arrived at angles of sight, angles from zero, reduction of range, because I was to use fifth charge, and so on.

Having been told always, when a cadet, that all calculations in the Royal Field Artillery (RFA) must be done without the aid of pencil and paper – after a very short interval I gave the following order to No. 1 gun by telephone:

'No. 1 gun ranging, target Dugout House, angle of sight 30 minutes, elevation angle 15 degrees, 20ft right of zero, range 4,350, charge V. ballistite, amatol, report when ready.'

I hoped I hadn't left anything out, but, apparently, I hadn't, for the colonel looked quite pleased, asked what I had allowed for wind, and I told him 10ft right, and 50yds extra elevation. He nodded, and the telephonist reporting 'No. 1 ready, sir,' I replied 'Fire!'

Immediately I heard the 'bump,' as the gun fired, and, for the thirty-five or so seconds the shell could be heard in flight I passed through thirty-five different shades of anxiety, as to where that 35lb shell filled with high-explosive would land. To my great relief, it made a splendid dark grey hillock of smoke a little to the left, and short of the target. The colonel then said, 'What correction are you giving?' I said quickly, '20 minutes more right, add 100yds.' He said, 'I should have said 10 minutes more right, and add 50yds.' I said, 'I prefer my correction.' He replied, 'Have it your own way,' so I corrected as I had suggested, and the next round went just as far over as the last had been short, and just as far right as the last had been left. This was a bit of luck as, in gunnery, a perfect 'bracket' is the ideal. By halving my correction, the next round should burst right on the target, and so it did.

I had hit my first enemy target in three rounds, and I knew enough about ranging to know that target in five rounds is considered good shooting.

After four or five further tests, which, naturally, were not up to the level of perfection of the Dugout House target – a very easy one, of course – the colonel said that would do, and we went back to the mess together.

On the way he remarked, quite casually, 'You have my permission to fire the battery at any time without reference to me.'

It was not until I knew my first CO a good deal better, together with the reputation enjoyed by his battery and the pride he took in it, I realised that, in that casual remark, he had paid me the greatest compliment I shall ever receive, and the greatest in his power to pay me.

After some days as battery officer, I went up to the infantry regions, about 2,500 yards nearer the Germans, under the guidance of one of the signallers, who, like myself, was next in turn for a tour of duty with the infantry.

D/303, being the howitzer battery of the 303rd Brigade, had defensive barrages to cover over a whole battalion front, whereas A, B, and C batteries, being 18-pounders, covered the fronts of individual company sectors. The FOO from each 18-pounder battery therefore lived with the commander of the company he covered with the fire of his battery, but the FOO of D battery had the distinction of living with the battalion commander at battalion headquarters.

I was, forthwith, introduced to the infantry colonel, his adjutant, and a brigadier general, who happened to be there. This was moving in high society with a vengeance, for a second lieutenant RA, with about a week's service in the line.

How those excellent footsloggers made me feel at home! How all the 'feet,' as we called them, treated the wandering FOO, provided, of course, he belonged to a really good battery! The relations between our battery and our 'feet' in both divisions in which I served, were simply ideal. A ready welcome was certain, whenever either of the different branches of the service had reason to visit one another, and our infantry knew that whatever difficulties of shortage of shells, broken, water-soaked, or shell-torn telephone wires might hinder us, in case of need, within half-a-minute or so of their asking the FOO, a certain number of our 'lazy lizzies' would be heard whining overhead, and bursting merrily somewhere on the far side of no-man's-land.

When men are being 'bumped' hour after hour with high explosive shell from 5.9-inch German guns, and trench mortars of all sizes, there comes a time when the sound or something going over the other way does wonders to cheer up the 'down-hearted'. That kind of firing was known as retaliation. It probably did very little damage amongst the enemy, but it certainly encouraged our own people in no small degree.

Owing to acute shortage of ammunition at that time, retaliation fire was forbidden, unless 'at the insistent demand of the battalion commander'. The battalion commander I lived with, an excellent and enthusiastic cooperator with artillery, said to me as soon as we became acquainted properly, 'When you feel a bit of retaliation would do my men good, get on with it, and I will do the insistent demanding in writing afterwards.'

The area we were holding had been famous (or infamous) for furious fighting when the French had held the sector. The notorious Souchez, at one time identifiable only by a noticeboard inscribed 'Ici fut Souchez', was a little to our north. It was mainly an area of trenches decorated by small wooden notices 'soldat francais mort pour la patrie' with a tattered kepi rotting on top of the wooden post, and usually nearby the body of the French soldier built into the parapet of the trench. In some places, where the sandbags had rotted with the rain, the bones of a foot would

15

project gruesomely. But the human mind gets used to grim sights of this kind very quickly, and to many other strange sights inseparable from stationary trench warfare: columns of rats moving about at dusk along the supports of the deep trenches, the night's casualties lying still on stretchers, covered incompletely with a blanket, waiting in neat rows round the officers' washing place for the burial party to take them away. How many times one wished that one's nose could learn as quickly as one's eyes to ignore the inevitable horrors!

The principal offensive operations in this area were raids on the craters which littered no-man's-land, and on the enemy trenches at night. In the night raids, the raiding parties were protected mostly by an artillery 'box-barrage', carefully timed and arranged so as to isolate the enemy trenches to be raided from reinforcements from other trenches. This was done by keeping up a steady bombardment on selected points along the main enemy trenches, to exclude interference from outside the area. Fire had to be extremely accurate, and could never be observed.

One night I was sitting on the roof of a small shed with the infantry colonel watching the progress of a raid being done by the battalion. Just as I was remarking on the apparent effectiveness of the box-barrage, the flashes of bursting shells making an almost perfect parallelogram round the section of trenches into which the raiding party had gone, a heavy trench mortar started firing from the north right over the artillery barrage, the huge bombs bursting in the area being raided.

The colonel said, 'My God! That'll wipe them out. Can't you shut that mortar up?'

When a trench mortar fired at night in the German lines, a telltale flash always gave away its position. From the flash it was quite evident that this trench mortar was situated quite half a mile north of the extreme limit of the area allotted to us for targets. As the night was pitch dark, I had not the vaguest idea where it was actually firing from. However, a good maxim for gunners is 'when anyone asks you to fire at anything, fire at something.' So I telephoned to the battery an enormous switch to the left of about 40 degrees, guessed a range at 5,200yds, and ordered, 'left section one salvo, fire when ready.' Naturally, my huge switch was queried, but I repeated it, and within less than a minute the lazy whine of my two shells came over far to the left. Marvellous to relate, the flash of the two bursts was quite near where we had seen the thin red streak of the enemy trench mortar firing, and equally marvellous it never fired again during the raid. If I hit it, it was certainly the biggest fluke that ever happened, except one in Salonica where we hit an impossibly small object in one round without knowing its range to half a mile.

I spent many hours in this sector sitting inside a tall steel tube, which had been erected by the French as an OP. It was an ingenious and clever imitation of the trunk of a big tree with the top blown off. It was constructed of steel plates riveted together with a small shuttered slit near the top to look through. The outside of this fake tree trunk was cleverly camouflaged with moss held in place by wire netting. The view was good, but the seat provided was a bicycle saddle made of iron. As there were no supports for one's feet, an hour or two up the tree was a kind of penance. At the bottom of the tree there was an opening at the side away from the enemy in which my telephonist used to sit with his instrument to transmit any firing orders I wished to give to the battery. Fortunately for him, the moment the enemy selected to put a small shell through the bottom of the tree was one afternoon when I had sent him off to get a mug of tea from some hospitable Infantry friends of his. It is true he was killed later on in France, but in the interval he had done magnificent service with the other battery in which we both served in Macedonia and Palestine.

The routine of duties for an officer on duty with this battery, in the line, was, generally speaking, two days as battery officer, two days at the battery OP (all day observation duty), and three days FOO with the infantry. The officer on duty with the infantry made a rule of going round the firing line at 'stand-to' at dawn, and spent the rest of his days on general observation, shooting at targets selected by himself, or by higher authority, and generally keeping an eye on the enemy trenches opposite, and being always where the battalion commander could communicate at once by telephone, should he desire artillery support at any moment day or night. The area was undermined in all directions. At any hour of the twenty-four, a mine might 'go up' and, in the struggle for the mine crater which invariably followed, artillery support would be essential. Unceasing vigilance was the price of holding the line in this sector. It formed a salient which the enemy might plan to abolish. Our battery commander's undertaking that he was prepared, and able, to fire on any selected point in his sector within thirty seconds, day or night, was a source of much confidence to the infantry whom we covered and with whom we were on the most friendly possible terms. Others, as well as I, often tested our colonel's thirty-second undertaking. The scarcity of ammunition, at that time, made frequent tests impossible, but D/303 never failed, as far as I heard, to put a round where it was asked for well inside the half minute.

The chief strain on the battery officers in my period in this sector was due to lack of sleep. It was a red-letter night when I, personally, managed to get more than five hours 'shut-eye'. Being one of those peculiar people who can exist with no more than five hours' sleep a night, I suffered from lack of sleep less than the others. But none of us could go on long without losing the necessary alertness of mind on so small a ration of rest, and so the colonel wisely arranged a week's turn of duty with the horses for each of us in rotation. The horse lines lay about three miles behind the gun positions, and a week at the wagon lines, riding every day, was a glorious change; it was like a holiday in the country to get away from trench life.

After some time, orders came along for the battery to move to a position further north. This was the first time I had been concerned in moving a battery in the face of the enemy. Nothing in the way of movement was possible before dark. I was given charge of the left section, and ordered to take charge, and report to the CO as soon as the section was on the road and ready to move. The two guns were manhandled by the detachments out of the gun pits, trundled along the grass, and the teams hooked-in ready to move off. I shouted in the dark for my horse, intending to ride along the front of the gun position and report in style to the CO that my section was 'all correct and ready'. But it did not turn out quite as I intended. The horse sent up for me by the sergeant major, a sour-tempered regular ex-corporal of the RHA, who had been left, temporarily, in charge of the wagon lines, reared up as soon as he felt my weight in the saddle, and went right over backwards in the dark. Fortunately, I had learned long ago what to do and, more fortunately, did it as quick as thought. By throwing my weight sideways over the horse's shoulder, I landed in the road with the result that, instead of a broken back, my injuries were confined to cut hands and knees full of gravel. My breeches were ruined, cut through at both knees, and streaked with scarlet from the blood which trickled from my fingers. After this misadventure, a stylish report from horseback was out of the question, so I ran along, and reported to the CO that I was ready to move off. He had expected me to report mounted as, normally, every decently trained field-gunner would. Hearing me speaking from the ground, he flashed his torch on me, and I must have looked a picture – my uniform was torn, I was covered with mud and blood, and looking, generally, like a 'dog's dinner'. After a word of explanation I went off and, finding another horse, I led my two guns to the crossroads and waited for the rest of the battery. Eventually, after marching a few miles, the guns were lifted on to trucks on a light railway and coasted down to the new position. Next day, the colonel, in a few well-chosen words, explained to the sergeant major the exact value of one who sent up, for an officer in the dark, a mount which had not been ridden for several months. I had to wear my hands in bandages for some time – not a pleasant addition to one's equipment in an area where much of one's duties was performed knee-deep in trenches half-filled with mud and water. An injection from the medical officer (MO) was obligatory, as the soil is so heavily manured in Picardy that, without an injection, tetanus is liable to follow any cut deeper than a scratch, should earth get into it.

The new position – an extraordinary one, originally constructed, we were told, by a French battery, whose gunners were professional miners – had beneath it almost a hotel excavated in the flint and chalk to a depth of, at least, 50ft. The interior of this gloomy cavern was as dark as the inside of a cow, and as damp as a sea fog. After the first night below, I instructed my servant, the faithful Buggins, to remove my belongings from the dungeon in which he had put them. After only one night, my blankets were like seaweed for dampness, and beginning to show signs of blue mould. Another camouflage steel tree was again my portion, and, of this one, the iron bicycle saddle seemed even harder. However, the colonel, having decided that he could do with my services permanently, wrote a request to the CRA (short for Brigadier General Commanding Royal Artillery) that I should be posted to D/303, instead of attached on approbation, as I had been up to date. The general – taking the colonel's request as a testimonial, as it undoubtedly was – posted me to another battery altogether, D/302, to my great regret at the time. My regrets were due to the fact that I had formed real ties of affection with the colonel and the other officers, and had come to realise that the CO was one in a thousand, and the ruling spirit of a battery which was, deservedly, a byword for efficiency. And so my first experience of a battery in the line came to an end, and I joined the unit with which I was to serve for the next three years continuously. But the short experience I had had with D/303 had taught me invaluable lessons of how a battery in action should be run to get the last ounce of efficiency out of it in trench warfare. Men like Colonel 'B' are rare, unfortunately, but their example is as widespread as the ripples from a stone thrown into a pond. The lessons I had learned stood me in good stead later. It was a most fortunate chance for such a green hand as I was to serve my apprenticeship with that battery.

After bidding goodbye to my good friends, officers, NCOs and men, who I hope reciprocated my feelings of regret on parting – and I am sure that some of them did – I studied my map, and soon found the map coordinates of my destination. My kit was to be transferred by sending it down to D/303 wagon lines, who would then send it along to D/302 wagon lines, presumably in the cook's cart, the two-wheeled vehicle with hood and shafts invariably used for transport of odds and ends in the British Army – it is, officially, known as a 'cart officers' mess'. My own journey would consist of a walk of, roughly, five miles. It rained all the way. Part of my route lay along disused trenches in bad repair, the rest of it across the abandoned fields, which extended in every direction, alive with stoats, half-wild cats, always tortoise and white in colour, busily engaged in hunting their prey among the thistles which, by then, had covered the countryside, and stood almost shoulder high on all sides. Far to my left rose the line of Vimy Ridge – in German occupation; to my right towered the ruined pinnacles of St Eloi, a gaunt white landmark, very useful for taking a compass bearing. My compass reassured me that I was travelling in the required direction and, at last, I arrived at a kind of dirt track, on the left of which were the gun positions of the 302nd Brigade. I passed by two batteries of 18-pounders and, finally, reached the battery position of my new unit at the end of the dirt road.

The contrast from what I had been used to was striking. The position of D/303 had been as compact and neat as anything possibly could be. The gun pits had opened at regular intervals off a trench floored with perfectly fitted duckboards, with ammunition dump handy on one side, and, on the other, in the order named, officers' mess, telephonists' dugout, CO's dugout, left section guns, officers' dugouts, right section guns, battery office and cookhouses. All had been as handy and clean as the quarterdeck of a warship and speed and efficiency in action were easy.

My new sphere of duties was in painful contrast. The battery position straggled all over the countryside. Officers' and men's dugouts had been excavated in front of the guns in the side of a gentle slope. Nos. 1, 2 and 3 guns lay in excellent gun pits at the usual intervals of 20yds, No. 4, for some ridiculous reason, was placed at a distance of 150yds or so on the left flank. The ammunition dump, which also contained the telephonists' dugout, was nearly a 100yds to the rear of the line of guns. The gun pits, while well constructed, were as obvious as they could possibly be; separating the men's and officers' quarters and the officers' mess (which in action serves as the battery headquarters) from the four guns was a slimy track flanked by a trench silted up with mud to more than waist deep.

It was evident, from the first glance, that rapidity in answering a call for fire was beyond hope in such a position. The guns were placed, with respect to the hill they fired over, in a position suitable, not to high-angle fire guns like howitzers, but to high-velocity low-trajectory quick firing guns, like the French 75mm and the English 18- and 60-pounder.

A glance round conveyed all the foregoing to a gunner even of so little experience as I then was. I slithered round to No. 1 gun pit, introduced myself to the obviously extremely competent and well-mannered sergeant in charge, who conducted me back through the slime to the officers' mess, where I shook hands with Major 'W'.

He was just what the battery position had led me to expect. I sized him up, correctly, as it turned out, as a very kindly, rather easy-going type of professional soldier. He was, obviously, conscientious and considerate, courteous, and thoughtful towards both officers and other ranks, but he had none of that electricity and devil without which no man can be a first class battery commander. During tea this estimate of my new CO's character was formed. I have found, all my life, that first impressions of character are those usually to be relied on. In this case they proved so, and while I think all the battery felt affection and respect for the CO there was in none of us that feeling of hero-worship for him that is felt for a real chief.

21

Compared with D/303, existence was uninteresting. Observation of the sector allotted to us was extremely difficult. Except from a disused French trench on a mound behind the infantry firing line, nothing much could be seen except heaps of mud – the parapets of German trenches. My time was spent living at company headquarters of the infantry when on duty as FOO toiling at digging out the mud round the battery position, and trying to help infuse some of the life and activity I had been used to into the detachments, at the impossible battery position in which I found myself.

I had been posted to the battery to take the place of 'K', an ex-sergeant of exceptional ability, whose knowledge of fuses and the more intricate mechanics of shells and guns, had caused him to be summoned from a battery in action to give advice to his superiors on matters upon which he was an undoubted expert.

The weeks went along, the monotony broken by the excitement of occasional barrages, arranged to protect raiding parties of infantry, until near the end of October rumours of an impending move became current.

The infantry were relieved by the Canadians, for whom the artillery FOO officers and their attendant telephonists were to act as guides whenever needed. The batteries remained in support of the Canadian infantry, as was wise, considering that we knew the danger spots of the line, and could, if needed, drop an annihilating barrage on any German raiding party who might venture to experiment with the newcomers.

These Canadians were the first colonial troops with whom I had cooperated. They were an amusing and sporting fraternity. They had just come out of the Somme fighting, and were far below strength. The company I lived with was commanded by a professional ice skater, with the rank of captain, the second-in-command was a major, who appeared to be a professor in civilian life, the only other officer in the company was a stout, middle-aged second lieutenant. They had an American sergeant, and some Japanese privates. The battalion commander, a Major 'O'D' – became a very great friend of mine. Our introduction was unusual. I slipped feet first down the 60ft staircase of battalion HQ, landed like a torpedo under his writing table, upset his papers, inkpots and private letters all over the floor, and immediately accepted his offer of a glass of excellent Canadian rye whisky. He was a charming personality, and after we had gone forth and removed from Ross Street an unexploded 8-inch German high explosive shell, which his men disliked walking past, we became on such friendly terms as were quite common amongst officers of similar ages, even in cases where one, myself, was of the rank indicated by one pip on the sleeve and one row of braid, and the other, being a field officer (why a major should be described by the ridiculous title of field officer, I have never yet discovered) wore sleeves embellished with a crown and three rows of braid. In some infantry units, officers with one pip were known as 'warts' and treated as such. Some of the 'warts' being in private life King's Counsels and men of considerable social and commercial importance, this appellation was as ridiculous as it was snobbish, but snobs and boors are to be met in all walks of life in uniform as often as anywhere else.

An extraordinary meeting took place just before the Canadian artillery arrived. One day when I was having a solitary cup of tea in the mess at the battery, Sergeant 'G', the most capable No. 1 of No. 1 gun, ran over, and, in great excitement, reported that two of his gunners had collared a suspected spy in the gun pit. We hailed the gun pit, and told the gunners to bring him across to the mess. When he had arrived, and had proved his ability to pronounce properly the word 'association', a stumbling-block to every German, however proficient in our language, I discovered him to be a chaplain of the Canadian division, a distinguished author, and a distant cousin of my own, Ralph Connor, author of *The Sky Pilot* and the *Parson of Crow's Nest*. So, having advised him to keep out of gun pits and wear a clerical collar, I invited him to share what remained of my tea, and enjoyed his company for the rest of the afternoon.

Then the Canadian artillery arrived. We held our breath as they came along. The position could be approached in daylight, so we had a full view of the column, most of the vehicles had only four horses, I think any pair of wheelers of ours could have easily pulled any of their six-horsed vehicles backwards, teams and all, such was the appalling condition of their horses. The men were, in appearance, no better. They had not had the luxury of a haircut for weeks, and most of them were obviously scrofulous. The detachments were below half strength, but this did not greatly matter, as only two of the guns were in a condition to fire, as they cheerfully explained to us. This was no dud battery, but a sample of the condition to which the field artillery was normally reduced in 1916 by a trick of duty on the Somme. The Canadian gunners were cheery and full of good spirits, an indication of which was the final vehicle of the column. This was an ancient four-wheeled cab, which had been salved somewhere and painted pale blue with a maple leaf to decorate the panel of each of the doors. One of the shafts stuck straight up in the air like an enormous fish hook, and the driver was wearing a disreputable top hat he had found on some rubbish heap. In this remarkable vehicle were stowed the valises of the officers. A battery whose line of march terminated with a spectacle of this kind, had obviously retained all of its morale in spite of the appalling conditions on the Somme, including thirty-six casualties – of the most demoralising of all, their own prematures – in addition to those due to enemy fire.

Two of the officers of each battery were left behind with twenty gunners and signallers to help the Canadians find their way about. This was absolutely essential, as this part of the trench system included that fortification which had appeared so often in the French communiqués under the name of the Labyrinth. The tangle of trenches in that sector deserved the name fully, and, on more than one occasion, I was lost for hours, and finally had to climb out of the 10ft deep communication trench, and find my way home across the open by compass bearing in the dusk.

Eventually the other officers departed, and I was ordered to conduct the details of our brigade out of the line. Here I had my first experience of the incredible lack of efficiency of the British staff. My orders were to march this nondescript collection of ninety men to the grande place of the village of Maroeuil, where motor buses were to convey the party to an unnamed destination. It was 7.00 pm of a November evening when we arrived, and we were as cold as torrents of chilly rain could make us. No vehicle of any kind was there to meet us, and no sign of a messenger to tell me why there were no buses, or where we were supposed to go.

The party did not contain a single NCO and I only knew one quarter of them by sight. They had no rations whatever, and signs of discontent were evident.

Three quarters of my first independent command had never seen me before, and, in the dark, they naturally felt little confidence in the ability of their unknown officer to do the right thing by them. I turned my torch on the disgruntled ninety, got them roughly into line, selected half a dozen sensible looking strangers, and created them acting unpaid bombardiers on the spot, left the man who said he was the senior soldier in command of the party, and told them I would find them shelter and rations as soon as might be.

My next job was to find someone responsible for the village. In the dark this was not very easy, especially as most of the village consisted of roofless ruins. However I found a Canadian town major whose sergeant major was accustomed to act on his own responsibility when his superior officer was not quite at his best. As the town major was, on that evening, very far from being at his best, I wasted no time with him, but fixed up a billet for my troops, in no time, in a barn with a weather-tight roof, and sent the Canadian sergeant major off to guide my soaking party to their shelter for the night.

Sometime before, I had done some shooting in cooperation with the SAHA (South African Heavy Artillery) who lived, as I remembered, at the chateau at Maroeuil. We had always found them excellent sportsmen in every way. So I went off there, and found a South African RSM, to whom I told my plight. As a matter of course, without any written authority, he had a wagon loaded with three days' rations for ninety men, and sent them along to my men's barn.

My troops had already lit a fire, and greeted the ration wagon with loud cheers, and myself with a warm welcome. The situation was now beginning to look less awkward. The food question was solved, thanks to the colonials (in the future I learned to make straight for a colonial unit whenever in dire straits, and I never asked for help in vain). It only remained to find a billet for myself. I had the luck to stumble in the dark upon a farm, where lived a trench mortar unit who possessed, of all marvels, a telephone with a line to our own divisional headquarters. By this means, I reported my predicament to our own Brigade Major 'P', and knew that my troubles were over, for Major 'P' was not the kind of officer to allow a second lieutenant to be messed about, as I had been, without the officer responsible finding out what kind of a worm he was in the eyes of the 60th Division artillery HQ. Having reported the matter, and fed at the expense of the trench mortars, I slept peacefully in the farmer's hereditary four-poster. Next morning at 6.00 am four perfectly good motor buses were waiting for us on the grande place.

The lack of ability shown by whatever brass hats were responsible for moving our division out of the line will be incredible to any who did not suffer from their monumental inefficiency. Troops moving into the line must naturally take precedence over troops moving out. As the troops coming up had been given the identical route to those going down, every single billet and road was packed with soldiers long before we arrived anywhere.

Into how many sections the artillery of our division had to be split, to divert small parties into unoccupied areas, I never heard, but I do know that our battery alone got split up into five separate fragments (one of which marched 20 miles in one day, and the next day marched back again to where it had come from). Rations for the men and forage for the horses only reached us owing to the untiring day and night efforts of our Staff Captain 'F', who careered all over the country on a commandeered motor bicycle.

This was the mess made of the simple operation of marching one division about 15 miles out of the line in the most peaceful possible area, occupied by a friendly and hospitable allied nation. It should not be forgotten that this was after two years of war. Can it be wondered that the men who did the fighting, had little use for what they called the gilded staff?

At last the battery became once more a unit. After a general clean up, we resumed our march. To my surprise and great pleasure, Major 'W' informed me that my future duties would be those of battery captain, not, of course, in any other sense than that I should ride at the tail of the column, and assist and supervise the quartermaster sergeant (QMS) in all matters relating to stores, rations and forage. There is no quarter master in the artillery. His duties are carried out by the QMS with such assistance as the captain of the battery has time to lend him. In moving warfare the captain and QMS find few opportunities for sleep or proper meals. Their hours of work average about twenty out of the twenty-four.

This was the first time I had seen my new battery as a whole, or any of its horses. The team horses of the right section were very good, those of the left section a very poor lot, with the exception of the gun teams which were excellent.

'M', the right section commander, and senior subaltern, was, obviously, a good horseman, and had had the pick of the horses for his section. The left section commander, 'H', could not have been described as a horseman of any known variety. He rode with his knees several inches from the saddle, and his teams were badly matched. Actually, however, the finest pair of wheelers in the whole battery were the roans in D sub-section gun team, and C sub-section gun team leaders were pictures, both in stamp and condition.

The riding horses baffle description. My own pair, which I had inherited from Lieutenant 'K', whose place I had filled, consisted of Big Bill, a well-bred Argentine bay, 16.3 hands high, famous for his mid-air gallop (his method of hailing the approach of a motor lorry) and a little round black cob, called Teddy, which went lame every march from incipient ringbone. The major's pair would have made respectable team horses, being obviously light draught in stamp, 'M's pair were Daisy, a black, ugly in the head, but with beautiful clean legs, and Sandy, a chestnut which had a considerable moustache, hair to the knees, and mulish ears. (Sandy was to prove a remarkable animal. I believe he must have been the offspring of some travelling thoroughbred stallion and a farmer's mare, probably presented with free service in exchange for a night's accommodation for the stud groom. Such arrangements are not unknown in country parts of England). Whatever Sandy's origin, any horse that could beat him over a mile course was worth racing, and, at full speed, the old chestnut's gait was as smooth as that of a racehorse. He looked, however, like a very humble farmer's nag, and did not lend an air of distinction to the right section.

'H's pair of chargers were of the class known in England as common cabbers; the battery staff, that is the signallers, were mounted on draught horses that would have been in the teams, except that they had been weeded out as useless for draught purposes. The only decent looking riding horse in the entire outfit, excluding Daisy, was that ridden by the sergeant major. It, however, was elderly, and cursed with a mouth like an iron railing.

The spare horses were, obviously, not fit for anything whatever, except to walk along a road unlade.

From the point of view of the horses, the prospect for me was

27

discouraging. Lieutenant 'H', the other subaltern who had joined the battery after I did, was provided with something to ride, of course – it was certainly a pair of horses, one for him, and one for his groom. In the historic words of David Harum, Banker, 'they must have been horses, for they were certainly nothin' else.'

After successive halts in pleasant country, and billets in farmhouses, we eventually reached our destination. I was sent forward to secure billets for our men, and was surprised to find that, at the trot, my Big Bill, while uncomfortable, had such a turn of speed that I easily outdistanced the billeting officers from the other batteries, and secured the best quarters for our men. First come, best served, is the invariable rule in billeting expeditions. Being the only officer in the brigade with a knowledge of French, and mounted on an equine giraffe that could trot 3yds while the other officers were covering two, it was the easiest of tasks to secure the choicest billets the local mayor had to offer.

The conditions of the competition being unequal, it was nothing to my credit that my first billeting operations were completely satisfactory, but I could see that the major was pleased.

The horses of the brigade were parked on a field of clover root, which had been mown so close that not a leaf, or stalk, was to be seen. Nevertheless, on the morning of our departure, the mayor, through his ajoint, presented his bill for damage done to crops on the bare ground which he had allotted us for our horse lines. My knowledge of French had, by then, somehow become known to our brigade commander, Colonel 'D', so I was deputed to settle the matter. Fortunately for our pockets, we had no French interpreter. I had previously dealt with several claims of this kind when OC wagon lines of D/303. I had found the mayors reasonable enough in making settlements, but evidently instructed not to be modest in claiming from the English. The principle I worked on, which proved its soundness in four different countries, was, in cases where some compensation seemed called for, to offer ten per cent, of the amount claimed. In the other cases, where the claim had, obviously, no other justification than a desire to benefit the commune at our expense, I directed the mayor, in the most vulgar idiom that his native tongue contained – and there are many most vulgar French idioms, not in common currency in country villages in France – to go and boil himself, or words to that effect. In this instance, the mayor fled for his life, and the claim for damage was not again presented. The system of ten per cent or nothing invariably succeeded, and left the mayor all smiles in those cases where payment had to be made.

On active service, even in a peaceful area far from war's alarms – we were then not far from Abbeville, and the scenery was unpolluted even by an Allied aeroplane – all operations were ordered for the middle of the night. The idea must be to make everything as difficult as possible, and to deprive hard-working soldiers of a night's rest in the name of the great fetish, secrecy.

It was, therefore, on the approved lines of the greater strategy that an officer, myself, was ordered by the adjutant (an ex-quartermaster sergeant, devoid of manners, brains, or elementary truthfulness) to report at brigade HQ at 11.30 pm mounted, lead a column of 140 drivers, with spare head collars and reins, to the railway station, and draw 140 horses from a remount train in a siding. That the locality of the station was quite unknown, either to the adjutant or myself, was, apparently, a matter of no importance. We possessed no maps of any kind, so I simply remounted my horse and rode off at the head of my long column in the dark.

It was not hard to find the station, or the remount train in the siding. The train was in the charge of an elderly remount sergeant with long, drooping moustaches. Knowing the correct methods among the old-time sergeants of the regular army, of which he was, beyond all question, a typical example, I found him asleep as expected, and slipped him a fifty franc note, innocently enquiring as I presented my order for horses, which truck had the best horses in it. He whispered in my ear, 'the last two trucks. Sixteen officers' chargers for the 12th Lancers.' Having sixteen drivers from my own battery with me, this was as easy as could be. Providence was solving the question of riding horses for my new battery. I led the column, now of 280 horses, back to brigade HQ, and sent off the drivers, each to his own unit, with the horses they were leading. By this simple means all of the officers' chargers landed in our lines, for the first night at any rate. In the morning the major and I could scarcely believe our eyes. On the spare line stood a row of sixteen well-bred, first class riding horses, of a type to which the battery had, hitherto, been quite a stranger. The general came round to see what I had brought to the brigade, and was obviously, pleased with what he saw. All the horses from the remount train were first class, and the general smiled in a most friendly fashion when he saw our portion of the spoils. The general was no fool, and he saw through my little plot and decreed that all the horses should remain in possession of the units on whose lines they then were, and, thus provided, our battery officers and NCOs appeared no more on the light draught Rocinantes of former days. 'M' wisely kept Daisy for his groom, and I kept Big Bill for mine, otherwise we all re-horsed ourselves magnificently, and everybody felt happier.

The process of entraining for Marseilles was my second experience of the staff work of the British Army, after more than two years of war. As usual, everybody was ordered to march to the station, Hangest, in the dark. 'M' and I had accompanied the previous battery for entrainment to the station, and had found that the arrangements were so inadequate, that the time schedule was already thirty-six hours out of gear.

We managed to persuade Major 'W' to start twelve hours late, so that we marched in daylight. He was very loth to treat brigade orders with such scant respect, but was over-persuaded, and, accordingly, we had only to wait a trifle of twenty-four hours outside the station in the rain.

The arrangements for loading 300 animals, and about twenty heavy vehicles, some weighing over two tons, all in pitch darkness, were such as would have disgraced the lowest paid outside porter in a wayside village station. The officer responsible for the arrangements was a staff officer with the rank of major, with beautifully cut breeches and riding boots, a monocle, and the usual red tabs. One ramp was provided for our 300 animals – several units were to travel on our train – which had, therefore, to be got into the trucks one horse at a time. Every vehicle had to be lifted bodily by manpower across the space between the platform and the flat trucks on which they were to travel. One hour's work of a platoon of Royal Engineers (if REs have platoons) and a small supply of 1½in planking would have sufficed to ensure end-loading (the only reasonable method of entraining guns and heavy vehicles), so that, instead of having to be lifted bodily, they are simply wheeled on to the end truck, and the wood gangway is transferred as each gun is wheeled from one truck to another. But staff officers are not paid to think of simple things like that. Common fighting troops are paid to toil, and sweat, while

30

ornamental non-combatants stand and watch their efforts, without doing the smallest trifle to lighten their unnecessary labours. When tired of watching the performance, our monocled major went off, accompanied, I am certain, by the silent contempt of every officer and man engaged in the quite unnecessary labour caused by the incompetence of this elegantly turned out railway officer of the general staff.

Eventually we moved off, not this time at the pace of the ordinary troop train. We travelled exceedingly fast; apparently so great was the haste that no stop whatever had been arranged to water the horses all the long journey from Abbeville to Marseilles. But, fortunately for the horses, an engine has to take in water at intervals, and, while the engine driver was filling his tanks, we had every driver rushing up and down the train filling our canvas buckets from the engine water-pumps, and passing them up to other drivers, who gave the water to the thirsty animals. In this way our horses, thanks to the untiring devotion of the men, got, probably, half rations for the two days which the journey lasted. One of the best of our new string of riding horses died of this treatment on the way. We dragged it out of the truck with the greatest difficulty – it had stiffened completely by the time the train stopped somewhere, and the seven other horses in the truck were standing across it – and we left it by the side of the railway lines.

At Marseilles, it was evident that the speed of the train was not because we were wanted in Salonica urgently, or, if we were wanted, Salonica would have to get along without us, as best they could. Occasionally a battery would leave the camp to embark. But day after day went by, and still we got no orders to move. After ten days in the camp, brightened by a few visits to Marseilles, our brigade, at last, received orders to embark on the SS *Manitou*, and left the harbour without any escort whatever. Our sole defence against the Austrian submarines was one 4.7-inch naval gun, and a pair of 18-pounders which were intended to damage any periscope observed by firing shrapnel at it. This did not seem likely to be effective. Obviously, any reasonable submarine would have sunk us with a torpedo long before any gunner could hope to smash the periscope by firing shrapnel at it. We were heartily glad that this sketchy anti-submarine defence was never tested. It could only have been a complete fiasco, and was probably intended for an amusement for the men, or else it was simply an example of 'eye-wash'.

The real defence against submarines was the zigzag course we steered and the proverbial luck of the SS *Manitou*, or rather the rigid light-discipline at night, insisted upon by her admirable captain.

No manure or dead horses were allowed to be thrown overboard, to avoid giving away our route to prowling submarines. The heat in the Mediterranean, even in November, is sometimes extreme. It was very hot during our voyage. The ship was fitted with horse boxes, but inadequately ventilated for the 600 animals we had on board. Down in the lower hold, where the mules lived, the only ventilation was provided by the canvas wind-scoops, which hung down from halfway up the masts. When the ship was stationary for a day off Valetta, and the wind-scoops ceased to function, the atmosphere in the hold was stifling. The smell of the piles of manure became almost intolerable in the semi-tropical heat, and the sweat ran off the mules' bellies in a steady trickle. The mules throve on it. How the drivers, who looked after them, fared was a different story. We had to organise spells on deck in the open air for these poor fellows to keep them going.

Here it was that I first learned the worth of Sergeant 'W', attached to our battery from the Army Veterinary Corps (AVC). He was a little, red-headed Glasgow Scotsman, devoted to horses. He had spent his life as a civilian looking after them and preparing them for the show ring. He went, untiringly, round the horses and mules on the whole ship, and, the other AVC sergeants being of little use, administered injections of strychnine with his hypodermic syringe, and kept dozens of failing animals on their feet. Whenever I hear the phrase 'devotion to duty' the picture of Sergeant 'W' comes into my mind. How we should have fared without his knowledge and attention to our animals, I cannot imagine. If any animal needed his help – in the bitter arctic cold of a Macedonian blizzard, in the scorching heat of the Suez Canal in August, in the cold in the high bills near Jerusalem, with ankle-deep torrents of muddy water cascading over the rocky hillsides, in shell-pocked areas round the Somme battlefields – regardless of his own comfort, or convenience, or safety, Sergeant 'W', AVC, was there, without having to be sent for, doing already everything his ingenious brain could think of, giving us and the animals the benefit of his expert knowledge, without expecting any reward of any kind except that greatest of all rewards – the knowledge, in his own devoted, loyal soul, that he had done everything to the limit of his powers of service. Sergeant 'W', AVC, had a diminutive stature, but he had 'a heart as big as a house'. He was fearless, determined, untiring, just what, in his own country, is meant by the term 'a guid mon', and, in Scotland, there is no higher praise for a man than that. If I knew of any words more expressive, I would use them here about him. The Scotch are a remarkable people, and the best of the Scotch are, in my experience, the people on whom a man can most rely when determination and selfless devotion are needed. Sergeant 'W' was just that type of Scotsman, and he won, and deserved to win, the admiration and respect of every driver, NCO and officer in the battery he served so well.

We recommended him for a decoration, but he was awarded nothing. I would have awarded him anything he asked for, at any time. But he wasn't the kind that asks. I don't suppose he wanted a medal any more than a 'cat wants a flag', to use another of the expressive phrases of David Harum, banker.

CHAPTER 3

BSF Salonica, Makukovo Salient

D/302 Brigade: feeling their feet

At last we sailed safely into the magnificent bay which forms the harbour at Salonica. The bay itself is large enough to give anchorage to a veritable armada. We landed, all our horses and mules being able to walk down the gangways, although one horse had to be left on the quay. Many of the animals were, as this one, by then down with septic pneumonia. It was believed that the infection had been spread either by the railway horse trucks in France, or by the horseboxes on the ship. Our battery landed without mishap. Guns are lowered from a troopship by being hoisted out of the hold by the ship's winches and ordinary derricks, by means of a hook which is passed through the trail-eye of the guns. One of the guns of one of the 18-pounder batteries of our brigade came down with a run, and landed on the dock on the muzzle. We heard that one of the pawls had broken on the forward winch. As a result one of the Greek dockside labourers lost his leg; the gun carriage and wheels were reduced to fragments.

We marched through the town with anxious eyes upon the team-horses, as we had no idea how they would manage the heavy vehicles, after eight or nine days on board ship, without proper exercise, and only hay and bran feeds. However, they managed the nine miles – part of it over the worst apologies for roads I had ever seen – without difficulty. Leaving Salonica, we waded through a lake of pale green slime about the size of a tennis court, and fully 2ft deep. Into this pond, natives were tipping lumps of rock from small carts, and the overflow was trickling into the deep ditches on either side of the road, as we waded through. The stone was green in colour and soft, so that the heavy vehicles ground up the stones into green porridge, as they went across. The life of a driver of an army motor lorry on this road, at that time, was reckoned to be six weeks; then he went to hospital. Macedonia normally uses only dirt tracks. To the natives' bullock wagons, streams, bogs, and swamps are matters of no importance. The ox wagons take no notice of such minor hindrances. It was a pretty sight to see the beautiful fawn oxen slowly marching to market, pulling the wagons, loaded with farm produce, at their slow, steady pace, urged on by the goad of the classics (a long pole with a broken nail in the end). The wheels were solid discs of wood, the axles, innocent of any grease, came through the centre of the disc wheels, and set up a continuous screaming that could be heard for miles. In Macedonia the oxen are costly, and cared for with the utmost solicitude. The cheaper beasts of burden – ponies and donkeys – are half-starved and brutally ill-treated. The oxen, however, are sleek, well-fed, and almost coddled. They are given straw for bedding at night when they lie down, in the open, behind the wagons; they have their forelocks and tails dyed orange, and like every other draught animal in Macedonia, wear a necklace of bright blue beads, as a protection against the evil eye. These oxen are not shod with the small twin, oval shoes of the French and Belgian working cattle. There are no clips to pass between the cleft of the foot. The shoe is a flat plate, rather like that of the Arab horse. The method of shoeing is as follows. The legs of the ox are tied together in pairs, foreleg to foreleg, and hind to hind, after which a stout pole is slipped between the pairs of legs from behind, and the huge fawn beast is turned upside down, and lies on its back, with its feet in the air, for the shoeing smith to work on at his ease. This is not for the greater safety of the blacksmith, as nothing could be more amiable and gentle than the Macedonian draught oxen. It is merely the easiest method of doing the job and, in Greece, the easiest way is the only way.

We finally reached our camping ground by branching off the Monastir Road to a muddy plain, known as Dudular. Why it had a name we never discovered. It was nothing better than a muddy stretch of land that had once been cultivated.

No one troubled to warn us that wind shelter for the horses was absolutely necessary. We selected the only bit of land that had a hard subsoil, and set up our tents, made horse lines, and encamped as best we could.

We stayed for nearly two months in that desolate spot, while the horses recovered from the sarcoptic mange they had caught on the journey from France.

The conditions of life at Dudular were very hard. Down from the snow mountains blows the wind known as the 'Vardar'. It blows with gale force for about three days, continuously each fortnight. The cold is intense, almost arctic, and the wind sweeps down the valleys driving with it particles of ice, gravel and small stones. During a Vardar later, sixteen horses, in our brigade, were frozen to death in one night. The cold in ordinary bell tents was terrible. There were very few tents at our disposal which was probably fortunate as the men had to sleep, fifteen to a tent, and so got some warmth. No floorboards were provided, nothing beyond bare rations and forage was supplied to us, and, as nobody from the local staff ever came near us, we had to fend for ourselves.

After a while it was quite obvious that the men must have something better, so we went foraging for ourselves. The Church Army came to our rescue, and, from one of their depots at the base, we collected a magnificent gift of comforts, games, cocoa, and a gramophone with records. I started an enterprising canteen, which I stocked with all kinds of things bought from the Salonica shops. In the shops I traded with the Spanish-speaking Jews aided by my broker, a smart young Jew of about thirteen years. I bought everything – charcoal, figs and blacking, ladies' blouses and beer, through my child broker, who, in return for his five per cent commission, enabled me to stock my canteen at wholesale prices at least forty per cent under shop prices. My canteen made large profits, and thereby we began to build up a battery fund to be used to provide prizes for the various competitions which we held amongst the men, and for other purposes proper for a battery fund. One of my best lines was the enormous tangerines called Mandarini. These I bought, in classical Greek, from the boatmen in the harbour by the thousand. My selling price for tangerines being one third that of the local hawkers – my figs were sold at half local prices – the canteen tent was resorted to by all units in the neighbourhood; I allowed any British soldier to buy at my shop, and, the prices being attractive, the stock was sold out in no time. I, therefore, had the interest of riding down to Salonica, with our cook's cart in attendance, quite frequently. The Grand Bazaar de Lyons, as the French canteen is called, was in those days open to the British, and there I bought the finest French chocolate in huge slabs, good wine for the officers' mess, and all sorts of things not usually to be found in army canteens.

The Church Army excepted, no one took the slightest interest in our little camp but the doctors of the Serbian Hospital. This was a curious unit. Its patients were Serbian soldiers, the doctors were English, and the nurses were French women, with the great Red Cross blazing on the front of their aprons. Their friendliness and kindness to a forlorn little camp like ours was as welcome as it could be.

The dreadful monotony was relieved by an occasional concert at the Serbian Hospital – one of their ambulance drivers was a tenor from the Paris Opera – now and then a brigade concert in the open air, and, at intervals, a bombing raid by a squadron of German aeroplanes.

Visits to, and from, the Serbian Hospital were only made possible by fording the rapid Galiko River, which lay between us. As the river had quicksands here and there and the water was girth deep, fording the river required a careful rider.

At last the mange was overcome, and we got orders to proceed up the line. We started to harness up and break camp in a Vardar wind. Hands got so cold that it took us hours above our normal time to harness up, after which it took another two hours to get the wretched horses to face the wind.

Our first march landed us at Topsin, the dirtiest camp we had seen yet, and reflecting no credit upon the French Army to whom it belonged. A broken-down vehicle delayed me for hours. I had to get a new shaft from somewhere on the way, and when at last I arrived I found my servant had secured me one of the wire-netting beds in a hut, and opened my valise on it. Insomnia is not a trouble of soldiers on active service, and it was not until I woke the next morning that I discovered that my mattress, in the valise, consisted of four pairs of heavy hob-nailed marching boots.

Next morning, we found the Vardar wind had finished. It was pleasant and sunny. An escort of the Lothian and Border Horse acted as guides to any unit travelling up the line by itself in Macedonia. The country is wild and scarcely populated, and maps were indefinite and far from reliable. As we marched across a hilly country covered with scrub and intersected by precipitous ravines (called Deres) some kind of escort was necessary, especially as the villages in the hills around were inhabited by people of extremely primitive and predatory habits.

These hill people living on the borders in the Balkans, like all border highlanders are a wild lot, the most handsome men I have ever seen, with faces like eagles, white kilts like circus girls, and with large wool balls on the points of their shoes. This native bill-costume has been adopted as the uniform of the Greek lifeguards, the Evzones.

After various misadventures, chiefly, if not entirely, due to the senseless orders we received – such as to march as a brigade in pitch darkness across a road-less moor with an interval of 1,500yds between batteries – we eventually arrived at Karasouli.

(When we came down the line, six months later, and the relative positions of the opposing armies were identical, we marched down in broad daylight, without any intervals whatever, and in perfect safety. By then, of course, we knew the line, and our own divisional staff were able to give rational orders without interference from the higher powers.)

Our poor horses, which, by that time, had only partially recovered, had to drag our heavy guns and wagons miles across yielding and boggy road-less country, because some unknown staff officer either could not, or would not, trouble to find out whether our route was hidden from the enemy. There was, in fact, no enemy observation on the entire route until far beyond Karasouli. After leaving there, we were eventually ordered to camp in a valley in full view of a Bulgar observation balloon, and were shelled out of it after two hours of daylight.

Incompetence could go no further, we thought, but subsequent experience proved that we were wrong.

Having extricated the battery from this unfortunate predicament, I led the entire unit out of the valley where we had been ordered to camp. The other officers with the battery staff – signallers on horseback – had ridden off to reconnoitre the hills to our left, where the battery was to come into action. By this time I had, of course, become aware of the direction where the enemy had fired their guns from, and selected another valley, which seemed likely to be hidden from hostile observation. It was all guesswork, as I had not the least information as to which range of hills was in enemy possession and which in our own. However, as no enemy fire followed us into the new valley, I judged it to be clear of observation, and constructed horse lines in the usual manner, and sent one of the shoeing smiths off on a horse to advise the other officers, now out of sight among the hills, where we had hidden ourselves. That evening I got orders to join the others, an extra officer having arrived to relieve me with the horses. I had to leave at 5.00 am to reach the position indicated at the time ordered.

And here, Driver 'W', attached from the Army Service Corps (ASC), proved his mettle. He was an old soldier, who, at one time, had held the rank of a senior NCO in the field artillery. He was now at least 45-years-old, had, I believe, earned his living in the boxing ring, and as a handyman in a racing stable. He was as tough as the sole of a boot, as dependable as a ship's chronometer, and the finest long-rein driver imaginable.

He woke me as ordered at 4.00 am in bright moonlight, in a temperature of certainly not more than 50°F. The two-wheeled conveyance I had ordered, the Maltese cart, was at the door of my tent, and, having swallowed a cup of welcome cocoa each, we started sitting side by side on my valise. A Maltese cart has neither seat nor springs, and, except for the shafts, is practically unbreakable. One of the shafts of this Maltese cart had been broken on the march, and the sergeant major and I had repaired it on the road, as best we could, with two strips of wood wrenched off a biscuit box, and many whippings of strong whipcord. The repair to the shaft was, however, strictly temporary in intention, and a mere makeshift.

Driver 'W', however, was no novice. He had harnessed the powerful, if clumsy, 16 hand pair of chestnuts from the water cart to the Maltese cart so that the sound shaft was between the horses. The broken shaft bent and gave with every stride of the team, as we went off at a sharp trot across the valley, fording a stream, following the rough dirt track through swamps and scrub, until we reached the range of hills up which the advance party had disappeared the day before. This was my first experience of travelling by compass in the day in completely unknown country. Beginner's luck stood me in good stead, and we arrived at the foot of the hills quite according to plan. We found a track up the face of the hill, which had a gradient of not less than one in four. Driver 'W' put our powerful horses at it at a hand-gallop. His uncannily skilful driving kept all the strain of our furious career on the one sound shaft, and we arrived safely, charging like wild Turcoman cavalry on to the proper dirt track which wound up among the hills above us.

It was then getting lighter, and we found the rest of the officers without difficulty. That day the guns came up and we occupied a retired position for a day or two. We were, nominally, in action, but as the enemy positions lay, at least, at double our extreme range, the position we occupied was utterly useless, and the guns might as well have been 40 miles away in Salonica town for all the good they were.

Our battery had, by then, a most curious command. The major had been promoted to colonel, and gone off to command a brigade somewhere. Our officers had none of them more than one star, so that we could now boast of no officer of higher rank than second lieutenant.

The right section commander, Second Lieutenant 'M' became de facto battery commander, and, at once, the battery improved out of all knowledge. He continued in command of the battery, with the exception of short periods when he was otherwise engaged, right up to the Armistice. For over two years, he led his battery in Salonica, Palestine and in France with continuous success, avoiding any semblance of a mistake. A good captain means a happy ship at sea. Thanks to the qualities of 'M', our battery was a happy battery. The shooting was extremely good, the telephone, and other signalling, was above the average, the horses, eventually, as good as any in the army (we won five first prizes in the First Army Horse Show, near Aire, in 1918), and, in short, the rather second-rate show I had joined in 1916, near Arras, became a unit of first class reputation, and one to which everyone of us was proud to belong.

In the meantime, the bachelor battery – all the officers were, from now onwards, bachelors – with its five second lieutenant officers, marched down the slopes of Baraka Hills to their new, and useful, position in the Cidemli Dere.

The Cidemli Dere, and its subsidiary ravines, contained practically the whole British Army in one part of the line. Had the enemy possessed the least imagination, or any reliable maps, or both, they could not have failed to realise that the troops could not be anywhere else. There was no other cover. But, apparently, the most efficient Austrian gunners who worked for the Bulgars were never ordered to 'search' the Cidemli Dere from end to end. Had they done so, the entire British force between Jumeau Ravine and the Vardar River would have been driven out of their tenable positions. Every day we lived there, we wondered when the obvious would occur to our friends the enemy. Accurate counter-battery work they understood, and executed with unpleasant results to us on more than one occasion. They had most efficiently handled 8-inch and 5.9-inch and 42-inch howitzer batteries whose shooting was, at least as good as that of any German gunners we came across, but no one in the Bulgar higher command seemed intelligent enough to realise that every single battery, battalions of infantry, machine gunners, and all the rest of the combatant units in our sector were, necessarily, huddled together by the river which flowed down the only valley deep enough to hide them from direct observation, from the commanding heights, called 'The Pips', which their own troops permanently occupied.

Every day I served as a soldier, Napoleon's famous dictum that 'Wars are won, not by the brilliance of the victors, but owing to the mistakes of the defeated' became more evidently true. Over and over again, lack of imagination, failure to form a picture of the obvious dispositions of the opposing forces, must have allowed both sides to occupy, and eventually extricate themselves from, most dangerous situations. It became quite clear to all thoughtful amateur soldiers of intelligence, that neither side understood the proper use and study of the contoured maps and aeroplane photographs, of which so lavish a supply was always at the disposal of higher commands.

Training in the proper use of maps is of the first importance in modern war. Excepting the artillery and engineers, where it is impossible to do anything right without accurate map work, we found no branch of the British Army which had been trained, adequately, in reading a map, and, without doubt, this was equally true of our opponents.

Orders came from brigade that we were to establish a forward section, and 'M' and I, accompanied by Colonel 'D', went off on foot, and finally selected an abandoned French position by the ruins of Bekerli village. 'M' then gave me command of the left section and orders to occupy the position. This was my first independent command of guns in action, and I was, naturally, most enthusiastic at the prospect.

'M' and I reconnoitred our route in daylight. As the whole area was under direct observation from the Bulgar OPs on the lofty Pip Range opposite, no guns, or columns of troops, ever moved except under cover of darkness, but small parties could safely go about in the open without fear of drawing shellfire.

The change from trench conditions in France was most welcome. Instead of trudging along deep communication trenches on slippery duckboards, we now could go down little pleasant glens on tracks beside little clear running streams. For scenery we had exchanged miles of the monotony of walls of mud and sandbags, for views of hills and mountains, similar to the scenery of the English Lake District. The hillsides were covered with scrub and flowering thorny creepers, which, although they quickly covered one's boots with a network of deep scratches, gave one the illusion of being a country gentleman inspecting the wilder portions of his estates. We felt that we were no longer living the rat-like semi-subterranean existence we had been driven to in the trench conditions in France.

After dark I set off on horseback, leading my section. Our drivers had not yet acquired fully their eventual ability to negotiate road-less broken country in pitch darkness, and, before long, we came to a sudden halt. What had happened was that, in a track which led between two high banks, the lead driver of my leading team, No. 3 gun, had driven too far to the right, the gun had slowly climbed the slope, and, eventually, turned over upside down. Two and a half tons was going to take some righting with the inadequate manpower at my disposal, no tackle, and no light to work by. However, nothing is impossible if it has to be done. By dismounting the wheel and centre drivers of the teams behind, and hooking the drag-ropes to the axle rings, my total manpower, including gunners, drivers, and cooks, and, of course, myself and groom, just sufficed to turn the gun right side up and hold it on the almost perpendicular bank, while the powerful gun team, reinforced with the willing pair of leaders from the following wagon, dragged it forward and down to the level track again, and we were able to continue our route.

The next, and most serious, obstacle, was Bekerli ford, where the track crossed a swiftly flowing river. I halted the column and rode my horse into the river to try the underwater conditions. I found that the going underwater was reasonably good, and that, with eight horses to a team, we ought to be able to get across safely. It was then absolutely dark, and a little to the left of the ford I had discovered that there was a hole in the bottom of the river deep enough to submerge an entire gun or wagon that was unlucky enough to get into it. Fortunately I had plenty of cigarettes with me. The method which I adopted proved successful. I lit a cigarette and rode into the river, having first instructed the lead drivers to drive straight at my red cigarette tip and follow me out of the river, keeping up a fast trot regardless of anything. As each team arrived I let them get as close as I dared; this was within about 4ft. Having as my mount one of the officers' chargers intended for the 12th Lancers, which we had acquired before leaving France, I could afford to take a chance. He was as handy and obedient as a cow-pony, and could turn on the proverbial sixpence. I tried him first, and found that, even in water up to the belly, and in pitch darkness, he could be trusted to do whatever I wanted. Team after team came charging through the river in showers of spray and managed to scramble up the steep muddy slope on the other side, which the passage of each dripping team made more slippery and difficult. The last two vehicles only just managed the slippery ascent, although we had increased their teams to twelve horses each. There was not much further to go, and, before daylight, my two guns were safely concealed in the deserted gun pits, which had been originally occupied by a pair of French 75s.

Very hard work had to be done to make the position reasonably secure. Sandbags, and other stores, were unobtainable. The position was far advanced, and the only troops in front of us were a company of the Queen's Westminsters, who occupied the near slopes of a hill called Mamelon Vert. The British line was not continuous. Our division was holding a front of, roughly 16 miles – instead of the 1,500yds or so they had been responsible for in France. No-man's-land was 2½ miles across, instead of the 80yds to 150yds customary near Arras. It was another kind of war altogether. With the exception of an occasional Bulgar raiding party which, now and again, did its best to capture isolated detachments occupying some lonely trench on a hilltop in front of our main lines, no target presented itself within range of infantry weapons.

On the other hand it was a gunner's paradise. OPs were the tops of easily climbed, isolated hills, instead of small holes in the ground exposed to trench mortar and machine gun fire. The enemy lines were a panorama of fortifications between hills and valleys, instead of a vague line of brown heaps of mud – all one could see of the parapets of the German trenches in France. Visibility was remarkable. From the top of Mamelon Vert in the clear, keen air I could distinguish, with certainty, cows. from horses at a distance of 15 miles, with my field glasses. Shooting, as in all hilly country, was as interesting as it was difficult. Problems of angle-of-sight arose every day. In shooting at long ranges, among hills and valleys, as every mountain battery gunner knows, a trifle of deflection, intentional or, caused by a puff of wind, may easily lengthen or shorten a range by hundreds of yards by bringing the line of fire to a higher or lower level. To shoot with accuracy in mountain country, the angle-of-sight (which is the relative level of gun and target) must be altered whenever deflection is altered, and a mental picture of the line of flight of the shell from gun to target has to be continuously kept before the observer. Gunnery among the mountains and gunnery in flat country have little, or no, connection. Gunnery problems on the flat are very simple arithmetic to the commander of a mountain battery. It was not long before we understood why the terms 'OC mountain battery', and 'gunnery expert' are synonymous in the British Army in India, and we realised, simultaneously, that shrapnel shell for the 18-pounders was sheer waste of transport. Effective air bursts (10 minutes above the line of sight) are an impossible ideal where the angle of sight varies several degrees between two successive rounds.

The gun pits, at the Bekerli position, had to be designed on novel lines. My extreme left target, a protective barrage, was fired at 880yds range, involving a kind of mashie-shot fired with first charge so as to clear the hill between gun and the valley where enemy attack was to be stopped by our bursting shells; my extreme right target had a line of fire at an angle of 196 degrees from my extreme left target. Most of the targets were at a range of 6,500yds to 7,200yds, our extreme range. The enormous switch, due to our position being actually in front of all the infantry, except one advanced company, involved an extraordinary opening in the front of the gun pits, and a correspondingly large platform to allow the trail of the gun to swing round through more than half a circle. As no approach to the position was safe in daylight, a minimum of 2,500 rounds had to be kept in the position.

When the gun pits were finished, dumps had to be constructed for all the ammunition. As any kind of hole in the ground fills up with water in Macedonia, all ammunition had to be stored above ground and protected from shellfire and aeroplane bombs with anything procurable. Our spades were kept busy.

I obtained fifty sandbags, otherwise unprocurable, in the following remarkable manner. One morning, about midday, I noticed a large party of Bulgars going to get their dinner in a ravine in the enemy lines. They were, roughly, 6,500yds from the hill top from which I saw them. Next day, at the same time, I climbed the same hill with a telephone and the company sergeant major of the local infantry. Soon we saw the same large party of Bulgars lining up for their dinner issue. I fired one round well over them on an earthwork I had previously registered, to get the wind correction for the day, then, dropping 450yds and altering my line, I landed a beautiful burst right among the lunch party. After watching the stretcher-bearers remove the casualties, the infantry company sergeant major (CSM) was so full of enthusiasm and admiration that he said I could have anything I wanted out of his company stores. Feeling somewhat like Salome dancing before Herod, I diffidently suggested a bale of sandbags – a treasure unheard of to gunners in Macedonia – and felt that I had asked for John the Baptist's head on a charger at least. But the CSM kept his word, and delivered the sandbags at the gun position the same afternoon.

This was good, if lucky, shooting. My first round at the target had to be a hit, or the target would disappear. As I built up my ammunition dump with my present of sandbags, I felt like the golf enthusiast who has done a hole-in-one. Undeniably lucky, but a good shot too.

About this time a perfectly delightful episode took place at a neighbouring battalion HQ where I happened to be at the time on some business errand. The night before an officer's patrol had captured and brought in the Bulgar sergeant who had been leading a party attempting to raid one of our posts.

The prisoner was brought down to battalion HQ during the morning for the colonel's inspection. The orderly officer, wishing to make a formal affair of the somewhat rare appearance of a Bulgar prisoner, paraded an armed guard which could only be composed of the odds and ends to be found at battalion HQ, such as cooks, servants, clerks, runners, and the usual rabble. Their buttons shone like planets, their boots were polished, and their clothes were newly issued from store. The orderly officer duly inspected arms in a perfunctory manner and concluded with the customary 'ease springs'. That one of the rifles must have been loaded remained unnoticed, and, when the triggers were pulled, it went off with a bang, and the little Bulgar sergeant in extreme apprehension bolted down the valley like a coursed rabbit. The entire guard and onlookers then pursued him, mostly completely unarmed, and a species of paper chase took place which ended in the Bulgar being brought back crestfallen. It was not easy to explain to a man, of whose language nobody knew one word, that the discharge of the rifle was an accident, and that we were not in the habit of shooting our prisoners. However, a pat on the shoulder and the offer of a cigarette is good Esperanto for 'don't worry', and soon the little prisoner was all smiles again.

Not long after we were shelled out of the Bekerli position. For all its good points, of which the chief was a 90ft deep well of pure, sparkling water alongside the guns, water so pure that no admixture of the abominable chlorine we hated so needed to be used with it, the position had one very serious drawback.

Trees in Macedonia are so uncommon that a large tree is marked on the maps. We knew that the Bulgar maps were the same in origin as the maps we used ourselves. Once our guns were spotted firing by an aeroplane, the position could be accurately marked down by the fact that there was a big tree marked on the map within 10yds of the guns. 'M' and I had regarded this tree as an imperative reason why we should not occupy the position. When we were overruled and ordered to put our forward guns there, we decided to double the aeroplane scouts who always swept the sky with field-glasses when the guns were firing, as, for all our cunning camouflage of the gun pits, the tree would give our position away to any aeroplane observer. The position was free of any ground observation, but, thanks to the tree being accurately marked on the map, artillery could strafe us easily by map shooting without observation.

Unfortunately, one morning an aeroplane, flying so low in the next valley that it was hidden by the hills between us and it, slid quietly over the ridge while we were firing. No blame could be attached to the aeroplane scout, Gunner 'L', the best in our battery; his sharp ears were not at fault as the aeroplane engine was not running, and the aeroplane glided suddenly over the ridge without warning. The next day we got it well and properly. Two counter-batteries, a 4.2-inch howitzer, and a 5.9-inch gun, fired at us continuously, each battery firing a gun at ten seconds interval for 1½ hours.

The guns were slightly damaged. Not one round of all our 2,500 was exploded, all the personnel was withdrawn unscratched, and the only casualty was my blue enamelled teapot, which had a splinter clean through it. The shooting of the Austrian counter-batteries was extremely good for map shooting. I watched, from a safe distance naturally, the 100lb shells from the 5.9-inch battery bursting all round my beautifully neat gun pits; I lay down on top of the ridge which the enemy aeroplane had slid so quietly over, and admired a piece of good shooting until the 4.2-inch battery began to drop a few beside me, after which I assembled my men and departed hurriedly.

After an interval in a dull locality half a mile west of the Bekerli position – the only thing of interest here was that a brace of partridges occupied a nest 20yds or so from the guns – the left section rejoined the right, and, once more, was ordered to occupy a dangerous position which had no proper flash cover. A 4.5-inch howitzer needs 16ft of cover to conceal its flash from ground observation. Here we had less than 10ft, and that only consisted of trees whose leaves were a far from complete screen.

We now had to have over five thousand rounds of high explosive with us, of which only eight hundred were able to be kept in a properly constructed shell-proof ammunition dump. The remainder were placed as best we could manage. We had nothing to use for protection, and all we could provide was cover from aeroplane observation. Two thousand four hundred rounds were piled in boxes under some trees which had overhanging branches.

I could see 'M' regarded the situation with considerable misgiving, and he was, as usual, right in his opinion.

While the left section, still under my command, was preparing to carry out a bombardment of a target, which we had registered the day before – 150 rounds were lying unboxed beside No. 4 gun – the 5.9-inch battery opened on us. After seeing that they had successfully bracketed the section in three rounds, I withdrew the men. My corporal and I had just got the dial-sights off the guns when the fourth round lifted the top off one of the big trees just in front of us. Corporal 'J' and I flopped into the river and ran down stream. We had only just left in time. The next 5.9-inch detonated right on top of the 150 rounds of high explosive beside No. 4 gun. The gun went up in the air about 60ft or 80ft and the whole valley was filled with soot-coloured smoke. The crash of 150 rounds of 4.5-inch high explosive exploding together was, literally, deafening. We were used to loud noises, as all gunners are, but this noise had a head-splitting quality of its own, and the explosion shook the ground like a small earthquake.

The 5.9-inch battery continued to plaster us unmercifully, and, from the top of the hill on which the village of Cidemli stood nearby, we watched the bombardment, and saw the most extraordinary things take place. The enemy shells were painted pale blue and were over 2ft long. One of them landed right on top of our ammunition dump and detonated beautifully. As dump builders, with plenty of experience but a shortage of material, we were entitled to feel proud that the roof of our dump stood the strain, and the burster of big stones out of the riverbed prevented every single round of the 900 inside from exploding.

Then we saw two miracles happen in quick succession. A couple of 5.9s landed right on our 2,400 rounds of ammunition in wooden boxes hidden under the trees by the riverbank. They detonated perfectly, and had our ammunition followed suit the result would have been comparable to a volcano. But nothing happened except that the wood of a couple of boxes was found later to be somewhat charred, and one charge in one of the boxes had caught fire.

The other miracle is hard to believe, but I saw it with my own eyes. One of these large 100-pound shells landed right in the stream, and did not explode. It bounced off the stony bottom of the stream at an angle of 90 degrees from its line of flight, and went whirling right over the Cidemli hill and village and landed again in the stream on the other side, where I saw it lying in the water like a pale torpedo as I walked past the next day.

This story of the bouncing 5.9-inch sounds like a travellers tale. It is, however, a literally accurate description of what happened under my own eyes at under 100yds distance.

After the somewhat hectic incidents above described we moved to a position higher up the river to our right, and occupied some abandoned gun pits on the right bank of the river.

This position gave evidences of much work on the part of the previous tenants. The quarters for the officers and men (especially the officers) had been rendered shellproof against bombardment by guns of the heaviest possible calibre. My own dugout was, probably, 15-inch proof, and provided with an excellent bedstead of the usual pit-prop and wire netting construction. When my servant the admirable Gunner 'C', who later died of wounds near Beersheba, had constructed an armchair of forty-five ammunition boxes, with the seat padded with a sand bag stuffed with grass, and a washstand of which the basin was a spare steel helmet, I had as fine a bedroom as any man could wish.

Unfortunately the energies of the former tenants of our new position had not included any protection whatever for the guns, and only the most elementary head cover for the telephonists' dugout, which did not appear to be proof against a shell of the smallest possible calibre. Our predecessors had, evidently, been of the 'let's be comfortable' school; their arrangements for fighting had clearly been in the nature of afterthoughts. Tactically, however, the position had been well selected, concealment was admirable and the field of fire was extensive, and under easy observation from Rook and Crow Hills a mile or so in front of the guns.

A few days after we had established ourselves in this new position, the general, or the commander Royal Artillery (CRA) as he is called, paid us a call. He congratulated 'M' – on the excellent behaviour of the battery under the most trying conditions, said that he was proud of our performance and had no intention of introducing a new battery commander to take over the command. Second Lieutenant 'M', therefore, the de facto commander of D/302, was to appear in the next list of Salonica honours and awards, as promoted to major. On the CRA asking 'M' which of his officers he preferred as his captain, he very kindly asked for myself, and so my promotion to captain appeared in the same Salonica list of honours.

I should imagine that 'M's rise from second lieutenant to major in one step was unique. It was, in my opinion, a tardy recognition of his exceptional qualities as a battery commander, which ought to have been recognised long before by the award of acting rank in accordance with his responsibilities. In congratulating me later on my promotion, the CRA, after a courteous handshake, said that he was certain that a rise from the rank of gunner to that of captain in seven months was a record in the history of the Royal Regiment of Artillery.

My excellent batman procured four extra stars and some braid from somewhere in the usual miraculous way of a good army servant. One does not enquire too closely on active service whence such things are obtained. They may have, originally, graced 'M's sleeves, for now his solitary star had given place to a crown. But the braid could not have been from that source of supply as his servant had to provide three rows per cuff, instead of the original solitary row which goes with the lonely star of a second lieutenant.

I do not propose to relate more details of our gunnery experiences on this front, or to recount our part in the offensive that failed, so tragically, in the Jumeau Ravine. In this enterprise, our division had the unenviable duty of making a demonstration in force against that impregnable stronghold of the Makukovo Salient which we called 'the Nose'. The object of this demonstration was to draw artillery fire away from the real objective, the high Belashitza mountain range. The demonstration failed in its object. The unreality of an attack on 'the Nose' must have been evident from the start. It was impregnable to troops advancing in the open across 2½ miles of no-man's-land under full observation, and the Bulgars confined their defensive fire against the 60th Division to a terrific trench mortar barrage, reserving the whole strength of their artillery fire for the main body of attackers who were conducting the real offensive further east, which became a small disaster. The British infantry were bombarded in the ravine with high explosive and gas from every battery of heavy artillery at the enemy's disposal. One battalion only of the division attacking reached its objective, commanded by the senior surviving NCO, a corporal – all the officers having become casualties. They eventually retired to their original positions.

The division on our right managed to advance rather more than halfway up the Belashitza mountains. They dug in on the green slopes, which were gradually shelled into what, from our sector, looked like a series of ploughed fields of red earth, and they also had to retire later in conformity with their neighbours on the right.

In its own small way, the Jumeau Ravine affair was a complete failure. The Bulgar defence line was far too strong to be captured by the limited opposing troops, and no further attempts were made to take it. It was a bitter experience for the troops who had suffered appalling casualties in the attack to hear that, at this particular period, a famous comedian was raising an easy laugh in a London music hall by singing a ditty with the refrain, 'If you don't want to fight, go to Salonica.'

The feelings of the men on the spot are beautifully, and truthfully, portrayed in Owen Rutter's 'Song of Tiadatha'. And we wondered 'How the birds could sing so sweetly, how the sun could shine so brightly, when so many British soldiers lay so still upon the hillside.'

Salonica (General)

A more deadly and persistent adversary than the Bulgar soldier was the climate of Macedonia. We had survived the intense cold of the winter. So extreme was the cold that one night sixteen horses in our brigade were frozen to death. A driver in my former battery died of cold in the saddle on the march, and a private of the 2/16 London Battalion died of the cold during a thirty minutes halt on the march. Almost all the British Salonica Force lived, or existed, through these winters in ordinary bell tents without floorboards. The physical hardships were extraordinary. Owing to the difficulties of transport, on dirt tracks and inadequate railway lines, forage was often below half rations in the winter, and in the winter of 1916-17 many units turned all the mules loose to fend for themselves and gave all the forage to their horses. The mules throve wonderfully, and in the spring great sport was obtainable in rounding up the mules, which had gone completely wild. I personally led a kind of cowboy squadron mounted on our best horses. We rounded up dozens of mules, and, after selecting the best and most law-abiding for our own use, we advertised a weekly mule market where anyone short of an animal could obtain a useful mule in exchange for anything we had need of.

We traded mules for sacks of potatoes, sacks of tea, a marquee tent, a field kitchen, and almost every conceivable piece of army equipment.

We lived a kind of backwoods life in Salonica. The civilians, mostly of mixed Greek-Bulgar-Serb-Turk origin, had been evacuated by the French military authorities; units did the best they could to remain alive without interference, or help, from higher authorities. In this one respect the Salonica Army was the best and easiest to live in. One had no visits from wandering staff officers, whose unwelcome attentions led, invariably, to trouble in the form of disapproval in writing from higher authorities, without exception and inevitably, completely out of touch with the fighting troops and with the conditions under which they had to live and fight.

After we had survived the winter, the weather grew rapidly warmer. With the beat of a semi-tropical spring arrived that more active and deadly enemy the insect.

The insect life of Macedonia deserves a chapter to itself. The leading martial race of the insects of Macedonia was of course anopheles, the malaria mosquito. He was responsible for many deaths amongst the troops and reduced many units of the British Army to well below half strength. In the malaria season, an officer or man, who went off to hospital with fever never got back to his own unit. There was always some other battalion or brigade of artillery more desperately in need of reinforcements than his own. To avoid losing our officers and men, we determined never to send anybody to hospital. This law-unto-yourself attitude was common in Macedonia. Distances from authority were so great, and isolation was so complete, that any CO could act as he judged the wisest and for the best interests of his command, without fear of effective interference from outside.

Our malaria patients were put in charge of Fitter 'E'. In his workshop in the battery position – which, over, the door, had the amusing notice-board, 'Fitter J.E.'; hours, twelve to one, and one to twelve' – our malaria patients lay in wire-netting bunks and received their ration of quinine and tinned milk under the kindly and conscientious supervision of the fitter.

A minor wound I received from a lump of high explosive (HE) shell, which hit me in the neck on the OP on top of Baraka Mountain, was dressed and attended to by our Sergeant 'W', AVC, at the horse lines. By these contrivances a unit in Salonica was able to keep up its numbers in the malaria season.

After the malaria mosquito, the chief enemy was a large blood-sucking fly, rather like an elongated bluebottle, but with a bead of brightest emerald green. These creatures could reduce horses and mules to extreme debility in a very short time. Fortunately they only flourished in certain low-lying localities, and the animals could be kept free from their attacks. We ourselves, wearing in the hot weather, of necessity, shorts instead of breeches, and a shirt with sleeves rolled up, instead of a tunic, were bitten every day by these green bluebottles. They do not sting, and the first warning we had that we were being bled was the sight of one of these creatures at work. A quick slap and a splash of one's own blood all over the limb indicated that that one was disposed of. We must each have lost a pint or so of blood each week in this way.

There were all sorts of other insects, but for numbers the common fly, in areas where horses lived, outnumbered them all. On a hot night near Kalinovo I once hung up my new duck tunic on a tent pole and slept outside for coolness. In the morning my new tunic was invisible. There was a coating of flies on it as thick as a swarm of bees. And when the flies had been brushed off the colour of the garment had changed. In one night a duck khaki – about café-au-lait originally – had changed to the colour of black earth. The fly-blow specks were so numerous as not to leave any of the original colour showing between them.

Fortunately, except the green bluebottle and some unknown insect whose bite caused biliary fever, none of these pests did serious damage to the horses. Horses do not suffer from malaria and, by some curious omission, providence has not seen fit to trouble this country with the sandfly, whose bite reduces horses to the same condition of utter debility as men who have been stung by them.

Just before our division left the line it was ordered to capture and fortify a locality marked on the map as Gridiron Hill. The map, however, as every unit in the neighbourhood knew, was quite incorrect in that particular area. 'Gridiron Hill' on the map was in reality a valley on the ground.

There is no more certain method of committing suicide than to capture and fortify a valley in full view of the enemy OPs on the top of a range of mountains directly opposite and commanding the whole valley.

Corps insisted that their orders should be carried out. Evidently those responsible for this insane operation order were not going to be taught their business by mere 'regimental' people. The situation seemed likely to develop into an impasse.

Our general officer commanding (GOC) division was saved from an unfortunate dilemma by orders to embark for Egypt. General Bulfin, soon to be promoted by General Allenby to the command of an army corps, would certainly have had the 'father and mother of a row' with someone over such an order. But providence intervened and saved us from an impossible situation.

Of the march down to Salonica, to embark for Egypt, I must relate a perfectly ridiculous incident.

Invariably in the army when a unit is ordered to transfer permanently any of the men or animals to another unit, the sergeant major is instructed to select the most worthless for despatch. This is regarded as a heaven sent opportunity to get rid of lazy, or troublesome, men and disgraceful-looking horses and mules.

Just as we were leaving Kalinovo for our 40-mile march to the sea, a note arrived that each battery was to receive one limbered wagon and a pair of mules from the ASC. Simultaneously our wagon and mules arrived. The mules looked like a pair of pantomime goats. In appearance they were undersized, half starved, and, in contrast to our horses which were then in first class condition of fat, their coats were rough and faded.

We had packed up everything ready to move off, but here was an extra vehicle and team. We hastily threw into the limbered wagon all our spare stock of horseshoes surplus shovels and picks, which we had intended to leave behind as we had no room for them. On top we loaded our portable forge and the chaff-cutter, neither of which look ornamental on the ammunition wagons of a battery on the march. By then the contents of the limbered wagon must have weighed over a ton. The track was uneven with small but stiff hills. As usual, I rode at the rear of the column, but this time a long way to the rear, as I had instructed the driver of the disreputable vehicle which had been wished on to us at the last moment to keep so far behind the smart battery column that nobody passing would even think it belonged to the same outfit. I expected the scarecrow mules to give it up at the first bit of hard going. But they walked steadily on as if the load was a hundredweight, instead of fully a ton, ignoring hills, rough pieces of track, small streams, or any obstructions customarily to be found on Macedonian dirt tracks. They were evidently not the worthless wrecks their appearance would have led one to think. The Maltese cart had a mule in the shafts with a somewhat heavier load than it could manage. I rode forward and halted it and, after transferring part of the load to the limbered wagon, continued the march with these two mule-drawn vehicles under my immediate eye.

Eventually we reached Kukus, on the outskirts of which the whole brigade encamped together on a large flat area of hard and dry earth innocent of any grass whatever. The first day's march to Kukus was a short one, but the second day the whole division was to march as one unit over the mountains to the outskirts of Salonica itself. We were warned that the march would be a long one, about 25-miles for the artillery, which included a long and very severe hill, and that an early start would be made, and each artillery brigade must move off promptly to time.

Our moving-off time was 7.00 am. We harnessed up in plenty of time, and while awaiting the order to march a heavy thundershower occurred. Exactly at 7.00 am the colonel gave the order, '302nd Brigade Headquarters, walk march!' Not a vehicle moved. The colonel said a few words, not congratulatory, to the brigade sergeant major, who then called out in his most brigade sergeant majory voice, 'A Battery, walk march!' Again not a vehicle moved. The thundershower had turned the dry earth on our camping ground into a slimy surface on which no horse could get a foothold. All the efforts of all the gunners manhandling the wheels proved useless. Next, 'B Battery, walk march!' with the same negative result. It was the same with C Battery. But with D Battery, ours, it was slightly different. Not one of our magnificent teams could move an inch, but the two disreputable vehicles we were so ashamed of quietly marched on to the road without any apparent effort, and so the 302nd Brigade RFA for a few minutes was represented solely by these disgraceful looking turnouts drawn by animals that would have been refused scornfully by any itinerant tinker, and, the road being narrow and occupied with traffic in the other direction, the whole brigade was led until the first halt by these two extremely homely turnouts. The little mules cannot, of course, have been as wretched as they looked. A mule is an animal that often

55

looks almost worthless when he is, in fact, a compact little machine of whalebone and whipcord.

This pair of scarecrows had probably been doing at least four times the work of any of the beautifully fat horses, and a trifle like greasy slime underfoot was a daily experience not to be regarded as worthy of notice by any reasonable mule in hard condition. The load these little mules were easily pulling was quite as heavy, per animal, as any that the big handsome horses had to draw. But, as every muleteer knows, the strength of a mule is far greater than that of a horse nearly double his size.

At length we arrived at Salonica, returned all our packsaddles to store, and embarked on the ill-fated SS *Cestrian*. I write ill-fated for, after carrying us safely to Alexandria, she returned to Salonica, loaded a cargo of selected mules for the artillery, and was torpedoed and sent to the bottom on her way to Egypt.

CHAPTER 4

EEF Palestine

C/268 Brigade: a competent battery

After arriving in Alexandria we went to a camp for one night and proceeded to entrain for Palestine. And at Alexandria we saw our first example of an RTO who knew his job and did it. The trucks provided by the Egyptian State Railways were perfectly equipped. End-loading was the method, and our vehicles were run on in no time. The RTO was a Scotch territorial with one sleeve empty. Nothing was left undone to make our job easy, and it was quickly finished. No sooner was a string of trucks loaded than a gang of several hundred Labour Corps wallahs appeared from somewhere, and they, singing merrily, in time but not in tune, hauled the loaded trucks into a siding.

Off we went. Whenever the train stopped at a station in Egypt big hawkers appeared selling 'eggs acook', twenty for five piastres (a shilling), little hard-boiled Egyptian eggs, and a very welcome addition to our rations. We left Egypt and reached the Suez Canal. And here the extraordinary methods of the general staff began again. Everyone except us and one other battery of the 60th Divisional artillery was to detrain at Moascar. We two batteries were to go on to El Ferdan, detrain there, and become the nucleus of the artillery of the 74th Division. This piece of astonishing news we got, by word of mouth only, from the RTO at Moascar. We thought he was having a joke at our expense. But no. He showed us his written instructions. So off we went, transferred from our old division without a scrap of explanation or written instructions, and at El Ferdan, a bit of sand on the edge of nowhere, we detrained without any other orders, and with no brigade to report to, or any idea of what we were supposed to do.

57

We found some huts of tattered matting and put our beds down there; we rigged up horse lines on the sand by running ropes through the wagon wheels as usual, unpacked the cooking utensils and, after a meal, went to sleep.

So far the Egyptian Expeditionary Force (EEF) gave me the impression of an army with a magnificent railway system, and no other system at all. Afterwards, when I heard all about the First and Second Battles of Gaza I realised that, as usual, our first impression was quite reasonably correct.

Bit by bit the 74th Divisional artillery accumulated at El Ferdan. Three batteries to a brigade was the new order of the day. We were re-christened C Battery, 268th Brigade, and found ourselves commanded by a fine soldier, Colonel 'C', DSO, a real fighting man, a retired regular with no less than fifteen years' active service to his credit. We had an ammunition column with Indian drivers. The infantry were all dismounted yeomanry, farmers' sons from all over Great Britain, and physically probably the equals of any infantry we ever saw in the whole of the Allied armies.

Our postal address now became C/268 74th (Yeo.) Division EEF. Our divisional sign, the broken spur, was a token that though our infantry now bore the names of famous regiments, Devons, Norfolks, Black Watch, Welsh Fusiliers, etc., their real allegiance was to the Yeomanry of Devon, Norfolk, Ayr and Lanark, Wales, and other counties. The appearance of the transport of our new division was clear evidence that these units were not ordinary infantry but real horsemen.

We marched to Kantara, and crossed the Suez Canal by the bridge (Kantara is the Arabic for a bridge), and marched to the biggest base camp I had ever seen. Possibly the base camp at Kantara was the largest in the whole British Army. It was like a great city, and to walk or ride down the main streets as an officer was to have one's right hand wagging up and down acknowledging salutes with the monotonous movement of the pendulum of a kitchen clock.

Then we entrained once more, this time for Belah, which was railhead, and on this trip we learned our first lesson about the Palestine coast, which is that at night the dew is so heavy that a man sleeping in the open will be soaked to the skin unless he sleeps under a waterproof. The trucks we travelled in on the Palestine Railway had no overhead cover. There were no seats whatever, and knowing nothing about the dew we lay down on the floor as we were. When daylight came all our belongings were as sopping as we were and as covered with smuts, the floor was half an inch deep in water, and our blankets were awash. Very temporary repairs were soon effected; we had long ago ceased to trouble about trifles, and we looked out with interest at the real desert ending to the left in the high ridge of sandhills on the coast. From time to time we watered the horses when the train stopped at little stations, sandbagged and loopholed and surrounded with barbed wire like blockhouses. This was good; evidently in the EEF, unlike the BEF, it was recognised that horses travelling by train need water. At last we arrived, after a train journey of nearly eighteen hours in open trucks, at railhead, having travelled 135 miles in this fashion.

Belah was a spot of singularly uninviting appearance. The entire prospect consisted of miles and miles of flat, dusty earth, for ornament there were a few tanks containing water for the engine, and a bell tent here and there, quivering in the heat of the baking sun. There was no platform. The whole railway track lay upon loose sand, and a ramp of earth had been raised to the level of the trucks so that vehicles and animals were easily unloaded. We hooked in, marched a mile or so away from railhead, and encamped in a dry watercourse. We had no tents whatever. The sun heat was terrific, and the best we could provide for the men was an issue of spare blankets propped up on anything to give them a bit of shade. Remarkably ingenious shelters were soon erected with the aid of shovels, swingletrees, draught poles and other props borrowed from the vehicles. Mindful of the dew, we covered the stores and the officers' mess with the large canvas gun sheets. Enough dew collected overnight in our gun sheet to provide each officer with half a canvas bucket of dirty water to wash in. Washing in the desert is simple, even if you have no water to waste. With a towel and your own perspiration even the dustiest face and hands soon assume the appearance of cleanliness. After the sun has been busy for three or four weeks and everyone is mahogany-coloured, the smears unavoidably left by this process are not noticeable.

Round about Belah we practised all kinds of manoeuvres for moving warfare. General Allenby arrived and became GOC, and it was quite evident that offensive operations were being planned. Far away on the horizon we could see, at ten miles distance, the great earth cone called a Tel which served as a lookout post for the Turks at Gaza. Camels were issued with native drivers for baggage and water transport. We gradually became acclimatised, and learned to do without water for long periods.

In the desert, whenever possible, troops march at night and sleep through the heat of the day. This is the ideal; marching at night is agreeable and interesting in a country with no roads or obstructions, where one finds one's way entirely by compass bearings marching on a selected star. Accurate bearings have to be taken, from the map, of the destination aimed at; while marching, the particular star selected must not be confused with the many millions of others visible, and a fresh star must be chosen every twenty minutes or the line of march will end up very far from where was originally intended. This art we practised diligently, and became so proficient that we could travel without fear of error long distances at the canter. For mounted work an oil-compass is essential, in the ordinary kind the needle takes far too long to settle down and much time is wasted as the slightest movement of the horse starts the needle waving in all directions.

We became really a mounted unit. We would walk half a mile to ride a mile, sooner than walk the whole distance. Living in the saddle is the healthiest way of taking the necessary exercise in tropical heat, and we became all of us as fit and hard as any cowboys.

Soon there were long reconnaissance rides to select gun positions for the attack on Beersheba. Parties of artillery officers rode out forty miles, and escorted by Australian cavalry – mostly of the magnificent Australian Light Horse – went right across the fifteen miles of no-man's-land and across the dry bed of the Wadi Saba. Squadrons of Turk Circassian cavalry were often to be seen moving about on their little white horses. They were not dangerous as any reasonably mounted English or Australian soldier could travel at twice their speed.

This was war in the open indeed. Forage, and rations, both for four days, were carried on the saddle. Bedding, reduced to a groundsheet and a blanket, was carried on the saddle in place of wallets, two bivouac sheets were strapped behind, and off we went 'into the blue' like Australian sundowners, except that we were well-mounted, and they usually have to pad the hoofs.

We always travelled from water to water. Our usual first stop for water was the Wadi Ghuzee at the bottom of which there are vast pools of water below the rocks. These were pumped up into canvas troughs by RE parties where the horses were watered. At other times we watered at wells of incredible antiquity, for example at Urn Gerar, where in Biblical times Abraham 'digged wells'. At last the great day came, and the 74th Division set out for Gamli-Shellal, a sector of the line then being held by the 60th Division. There we remained for about a week while operation orders for the attack on Beersheba were issued and thoroughly digested. The day of the attack drew nearer. Our brigade had been allotted the task of bombarding the trenches of the outlying work which must be carried before the main Beersheba positions could be attacked. Unless machine gun fire was kept under by the artillery this preliminary attack would inevitably only succeed at the cost of very heavy casualties to the attacking troops.

It will hardly be believed that our brigade – responsible for this most important duty on which the success of the entire operation depended – never received any orders to march to the attack. But such was the case. One afternoon our major's brother, at that time orderly officer to the colonel, went out for a ride solely for a little exercise. About three o'clock he arrived back at brigade headquarters at full gallop, and reported that everybody had gone from the entire neighbourhood.

Colonel 'R' was just the man to deal with an emergency of this kind. Realising that someone had blundered he ordered the brigade to break camp and hook in. This we had practised until we could pack up and be ready in under half an hour. This time all previous records were broken. The colonel sent for me and ordered me to take charge of all the baggage and water camels, sick men and lame animals, and come along after the brigade as fast as I could get them along. The brigade set off on a forced march, and travelled all night to the wadi where their gun positions had been selected, and arrived in time for the attack at dawn next morning.

This march was a fearful strain on men and horses. Luckily both men and horses were 'fighting fit' and managed to arrive in time in spite of the heavy going. They had to march all night at the utmost speed they could manage. I came along at my leisure in the starlight, having to find my way by compass and memory. No forced march was possible for my column of heavily laden camels and invalids. But we got there by good luck and determination just before the battle started, in time for me to take charge of the supply of ammunition and water to our battery.

It was well for the operation that the command of the brigade was in the hands of a soldier of our colonel's experience. Many brigade commanders would have hesitated to move without orders, in which case the preliminary attack would have been held up with consequences most serious to the entire operation, and undoubtedly most serious for those who had failed to ensure that orders to move forward had reached our brigade.

Our confidence in the RA staff of our division was badly shaken by this inexcusable blunder.

The Beersheba attack was a complete success. The whole position fell to our attacking troops, and we were, as a brigade, extremely proud to hear from the infantry, with some of whom we inspected the position which we had bombarded, that machine gun fire from the Turkish outwork had been negligible. Shooting had been extraordinarily difficult for the artillery, as we were attacking east at dawn and shooting into the glare of the rising sun. An ingenious device was adopted by the infantry so that we could see their advancing troops. A biscuit tin lid was fastened to the back of every tenth man, and the flashing of these tins could be readily seen even in the half-light when the attack took place. Although every machine gun in our target had been put out of action by shellfire – every machine gun was completely ruined – it is an interesting fact, showing how rarely a direct hit can be obtained, that only one machine gun had been damaged by anything but splinters, and that had been knocked over by a dud shell from our own battery. The brigade must have fired several thousand shells on this advanced work; machine gun fire had been completely overcome, and yet no direct hit was registered, except in the case of this one shell which had failed to explode. The flying splinters are what do all the damage in a bombardment, especially with high explosive shell fitted with direct action (now 106) fuses.

Aeroplane Bombs

The day following the battle of Beersheba our battery met with its first serious casualties. We officers had breakfasted as usual outside our bivouac tent and had left not more than a minute when an enemy aeroplane appeared high up over us and dropped, from a great height, several bombs aimed at the large number of troops scattered over the hillside. By sheer bad luck the bombs dropped exactly where our five servants and our cook were breakfasting at the biscuit box table we had just left. One servant, the major's, was killed outright, the cook and my faithful batman had their legs blown off, and died before the mule ambulance could remove them, two others died soon after, and 'T', one of the officers, who had one leg ground to pulp, and two others, died in hospital or on the way there. Four or five of our horses were seriously injured by the flying splinters, and there were some casualties among the nearest infantry. Our cook's cart was blown to pieces, and my Sam Browne belt and priceless Zeiss field glasses were peppered as if by a shotgun and ruined. My valise, which was lying near, although tightly rolled up and strapped, had pieces of bomb all through it. We all felt the loss of our servants. The relation between an officer on active service and his batman is closer probably than any human relationship, except husband and wife. An officer has, and can have, no secrets from his servant, he depends on him for all those little comforts that devoted service can offer, and my faithful Gunner 'C' had been all that was devoted, unselfish and loyal. How much I missed his cheerful company for the next year!

The problem of water supply for men and animals now became acute. Apart from the Desert Corps of Australian New Zealand and Yeomanry mounted divisions, and the Imperial Camel Corps, the XXth Corps under Sir Philip Chetwode consisted of the 10th, 53rd, 60th and 74th divisions, and twenty-three batteries of corps artillery (mountain, heavy and siege). The full water ration for mules, horses and camels is ten gallons a day per animal. It had been hoped that the seventeen wells of Beersheba would have sufficed to supply the water for all the thousands of men and animals composing the XXth Corps. This expectation proved false. On their retirement from Beersheba the Turks had deliberately ruined the wells, and the thousands of thirsty animals, which were sent to Beersheba to be watered, waited there hour after hour while frantic efforts of the REs succeeded in getting some of the wells cleaned out and in working order. Evidently Beersheba as a water base for the further advance of the XXth Corps was hopeless.

The Turk action in spoiling the wells at Beersheba was probably a legitimate defensive operation. The capture of Beersheba and its water supply was designed as the first step in rolling up the Turk defensive system from its eastern extremity. From the capture of Beersheba the British could advance to attempt the capture of the ample water supplies at Sheria. But the destruction, or pollution, of wells in a desert country is regarded as little better than a crime against humanity. It is one of the things that are not done by desert peoples. Wells are the means of life for men and animals in the desert, they are sacred and the objects of primitive worship, not only for being the sole means of life for crops, animals and men, but because they are monuments of antiquity, and in the long memories of the people recall the names of the legendary benefactors of the locality. Taught by their German masters that 'necessity knows no law', the Turks gained temporary advantage by what they did to the famous wells of Beersheba. Politically it was a blunder like the shelling of Scarborough and the unrestricted submarine campaign. The Arabs are a desert people, and much of the enthusiasm of the Arabs in their revolt against the Turks can be attributed to this, in their eyes, criminal destruction of the sacred wells of Beersheba

The military advantage they gained was altogether temporary. After consultation by our generals, it was decided to risk all in an attack on the water supply of Sheria. Thirty thousand camels, each carrying thirty gallons, immediately started to transport water from the Wadi Ghuzee. Water rations were reduced relentlessly to one water bottle per man per day, for cooking and drinking and one and a half minutes' drink per day for horses and mules. The famous Army Order was issued, 'that officers and other ranks will not wash or shave for eight days', water officers were put in charge of all watering places, and the XXth Corps prepared to attack Sheria. The men probably did not guess the truth, but the thoughtful of the officers could see plainly that the consequences of failure in the Sheria attack would be that XXth Corps would die of thirst in the desert.

The arrangement involved a daily march for camels and their native drivers lasting twenty hours in each twenty-four. It is not possible to get more out of either man or beast than that.

The effect of the no washing and shaving order was comical. To see a subaltern, chalk-faced with dust saluting a colonel or general with the same chalky complexion, ornamented with half an inch of bristles, which varied in colour according to the age of the wearer, was a sight for gods and men. As I personally had not had my shirt, boots, or breeches off for more than a week the no washing order made little difference, especially as there seemed little prospect of my removing them in the immediate future.

Colonel 'R' upon this appointed me water and ammunition supply officer for the 268th Brigade. From now on, until Sheria was captured (or an attack failed), the responsibility for water, which was five hundred horses, was to rest upon my shoulders. If I made one mistake in map reading, or my compass went out of order, or both my horses went lame, or I collapsed from exhaustion, five hundred men would go thirsty and also five hundred horses and twelve guns would remain unfed.

Habits of discipline won. It wasn't really my job, which was to be second-in-command of C/268, my own battery; it was an arduous duty involving more responsibility than I cared for. It deprived me of all opportunity of shooting our guns; I was proud of my shooting, and having a gift for shooting field guns was fond of exercising it. However, there it was, and it had to be done, so I checked my compass, wangled a supply of duplicate maps, and started off for a week of suffocating dust. On one occasion I had to be out for seventy-two hours on end, of which I spent sixty in the saddle. On another I was posted as missing for two days. On another, failing to find any traces of our Divisional Ammunition Column, who, like most people in an advance, had lost themselves and marched to a place miles away from their assigned area, I relieved a distressed sergeant from quite another division of 250 camel loads of ammunition, and, by this means, kept the guns supplied with shells in the absence of any legitimate supply.

Delivering these shells, I found our battery on the edge of a slope facing Tel El Sheria. I had been temporarily, lending a hand with the guns earlier in the day. We had occupied four positions by ten o'clock in the morning.

The country being featureless the question of aiming points had to be dealt with on original lines. Our next neighbours B Battery had dropped into action beside us. It was exactly like a field day except that enemy shrapnel was bursting high overhead. The twelve guns advanced in line at the trot. At the order 'halt action front', everything was done exactly as in the training manuals, probably for the only occasion in the whole war. The twelve guns swung round together. Major 'B' of B Battery ran up the slope in front of his guns, and gave the following original order, 'All guns lay on me. Range 3,000, one round battery fire.' We sent a man up on to a mound behind with a flag to act as our aiming point. Range was impossible to estimate, so we used the finest rangefinder of all, our newest gun. The major's order was, 'No. 1 gun fire one round at the following ranges: 1,000yds, 2,000yds, 3,000yds, 4,000yds, 5,000yds, 6,000yds, and 7,000yds.' As the infantry were less than 200yds in front of us they were quite safe. We watched the fall of each shell to get the range on the ground for future use, and the 7,000yds shell was easily identified. It went slap into a marquee tent a little beyond, and to the right of the great earth mound called Tel El Sheria, the only feature on the entire map.

When I returned with the ammunition the major had had about all any man can stand. His horse had gone mad with want of water. I reported it, and that it had had to be shot. The major's brother had been mortally wounded within 10yds of him. His only possible OP was a trench filled nearly to the top with the bodies of dead Turks. Seeing that he was very near the cracking point I persuaded him to take a rest, and occupied his seat on top of the heap of bodies of our late gallant enemies, from where I finished the day's shooting.

The Turks, as always, fought with the utmost determination and courage. In equipment, training and artillery, as well as numbers, they were hopelessly inferior. They made desperate counter-attacks, and their machine gunners stood their ground to the last and died beside their guns to a man, almost invariably of bayonet wounds. Johnny Turk, with the worst of equipment and clothing (many of their infantry had one boot and a sack round the other foot; some of the guns we captured at Sheria were drawn by four small cows) and starvation rations, proved himself, as the Scotch used to say, 'a bonny fechter'. I am quite sure that no troops that ever came to handgrips with the Turks thought otherwise.

Like the Bulgars, the Turks were on the wrong side in the Great War. They had probably realised it long before the days I write of, they certainly realise it now; their folly cost them Egypt, Palestine, Iraq, Arabia and the headship of the Moslem world, not to mention such famous oriental cities of the most ancient renown as Baghdad, Damascus, Cairo, Mecca, and finally Jerusalem. Their present capital Angora, the site of the capital of the forgotten empire of the Hittites, has no renown comparable with that of any of these centres of the civilisations of the ancient world. Besides ruining Germany the war-lords of Germany destroyed for ever the prestige of the Osmanli Turk throughout the East.

After the capture of Beersheba and Sheria the Turks could no longer dare to resist at Gaza, and they retired in haste northwards, withdrawing their defensive lines with repeated rearguard actions, until the broken weather and the broken country of the Judean Hills checked the rapid advance of the British.

The remainder of our adventures in Palestine are fully described, as regards the military operations, in the accounts which have been published regarding the capture of Jerusalem. In the final rout of the Turks, concluding with the capture of Damascus, we took no part, as we returned to France as a division in May 1918.

Some account, however, of the difficulties due to climate and weather should be included in the story of our adventures.

Shortly after the capture of the Sheria water supply from the Turks the lengthening line of communications of the XXth Corps caused insuperable difficulties, and evidently so large a force could not be kept supplied. The 268th Brigade therefore, with an infantry brigade halted at Karm, where we had an experience of a khamsin, or dust storm. These storms begin with a hot wind. As soon as the hot wind started the camel drivers tied up their recumbent animals' heads in sacks, and themselves lay down on the sheltered side of their camels. We saw that something serious was about to happen, and wondered how the horses would fare. We could do nothing for them, as we were in an exposed position in an open plain. Quickly the wind grew into half a gale and the heat was almost intolerable. The air was filled with particles of fine dust, until a man who breathed otherwise than through the nose would have been suffocated. Great spirals of dust with rubbish swept up by the wind and whirling

67

round and round, scooping up sticks and straw, raced across the plain. These dust devils have the appearance of waterspouts at sea, and are quite alarming and, as we were told afterwards, very dangerous if one should be caught in their course. After some hours the khamsin departed. But for several days every mouthful of food was full of grit, shaving soap made no lather on the face, but only a grey smear, and everything we possessed was peppered with this alkali dust which seemed able to penetrate even into a tightly strapped up sleeping bag.

The next hardships were the extreme opposite. For the battle for Jerusalem our position was near the top of a rocky hill, about 3,000ft above sea level. The whole battery was clothed for the desert in cotton uniforms; we had no tents, and no overcoats. Our heads were covered with pith helmets. The month was December. It was as cold as an English December; the weather included sleet, hail, and tropical rain, which one day reached the extraordinary figure of ten inches in eight hours. About Christmas time food and forage for men and animals almost failed altogether. Nobody had built a bridge across the Wadi Ghuzee forty or fifty miles south of us. This dry wadi after the rains becomes a raging torrent.

For a few days trains struggled across this river on lines laid on a sandbag causeway, and then the causeway was carried away and no more trains could cross. Meanwhile, mountains of supplies piled up and rotted in the rain on the far side of the river.

On one day the forage for a brigade of artillery (500 horses) consisted solely of 100lbs of hay; that is, the official issue was, in round figures, one-fifth of a pound of hay for a horse with no corn whatever. On Christmas Day, 1917, the official rations for our men, for the day, were one tin of bully beef to four men, one biscuit, and one small tin of jam to twenty-four men. One mug of hot tea, boiled on cordite, as we had no fuel whatever, was just possible. These were the official rations. By various fraudulent subterfuges I contrived that our battery did better than that. I had heard about the total failure of the forage supplies the day before, and contrived to draw our forage twice over on that day. Somebody else had to go short, of course, but our animals got their usual standard ration of wet and mouldy provender. Jerusalem had been captured by then, but, except for a battalion on guard, none of the troops who had done the fighting were officially allowed to go inside, even the suburbs. This is a privilege almost invariably reserved in war for those who have taken no part in the actual fighting.

But there are unofficial ways of doing almost anything in the army. A note or coin here, a bluff there, possibly a friend at court, if one is very lucky; *laudace toujours l'audace* is a good motto for a soldier in search of something for the men to eat. I took with me on the four-mile ride six mules with packsaddles. And these mules returned from Jerusalem loaded with eatables. It was mainly bread, but not altogether. There was a skinny leg of mutton that cost me a pound, two tins of Bordeaux asparagus excavated that morning by the Armenian greengrocer. By what means I got past the sentry and found my way into the Holy City I shall not now disclose.

It was not bribery or corruption of any kind, it was simply low cunning. And the same trick worked perfectly on a second occasion. On my way home to the guns I saw a wooden box lying on the hillside. Fuel! To my amazement my groom said it was too heavy to lift, so he was ordered to sit on it, and kill anyone who tried to take it from him. As a groom has no lethal weapon but his issue jackknife and mine weighed no more than six or seven stone, and was a most unwarlike person, this order was purely formal. Soon I sent a pack mule back and the box was brought in. When opened it contained a tin of quails, a bottle of whisky, a tin of asparagus, a tin of plums and various other quite unobtainable, at any price whatever, luxuries, on the side of a mountain in Judea. This box must have fallen off a mess cart belonging to some dignitary of a very high military rank. So ended the most successful day's foraging of my army career. Double forage for our animals drawn in the morning, a general's tuck box at night, and an unauthorised day's shopping in Jerusalem in between. That day I certainly earned my pay.

I think I may mention here that by some chicanery at the War Office the establishment of a four-gun howitzer battery had been reduced from a major and a captain and three subalterns, to a major or a captain and four subalterns. By this simple substitution of the word 'or' for the word 'and' the rank and pay of the major was reduced to that of captain, while my rank and pay became those of lieutenant. This, despite the fact that both of us were performing the same somewhat arduous duties as we had performed for over eighteen months in the same battery. As a crowning piece of injustice both our 'demotions' were antedated several months. No doubt somebody at the War Office, who had thought out this ingenious plan and was drawing a rate of pay far higher than that of any officer of any battery, went home to his comfortable flat in London feeling that that day he had deserved well of his country, and qualified for the letters OBE after his name. We didn't worry, but enjoyed the unusual luxury of tinned quails, crouching under shelter of a big rock on the lee side of our Judean hill.

After a counter-attack which failed disastrously the Turks abandoned all hope of recapturing Jerusalem, and retreated northwards up the Nablus road. (Nablus, a corruption of the Greek Neapolis, is the modern name of Shechem.) This was the only road north of Jerusalem and was no more than a rough track across the hills, consequently an army in retreat with guns and wagons had to march that way and the advance of the pursuing troops must follow the same route. The sidetracks being only suitable for skirmishing parties the retreating Turks were not in any danger of being cut off from their base at Nablus.

Most of our division had now been withdrawn for rest and refitting of which all units were in urgent need, but our battery was lent to the 53rd Division to strengthen their artillery. We were in action at Beitin (Bethel) Sheik Yusuf, Ain Yebrud and Selwad where I received orders to attend a refresher course at the School of Gunnery at Heliopolis near Cairo and was away from the battery for about a month.

These refresher courses were of value in that they afforded people an opportunity of exercising their brains solving theoretical problems and getting necessary repairs done to clothing and equipment. As instruction in problems likely to confront officers engaged in actual fighting the course at Heliopolis was beyond a joke. The two instructors in charge of us appeared to have no experience of practical matters behind them and many of the problems given us to solve were so divorced from the possibilities of actual war as to give rise to roars of laughter among the students, whose experience of the 'real thing' entitled them to treat the theoretical rubbish solemnly discoursed from the platform as the useless nonsense it actually was.

All the students knew very well, even if their instructors did not, that the subaltern a battery commander on active service prays for is not the man who can solve odd-shaped TOB triangles by trigonometry and logarithms, but the lad who can get a gun up a mountain behind a beaten gun team, can get another two hours' willing work out of men who have already done twenty hours heart breaking labour on end, and can hit a target in a gale of wind by instinct long before the expert of the barrack square and lecture room has even adjusted his slide rule.

Before the refresher course was finished the 74th Division was ordered back to France. I was, therefore, spared the mournful task of handing over our guns and the faithful horses who had dragged them for over two thousand miles, over French pavé roads, Macedonian bogs and mountains, scorching dust and sand in the deserts of Southern Palestine, and the rocky hills of Judea.

The battery was now under command of an absolute novice, a Major 'B' just out from England; our own Major 'M' had been sent away to England to take a battery commander's course. Everything had been handed over to the 7th Lahore Division except the men and their small kits, and the remnants had travelled down by railway to Kantara Base Camp where I joined them.

The new commander of the battery must have had real moral courage. He saw that his knowledge of the duties of a battery commander was literally nothing. He also was quick to recognise that good luck had placed him in charge of a unit quite capable of running itself.

Socrates long ago described himself as the wisest of all men because 'he knew that he knew nothing'. Major 'B' was wise in the same way. As soon as camp was pitched at Kantara, he assembled the officers and sergeant major and asked us to carry on running the battery as we had before his arrival, saying that he was fully convinced that the battery was competent to manage itself without his assistance. There are not many men who would have had the moral courage to act in this way. Dumped without any knowledge whatever of his job into the command of a unit as experienced as ours, his position was absurd and impossible. We all of us recognised and appreciated the honesty of his action and did our utmost to maintain the very high level of efficiency we had been accustomed to keep up.

We drew from ordnance six new 4.5-inch howitzers, complete equipment of new harness and stores for a six-gun battery, and the most magnificent lot of horses, all of Australian breeding, that I ever saw in the army.

After this Major 'B' retired to his tent and subsequently to hospital and we never saw him again.

71

AMATEUR GUNNERS

We entrained eventually for Alexandria without a battery commander, and on 2 May 1918, embarked for Marseilles. Owing to transport difficulties we could not be accommodated all on one ship. Two subalterns and the sergeant major with the drivers took charge of the horses on a captured German ship re-named the '*Huntscastle*'. The gunners travelled on another ship under another subaltern; on the third ship, our old friend the SS *Manitou*, were to travel two officers with their servants without other responsibilities. Those for the various duties were appointed by the spin of an Egyptian five-piastre piece. In some units without a titular head this allotment of ships would have led to dissension. The heaviest duties obviously would be the lot of those in charge of the horses. The one officer in charge of the gunners would have heavy responsibility without anyone to share it. The other two officers would travel as first class passengers at their ease. But in the old battery we settled such problems without rancour or dispute. By a spin of the coin 'B' and 'H' got the worst ship and the hardest work; 'LH' got the men, and 'K' and I won the 'gros lot', a first class cabin on the best ship in the convoy with no work whatever except the ordinary routine duties of a military transport. This decision of chance was accepted by all concerned without a grumble, a trifling indication of the 'band of brothers' spirit of our battery officers.

We set sail on a cruise to last nine days. The convoy of thirty-two ships was led by the *Manitou*, the escort consisted of eight Japanese destroyers (part of an independent Japanese flotilla based on Alexandria, and described by our convoy commodore, the captain of the *Manitou*, as equally efficient with any destroyer flotilla in the British navy).

With the exception of rough weather off Sardinia, and a submarine attack in the middle of the storm, in which a French transport in the convoy was torpedoed and had to be beached on the shore of the island, the voyage passed without incident.

At Marseilles, without any official organisation, every member of the crew and troops aboard the *Manitou* lined the side of the ship and cheered the captain down the companion way, a remarkable and unrehearsed tribute to the strictest of disciplinarians, spontaneously expressing the gratitude of the rank and file for his tireless devotion to duty, and success in ensuring the safety of the many lives committed to his care.

CHAPTER 5

BEF France 1918

D/44 Brigade: Hardshell Gunners

It was a 'hard boiled' unit that landed at Marseilles in the summer of 1918. We were all burnt to a mahogany colour by the desert sun; we were practised in gunnery of all possible varieties, gunners and drivers were skilled workmen who knew their jobs and were proud of their skill.

No one who had seen us sail away from the same port in November 1916, would have taken us for the same battery. I do not think I exaggerate when I say that as a fighting machine we were ten times the value of the inexperienced organisation that had left the Western Front two and a half years before.

This time we had no leisure to sample the delights(!!) of Marseilles; we entrained promptly and, in contrast to our former experience, we were given proper opportunities to water our animals at intervals. We ended our long train journey at Noyelles Station near Abbeville where we detrained. Even after four years of war railway arrangements for the movements of troops in France were as primitive as ever. There was no platform, no ramp was provided. Guns and other vehicles, none of less weight than four tons, had to be lifted bodily from the trucks to ground level by human muscles unassisted by even a porter.

We marched off and concealed the horses in a wood near Noyelles, where three incidents occurred, none of which I shall ever forget. The first was good, the second was most alarming, the third was so good that nothing could have been better.

The first incident was an inspection of our horses by an artillery general of very high rank. Lieutenant General 'M' closely inspected our Australians and remarked to me with a friendly smile as we left the horse lines, 'And do you seriously tell me that these animals have just come off a transport after nine days' sea voyage?' I replied, 'Yes, sir, and two days in a railway train after that.' 'Well,' he said, 'I've never seen anything like it in all my experience. Will you please tell your major and sergeant major from me that the condition of your horses after eleven days' travelling is superior to anything that I would have believed possible.'

The second event was a German night air raid on Abbeville. In this raid a huge petrol dump was set on fire, splinters from our anti-aircraft shells wounded several of the horses and broke the tiles on most of the roofs of the houses in our neighbourhood. The German bombs dropped on Abbeville, did heavy damage in the town and killed numerous women and children, while the blaze of the burning petrol dump lit up the entire surrounding country and illuminated the sky for miles around so that the movements of the hostile planes and the British war planes attacking them were as visible as if it had been midday instead of the middle of a dark night.

The third and best occurrence was the return of Major 'M' to take command of us. At Colonel 'R's request he had been summoned from the school of gunnery, where he was acting as instructor, to return and take command of his old battery, now for the first time of six guns and renumbered D/44. (The former 268th Brigade of Palestine had become the 44th Brigade; it now consisted of four six-gun batteries and was still commanded by that experienced soldier Colonel 'R'.) This was our last change of title. Up to now our battery had been numbered 2/22nd County of London, D/302, C/268, and now finally D/44.

The whole battery, officers, NCOs and men, rejoiced unfeignedly at the return of Major 'M'. Even the centre section, strangers who had been posted to us when we became a six-gun battery at Kantara on the Suez Canal, celebrated the occasion with enthusiasm and soon had good reason to know that their celebration was justified.

Major 'M' was a battery commander second to none. He knew from personal experience the hardships and troubles of the rank and file on active service. He set an example to everyone of cheerful endurance, tireless energy, and an intelligent grasp of a situation however difficult and dangerous.

The efficiency or otherwise of a battery is at least fifty per cent in accordance with the confidence felt in the battery commander. The confidence we all had in Major 'M' was absolute, the NCOs and men in his courage, fairness, and consideration, the officers in all those things, and in addition we had had innumerable examples of his coolness in action, resource in emergencies and exceptional ability as a gunner. And we all liked him as a man, no unimportant matter.

We felt that the old luck of the battery had come back again and I, for one, looked forward to whatever was to be our destiny with a confidence I had not known since he had left us in Palestine.

By now the personnel of the old battery fully deserved the description of veterans. We had successfully unloaded all our 'stiffs' onto another artillery unit at Kantara, where we had been ordered to send our surplus numbers to another battery. Such an order is regarded in the army as a heaven-sent opportunity to get rid of useless and troublesome men and we had made the fullest possible use of it. We had still with us all our old and proved 'standbys' such as the limber-gunners and gun-layers, we had NCOs whose abilities had been fully tested in trench, mountain and desert warfare, the officers were truly a 'band of brothers', the horses were a superb lot of Walers, and, most important of all, we had a CO who had led us with invariable success in situations of the utmost difficulty. I knew for certain, too, that our major was valued at his true worth both at brigade and divisional headquarters.

I make this statement as a bare record of fact. It is in no sense a flattering description of a close friend by one who owed him every expression of affectionate esteem, I set it down as the considered estimate of a critical mind after many years have elapsed. Readers of this record will, I hope, have put me down by now correctly as one not easily satisfied, unaccustomed to hand round bouquets to the undeserving, but appreciative of worth and merit wherever I found it.

In these circumstances the 'cook's tour' we officers were given as an introduction to the conditions of warfare obtaining in France was interesting but entirely superfluous; especially as the area to which we were sent was practically the same spot as that in which we had served our apprenticeship in 1916. The field days too, for practice in open warfare under the eye of inspecting generals, were sheer waste of time, corresponding to make believe contests with buttoned foils for a duellist experienced with a sharpened rapier.

The training, however, which we received in the use of gas protective equipment was most valuable and absolutely necessary. Neither we nor the Turks had used gas in Palestine and the protective equipment we had used in 1916 was utterly out of date now.

After a pleasant period spent in these various exercises in back areas we went into action at Robecq in the Lys Sector, where I found the names of places such as Lillers, Aire, Armentières familiar from recollections of the final chapters of Dumas' The Three Musketeers, the action of which is placed in these regions.

At Robecq we had three positions, the left section was in action in a farm with excellent rooms on the ground floor but no tiles on the roof; the centre section, of which I was nominally section-commander, was further forward in Laleau Farm, where the cherry trees were laden with ripe fruit. At Laleau the gunners had to be summoned by whistle out of the cherry trees whenever the section was ordered to fire. The dugouts in the cellars of the farm had been constructed on such insecure principles that the men preferred the risk of shells in the open to sleeping in sandbagged cellars which would certainly have become death traps if one small shell had hit the farmhouse.

The forward section, under charge of 'B', consisted of the two guns of the right section placed about level with the infantry front line; they could only be fired at night when other guns were firing and the sky was illuminated as otherwise their flashes were fully visible to the enemy. This forward section was so placed that rounds fired at any range were bound to fall at some point on the mathematically straight road which transport had to use in bringing up supplies to the German support and front line troops. Gunnery for this section consisted therefore in firing unobserved rounds on one line only but at varying ranges; the most uninteresting gunnery imaginable, but probably the damage inflicted upon enemy transport was serious.

The contrast of the ammunition supply with that of our former period of service in France was amazing. In the old days shells had been treasured as if they were diamonds and a battery had been limited to an expenditure of fifteen rounds a day. Now, so enormous had become the output of the munition factories, that harassing fire was almost continuous and we had the greatest difficulty in expending the minimum of rounds ordered to be fired in each twenty-four hours if the gunners were to have any sleep at all.

The Robecq area – which we had taken over from a most unwarlike Midland division which, in turn, had relieved the Portuguese – was not an attractive one to a gunner. The country was as flat as the proverbial pancake, effective observation was extremely difficult, from the front line trenches standing corn obstructed a view of the nearer targets and the further view was obscured by the undamaged trees which were in full leaf.

I spent most of my observing hours upon a platform perched high up in a slender tree which swayed with every puff of wind, or lying on a heap of wheat peering through a hole in the wall of a ruined barn or spotting flashes from a platform high up inside the spire of Robecq Church. The other OP was in the attic of St Venant Asylum, too far back to be of any useful purpose to field gunners except the registration of the correction of the day with a few rounds on the ruined tower of Calonne Church. On this sector our infantry patrols and artillery FOO parties made the astonishing discovery that standing corn has the property of diverting rifle and machine gun bullets from their original course.

We did one magnificent feat of gunnery in the Robecq position, most of the credit for which was due to 'MP', the kite-balloon officer (we called them balloonatics) who did the observation. This shoot is worth recording in detail as an example of devotion to duty in a kite-balloonist.

The division on our right, in the line in front of Nieppe Forest, notorious for intensive enemy gas bombardments, proposed to make a battalion raid on the German lines in daylight. On the right flank of the line chosen for the route of the raiding battalion was a line of concrete machine gun posts, whose fire would enfilade and decimate the raiders unless kept under by continuous howitzer bombardment. Observation on these machine gun posts was only possible from the air, and our rear section was called upon to undertake the task with the assistance of the kite-balloon observer.

The day of the raid drew nearer, and a high wind made balloon observation difficult and uncomfortable; because at over 40mph the wind causes a captive balloon to sway frantically to and fro, so that seasickness in the observer is inevitable and both hands are needed for safety. On the last day for registration, that is the day before the raid, in spite of half a gale, wind velocity being 55mph, 'MP' succeeded in doing the registration notwithstanding the gyrations of his balloon and the consequent seasickness that attacked him.

Next day the raid took place and was entirely successful. The GOC raiding division sent our battery a most congratulatory note, in which he stated that the raid had been a complete success, instead of a total failure, solely owing to the accurate fire of our guns. I believe, in acknowledgment of this compliment, our battery commander duly reported that most of the credit was due to the efficiency and devotion to duty of 'MP', our kite-balloon observer. Anyhow when, as usual, our air observer dined with us on the evening of the raid, we drank one another's health enthusiastically in whatever fluid the local canteen would part with.

After winning five first prizes in the First Army Horse Show our pride in our battery rose to even higher levels. The general who presented the prizes congratulated 'M' on the wonderful record of one battery winning five firsts in competition with the whole of the First Army, and remarked, 'a regular battery, of course'. But when 'M' replied, 'No sir, Second Line Territorial,' the general showed such symptoms of apoplexy that our CO added as a palliative to the shock, 'but my sergeant major is a regular,' which, of course, accounted for everything and rendered medical aid unnecessary.

After that we entrained for the Somme at Lillers on 18 August, and became part of the Fourth Army occupying positions at Bouchavesnes, Moislains, Villers Faucon, Templeux Le Guèrard, two positions at Epéhy, Tombois Valley near Ronssoy, and assisted in attacks on Templeux Le Guèrard, Gouy, Le Catelet, and the breaking of the Hindenburg Line at Vendhuile. We supported with our fire the 74th, 58th, 12th, 18th, 50th and 38th divisions, as after our own 74th (Yeomanry) Division was reduced by casualties below the strength entitling it to remain in the Fourth Army, we became an army unit and engaged in any battle that took place in our neighbourhood, cooperating with Australian and American troops.

In a book of this kind it would be superfluous to attempt to describe in detail all our adventures in this, the greatest battle of the world's history. A few incidents will, however, be recorded as noteworthy.

Amid endless responsibilities and efforts I had to invent expedients and ingenious arrangements so that the toil worn drivers should have at least five hours sleep in the twenty-four, and the gallant horses should have some little rest.

The duties of a battery captain in the Somme area at this time were distracting and endless. Water for the horses was invariably several miles away. Batteries, whose animals were used to being watered at least three times a day, had at times to send their horses as much as 50 miles a day on their way to the watering places and back again. Our horses, used to desert conditions, only had to make the trip there and back once a day for water, and soon showed by their superior condition how much they gained over the animals used to the French war front only. Both were toiling to take ammunition to the guns at all hours of the day and night, but my charges, having only to spend one third of their rest period in journey to water, enjoyed double the amount of rest that the others did, and so did their drivers.

In spite of the fact that the condition of our animals was fifty per cent superior to that of any other battery on the Somme front, I was adversely reported on by one of the horse adviser colonels, who was also a peer, for only watering my animals once a day; my written reply in explanation of my methods finished the interference for good. I replied, 'Reference your criticism of watering arrangements of these wagon lines, these horses have been accustomed to one watering a day only for the past three years, and their condition speaks for itself.' I heard nothing further on this subject.

During this period I had my meals whenever possible from the drivers' kitchen, sleep amounted to four hours at the best, and my days, apart from attending to urgent calls for more ammunition and teams to move the guns from time to time, were spent in trying to extract our legitimate rations and forage from the supply departments of the various divisions to whom we were temporarily attached. This was seldom given us honestly without indignant application by me in person to the senior supply officer concerned.

An attached battery serving away from its own organisation is nobody's child, and there was a singular and unpleasant unanimity among the divisions to whom we gave our assistance that our forage and rations were not to be fully delivered to us until all their own units were supplied.

This meant that our men and horses were to live on all the underweight and inferior food and forage supplies which came up to the divisional dump, a most serious matter in days like these when the British scale had to be cut down to make up the deficiencies in the supplies for our American allies, whose own service of supply had failed completely in its organisation, and to whose rescue the British supply department had manfully come, necessarily at the expense of the British divisions in the line. But these unsporting gentry soon learned that D Battery, 44th Brigade, had to be at least as well treated in the matter of rations and forage as units of their own division, or a certain Scotch-American amateur gunner would raise such a strafe as would very likely cost them their jobs. I had learned how to put the wind up gentlemen of their kidney, and the scurvy treatment, invariably handed out on the first day that we came under their organisation, as regularly changed to satisfactory quantities on the next. On the Somme battle front in 1918 the meek did not 'inherit the earth' or any part of it, and as I wore an overcoat without badges of rank, and through lack of sleep and regular food, and Palestine sunburn, presented a somewhat worn and elderly appearance, many of these warriors of the Army Service Corps (facetiously known throughout the army as Ally Sloper's Cavalry) treated me with a respect and deference due to my supposed years, and to a temper and language associated with livers and Indian curry. Had they known that only two stars decorated the sleeve beneath my raincoat, and that I had never been near India in my whole life, I should certainly have been placed in arrest for addressing my superiors in rank with such scant ceremony.

There was a great deal of gas shelling on both sides, and all one night near the Canal du Nord when I was compelled to hang about in the ruins of a village, trying to disentangle our vehicles from the steady stream of transport which blocked all roads behind the firing line day and night, I became quite seriously affected. The whole area had recently been drenched with gas by the British heavy artillery. All the village reeked of it, although hours had elapsed since the Germans had retreated, and I learned from painful experience how very effective was the lethal gas contained in British ammunition.

Gas does not affect horses as seriously as human beings. Although horses' stomachs are delicate organs very easily deranged, the lungs and heart of these animals are much more resistant to gas poisoning than men's, and on most occasions a nosebag of damp hay provided adequate protection.

While on the subject of gas bombardments I am bound to relate one incident which displays a magnificent spirit of devotion to duty. The reinforcements which reached us in the big Somme battle were totally untrained. We had actually, on many occasions, to give lessons in elementary gun-laying, in the middle of a serious attack, to so-called gunners who had come up to replace casualties. One of these untrained reinforcements was a middle-aged German Jew, Gunner 'R', who was so unlikely a recruit that I made him extra assistant cook and part-time boot repairer, as in civil life he had been a cobbler in the East End.

In the course of a severe gas bombardment many of our best men were seriously gassed and had to be forthwith evacuated to hospital. I sorted out the less seriously disabled as they arrived at the wagon lines riding on the ammunition wagons, and ordered them, if they were able, to sit by the fire in the cookhouse until morning. They choked if they attempted to lie down.

When daylight came a pitiable group of men, hoarse and with streaming eyes, coughing and spluttering, were still sitting round the cookhouse fire. With the exception of the Jewish cobbler they were our most valuable gunners, layers and limber-gunners, and these I begged to try and stick it out, and they all agreed like the willing sportsmen they were. We could not afford to lose them, and they knew it, and I knew that not one of them would fail in loyalty to the battery they had served so long and well.

Gunner 'R' was different. He was a newcomer, able, through lack of experience, to do only the simplest tasks, a grey-haired foreign Jew, and, by birth, presumably not interested in a British victory. I thought it unnecessary even to ask him to stay with us (one does not order men in the plight of these poor fellows to go or stay) and told him he'd better get off to hospital. But this middle-aged German Jew stranger would not hear of it. He staggered to his feet, and waving his hands up and down palms upward, whispered in an almost inaudible voice, such was his hoarseness, 'No, zir, I don't vant to go. I could still go on helping mit der cooking.' I believe, in an alien Jew, this episode was unmatched in all the war.

Next I want to relate a story of a water cart. Water for all purposes was conveyed to the gun line by means of the water cart, a clumsy vehicle on two wheels of incredible weight and warranted to break the hearts of any pair of horses harnessed to it when travelling over soft ground. One day the water cart was hit by a shell on its journey back from the guns. One wheel was broken, and there was a hole in the side of the tank the size of a football. I reported the casualty to our CO and promised that I would, without fail, get a new water cart from somewhere before next evening.

We bound up the broken wheel with rope and bits of wood, and I set off, leading the ruin of which one wheel was almost triangular in shape. (Our water cart horses in those days were a splendid pair of greys, which could and would have dragged along a small cottage if we had asked them to do so.)

Ultimately I arrived at divisional headquarters and found DADOS (Deputy Assistant Director of Ordnance Stores) seated at a table, surrounded with papers all neatly filed, the whole office a model of order and only lacking a ball of red tape to complete it.

I explained to DADOS, who was plump, short, and smug, that I had to have a new water cart at once, or the gun line of the battery would be waterless in about four hours. He was quite unmoved, almost peevish at being disturbed on account of such a trifle. Pompously and in his best civil service manner he dismissed me with the words, 'Indent for it, as usual, in triplicate, and I will give the matter my personal attention.' He then returned to his regular duty of filling in forms and posting ledgers which I had so thoughtlessly interrupted.

I hadn't expected anything better of DADOS, and so was not seriously disappointed. What he imagined would become of the gun line who would have no water for a fortnight, while these triplicated indents were wandering all over the north of France for the usual approvals, I have no idea. Probably he was not worried about it.

I led the limping water cart away from these infernal regions and by a sheer miracle found a small wood in which stood a couple of bell tents labelled 'Ordnance Workshops'. In one of the tents I found an angel from heaven in the form of a very stout officer, far over military age, to whom troops in the firing line were not common fellows of no social importance, but people who deserved all the help and consideration a non-combatant could give them. On hearing my tale of woe, he inspected the ruin, ascertained that one wheel was still in good order, and said he'd fit me up in half an hour. He explained that he had in stock a perfectly good water cart with one broken wheel belonging to one of these 'blasted non-combatant base-people'. Once my sound wheel was changed to their cart, 'there I was,' he said, 'with a new cart.' When I enquired what about the other people who would then have a smashed cart with two broken wheels, he said, 'What of it? You fighting people come first.' Well, we did that time, but hitherto we had found that all non-fighting people in beautiful fancy dress came a long way before us dirty troglodytes with muddy boots and shabby tunics.

This was a new attitude of mind to find in the regions behind the lines. I thanked God for it and him, lent him my pair of greys to take his own water cart to the well, accepted gratefully his cordial invitation to lunch, and set off in triumph, having kept my impossible promise to the major about getting a new water cart in one day.

Probably this stout sportsman was one of those who really regretted the years which had deprived him of his chance of being a real soldier. This episode the major correctly described as miraculous beyond belief.

In the late summer and autumn of 1918 the Somme sector was no place for novices or incompetents.

During the great offensive, units in the Fourth Army were provided with a steady supply of reinforcements, without which the heavy daily casualties would soon have reduced a battery below fighting strength. These reinforcements, combed out of non-combatant departments and hurried out from England, were of very inferior value as regards training. In the case of drivers and gunners the men had received little or no instruction in the elements of their duties, and had to be employed largely as unskilled labourers to relieve our hard-worked veterans of such jobs as could be tackled by willing ignorance.

In the case of NCOs and officers this pitiful lack of training and experience was very serious, and the utmost tact had to be used in their employment. You cannot put novices in charge of veterans without seriously impairing discipline and efficiency. Experience in actual war, acquired in several years' continuous fighting, does not easily accept superiors whose simplest orders betray lack of knowledge of the business in hand. It meant, of course, that the more experienced had to carry out most of the duties of the novices in addition to their own. Fortunately for us few of our novices were of the awkward type. Mostly they readily admitted their inability to direct subordinates of such long experience as those under their authority, and they wisely left those who knew how to do the job to carry on without interference.

The story of our destruction of an entire German battalion is a perfect illustration of the result of inexperience in command in the middle of a big battle.

One misty September morning 'M' and I went to the OP just before dawn. As the British had captured enemy positions the day before and counter-attacks were to be expected before dark, 'M' had, as usual, carefully registered the chief points in the sector we covered and selected his OP.

To our astonishment as the day broke we could see an entire German infantry battalion drawn up on a forward slope facing us, evidently preparing for a counter-attack. Range and line of the target was immediately telephoned to the battery, and orders given to fire as rapidly as possible. I ran down to the guns, so as to urge the gunners to keep up the most rapid rate of fire consistent with accurate laying.

For fully half an hour each gun fired ten rounds per minute of high explosive, fused with the deadly instantaneous 106 Fuse, right into the massed ranks of the unlucky German battalion. The effect upon these wretched men of sixty rounds a minute bursting right among their ranks for half an hour must have been appalling. Probably not one man was alive after the first ten minutes. It was impossible to see the effect as in less than a minute the whole valley was black with the smoke of our bursting shells. When the smoke finally cleared away there was not a living or moving creature to be seen where we had caught this thousand enemy infantry in the open without enough cover to hide a rabbit. No other battery fired, nor did any small arms weapons engage this remarkable target.

This German battalion had massed for a counter-attack on the American 27th Division.

After we had completed this slaughter of the innocents we naturally discussed the affair, and decided either that the German battalion commander had massed his men for the counter-attack without realising that his assembly position was in full view of the enemy, or else that, having properly assembled his troops under cover of darkness and been ordered to await further instructions before making the attack, the order had failed to reach him, and he had not had the experience to be bold enough to withdraw his men without orders to a less conspicuous place on the arrival of daylight.

Evidently the lack of training in the British Army reinforcements was also troubling the Germans. In this case, as always, the incompetence of the commander was paid for by the rank and file. It was a piece of cruel bad luck that the area selected for this terrible blunder happened to be directly opposite to so competent a man-killing machine as D Battery, 44th Brigade, RFA. The feat was not one of gunnery. It was due to three of the main grounds for our claim to be a first class battery: accurate registration, intelligent observation, and machine-like proficiency in gun drill. Not many batteries on any front met with so helpless a target. The full price of incompetence was exacted, as it should have been, without mercy.

I must now relate the sad story of Lempire, and how we had our one disaster of the war. We had to move forward as a complete battery and occupy a position for the assault on the Hindenburg Line at Vendhuile. I started off from the wagon lines at 4.00 pm with all the teams, hooked into the guns at Épehy, and led the battery along the main road past Ronssoy. There the colonel and 'M' galloped forward to select a gun position in an area which was being steadily shelled by enemy 5.9s. The prospect looked most unpleasant. I had orders to halt the column somewhere on the road near the remains of Lempire. I did so, and as the German guns were searching the neighbourhood I galloped forward to find if the position had been chosen, and get the teams away from the risk of shells with as little delay as possible.

I met the major about a thousand yards from the column, riding back to lead the guns and wagons to the position he had selected. Just as we met, a salvo of 5.9s exploded right on the road where I had left the column in charge of a very junior and inexperienced officer.

'M' and I galloped back as fast as we could, and met the remains of the battery streaming down the road. Only two guns out of six and four or five ammunition wagons, the water cart and the GS wagon were coming along. 'M' led the remains to the position selected, and I went on to find on the road a mound of dead and wounded men and horses and broken vehicles. In the meantime the baggage wagon had run over a land mine which killed both the ASC horses, blew the wagon in half, and the driver, a Canadian, 30 or 40yds through the air. I patched up teams, drivers and harness for the two other guns which were still serviceable, shot the hopelessly wounded horses (one of which was calmly grazing although one leg was missing and blood was pouring out of the place where the leg had been) with a revolver I borrowed from an American infantry sergeant, got the wounded away to hospital, identified the dead, rescued the one survivor of E sub-section gun team, our show team, which a local brigand was endeavouring to make away with, and led the vehicles I had been able to patch up with slightly wounded horses and drivers up to the gun position.

Shells were falling steadily all round the guns so as each team unhooked it was sent away at the gallop, and eventually I arrived at the horse lines, which had been selected quite by chance, and fortunately in a well covered place, to find that, in the confusion, rations had not been sent up to the guns. So off I went again to lead the ration cart. By the time that was delivered, and I had reached the scene of our calamity, it was twilight.

The only way I could be certain, in the half-light, whether any of our men in the mound of apparently dead were alive, was to prod them with my jackknife. None were alive, and I then had the gruesome task of dragging the dead horses off them, and collecting their various identity discs, and pay books. As by this time my groom and I had been hard at it for sixteen hours continuously, we were not sorry when at last we arrived at the horse lines, and got to sleep. Before leaving this disastrous incident, I must record the gallantry of Driver 'D'.

He was a Welshman, short and thick set. He drove the finest pair of wheelers we then had, in the wheel of No. 4 gun. Dick, the riding wheeler, was slightly wounded on the rump above the tail, Maggie, the hand wheeler, had a shell splinter inside her off flank. Driver 'D' himself had a small hole in the back of his tunic through which blood was oozing from the small of his back, the centre horses and driver were undamaged, the lead horses and driver were all hors de combat. All the gunners and NCOs of No. 4 gun were killed or wounded, the other vehicles had disappeared, and no one remained to lead the gun up to the position. Driver 'D', however, offered, wounded as he was, to take charge and find the gun position, so I sent him off.

This wounded boy of nineteen – he had been on active service for nearly four years already – took charge of the gun, arrived safely at the gun position, brought the team safely to the wagon lines, handed over his horses, checked and got a receipt for his harness, and then collected his belongings and reported himself wounded, and went off to hospital.

Driver 'D' had come to us at Kantara, one of the unwanteds sent from the 10th Division. Besides this stout-hearted performance he drove in the wheel of the team when it won the battery driving prize at Robecq, defeating the A sub-section gun team which had won the driving test repeatedly for over three years.

The battery that discarded Driver 'D' must have been a very queer unit.

The horses at this time were putting in very hard work, as the enormous quantity of rounds we fired involved ceaseless relays of ammunition wagons travelling up and down from wagon line to battery position at all hours of the night. It was impossible to use the roads, which were blocked with traffic, and the state of the land, pockmarked with shell holes dating from the battles of 1916, made the risk of accidents on country journeys in the dark considerable, as many of the shell holes were over 6ft deep, and others were so full of weeds as to be hard to identify until horse or wagon had fallen into them. The journeys had to be long as horse lines could not safely be established nearer than three or four miles in rear of the battery positions.

When the time came to move the guns from the first position at Épehy to the second position, which lay about a mile further south, the horse lines were near Longueval, about five miles to the rear. I got early warning of the move from 'M' and had all the teams harnessed up ready by afternoon, and arrived about dusk at the gun line, leading a column of eighteen wagons and gun limbers and the GS wagon for the telephone equipment. We had had to adopt a long and roundabout route for traffic to the gun line, involving a march of roughly ten or twelve miles round a hill to avoid enemy observation and rows of rusty barbed wire entanglements that littered the slopes of the higher ground on our side of the hill.

The moving of our six guns to the new position was a ticklish job. Most of the way the shell holes, some deep enough to hold a cottage, were as close together as cells in a honeycomb. Remains of blown-in trenches and barbed wire defences presented ugly obstacles for the teams straining at the heavy vehicles in the half-light. The safest way to avoid accident was to detail an officer or sergeant to lead each team on foot, and this was the method we adopted.

My charger being very clever in the dark, I led the first gun mounted, having first instructed the lead drivers of all the teams to meet me, when the job was done, at a place easily recognised where two earth-tracks crossed beside a hillock. As soon as I had safely delivered my gun into position, I rode off and dismounted, and sat on the ground to await the other teams, and then took place the most wonderful display a waiting man could ask for to pass away the time.

As I sat on the ground enjoying a pipe, and holding my horse by the reins, the moon rose slowly over the horizon. It must have been an exceptionally quiet night, as the gun-flashes were only visible here and there, and did not light up the countryside as they did in an intensive bombardment. When the moon was fully up a squadron of enemy aeroplanes could be heard overhead. (The note of the German aeroplane engines was easily distinguishable from that of the allied machines. The latter made a sound like the regular rumble of a circular iron cylinder on a road, whereas the enemy machine had an elliptical effect.) The sky was immediately stabbed with brilliant beams from the British searchlights, great bands of light wandered across the sky, and, as any searchlight lit up the machine of an enemy airman, the beam followed, holding the aeroplane in its grip while, anti-aircraft guns filled the sky with high bursting shells. Brock never staged such a firework display as this, it was awe-inspiring, but magnificent as a spectacle.

The next entertainment provided for me and my three waiting drivers was, to my horse-lover's eye, the finest picture of strength and energy an artist could imagine. Over the crest of the hill on my right, silhouetted against the moon, marched two complete batteries of 60-pounder guns, each vehicle drawn by a magnificent team of eight heavy draught horses, beautifully handled, every animal pulling his full share of the load. A more perfect picture of willing energy was never seen, and a great animal artist like Lucy Kemp-Welch could have made a picture of it unmatched even by the famous horse fair.

It was about 3.00 am when the teams began to arrive. The 'place of assembly' that I had chosen proved to be a good one. Not a team had missed its way and there was ample space for my nineteen vehicles to line up 'shipshape and Bristol fashion'.

'Column of route from the right,' and off we went, B sub-section firing battery wagon leading, because the lead driver of that team was my night vision specialist.

This time I decided to take a risk and try a short cut to save the men and horses several miles of their homeward march. Instead of returning by the semi-circular route we had followed in the afternoon I determined to trust to my sense of direction, and, although the march was in pitch darkness, I left the track and struck off boldly across country at an angle of about 45 degrees to the left of it.

The risk was considerable but not unjustified because, having unloaded at the gun line the shells we had carried on the way up, the vehicles were light and our indomitable horses would manage to haul them out of any probable obstacle. The chief risk was barbed wire, but my own charger could be trusted to see a single strand of it in the dark before his forelegs touched it.

When we had travelled a quarter of a mile Sergeant 'G', the most intelligent and wide awake of our No.1s, trotted up and most respectfully said, 'Excuse me, sir, but are you sure we're going the right way?' I replied, 'I hope so, I'm trying to save about four miles by striking across the diameter of a circle instead of crawling round the circumference.'

Sergeant 'G' thought I was taking too big a risk in unknown country and exclaimed, 'Don't you do it, sir.' But we had been on the job for quite ten hours by then, the men were very tired, the horses were far from fresh, and so I held on.

After another four or five miles we passed in the dark through the remains of a ruined village. As we were not expecting any village on our way, I resigned myself to the probability that I had put my boasted sense of direction to too severe a test and we were lost.

That night, however, my luck held good. Less than two miles beyond the village we dropped into a valley at the far end of which we found our horse lines. We unharnessed and found our beds, and as I was taking my usual walk round to see, as I did every night, that all the horses and men were as comfortable as possible, I overheard several comments on my 'ruddy skill as a night pilot'. Evidently others beside Sergeant 'G' had felt misgivings about my short cut.

We left the Fourth Army and returned to the northern area on 18 October. Having been detailed with another officer to collect the canteen allotment of the 74th Division I did not entrain with the battery.

Our three-ton lorry loaded up at Peronne and we travelled in it all the way from there to Béthune. It was a most interesting journey and I learned the advantages of a three-ton motor lorry as a travelling conveyance.

There were six of us on board, two officers, two ASC drivers and our two servants. The lorry served as a travelling caravan, it was our bedroom, kitchen, dining room and lounge. It also became our warehouse, whenever we saw anything of value lying abandoned by the roadside (among other articles we salved were the useful parts of a kitchen range, on which, having fitted an improvised chimney, we cooked our various meals as the powerful lorry bowled along the main roads).

We passed through Bapaume, now a mass of ruins, Arras, more dilapidated than it had been when last I had visited it, and thence we travelled along the road Liévin, Nœux-les-Mines, Béthune.

From Arras to Liévin the excellent road ran through the region where the gun positions had been in the summer of 1916. Since that time Vimy Ridge had been captured and now the old gun line and even Madagascar Corner, once the terror of transport columns, were occupied by the horse lines of the ASC and other peaceful and peace-loving branches of the Army. The guns now occupied regions which had formerly been our favourite targets, and the scenes of our frantic efforts to keep up the rate of fire required for SOS and barrage bombardments had now become semi-pastoral areas where horses grazed and wagons and harness were washed and polished in full daylight, and perfect security.

After leaving the lorry and canteen stores with divisional headquarters I rejoined the battery near La Bassée. We advanced next morning, came into action at Fournes where we fired a few rounds, and occupied positions at Wattigny, Sainghin, Gruson and Camphin.

All this time the defeated German Army was retiring as rapidly as it could march and the first serious opposition was met with in front of Tournai. The enemy resumed his retirement on 8 November and we reached Ostiches at 11.00 am on 11 November when the Armistice took effect.

During the last days of the war, Belgian civilians, having seen the last of their German oppressors only an hour or two before our arrival, welcomed us with tears streaming down their cheeks. They offered us all the humble hospitality that they could, sometimes an apple, sometimes a last bottle of wine, sometimes a kilo of butter. They decorated our horses and guns with wild flowers and little cotton Belgian flags whenever we passed through a village.

It was utterly pathetic. The gratitude of these simple people was so genuine and unashamed. Unlike the population at home in England the war had been one long history of privation and hardship to them. Oppression instead of fantastic war wages had been their lot, and our coming was the realisation of a hope that had faded so often and almost died of despair.

We wondered where they had got the little Belgian flags from and they told us how, immediately before they had scrambled away to safety, the German soldiers had hawked these flags from door to door. How much truth there may be in this statement I do not know; to one who knows the meaning of the word 'profitieren' it is not incredible and if it is true, it presents to the world the supreme instance of the triumph of the commercial instinct over national disaster.

At this time our infantry were days behind the artillery, ASC supply wagons were marching continuously day and night with horses on the verge of collapse and drivers asleep on the box. Our corps cavalry were half a day behind the guns and the only section of our division which preceded the artillery was a party of enterprising machine gunners mounted on mules.

This picture of the last days of the war exposes the tale, now being carefully spread abroad in Germany, that 'The German Army was undefeated in the war', as the utterly absurd fiction, that it really is, on the same ludicrous level as the other fairy story that 'America won the war'. Any German soldier who took part in the final struggle and the very small proportion of the American Army that took any active part in the actual fighting must hear these fairy tales with utter shame and confusion.

The German Army was not merely defeated. It was totally demoralised and most of it fled from the battle area as a disorderly rabble, some of whom sold their horses and others their field guns to any Belgian who cared to make a contemptuous offer for them.

This, the literal truth, is written in no disparagement of the soldiers of a nation in arms, which displayed magnificent courage and formed in the words of Marshal Foch, 'the finest army that ever went to war.'

It was the old story of the willing horse that was spurred until it foundered. When the end came it was collapse, final and complete.

CHAPTER 6

Armistice

Goodbye to all that

November 11th found us marching eastward in the direction of Ath. Our teams, long reduced to four animals each, managed the heavy vehicles fairly well, in spite of their worn out condition, so long as the roads were reasonably level.

On 11 November at about 10.30 am with the exception of our weakest team, the first line wagon of E sub-section, the battery had successfully negotiated a very stiff hill.

As we were leaving the Somme area we had passed a senior officer who was horse adviser to the corps in whose area we had been operating. He had told us that our Australian horses were far and away the finest team horses he had ever seen on the Somme front and he had said that it was absurd that such splendid animals should be going out of it. The said splendid animals had lately been working all day and most of the night, for nearly two months on end, hauling ammunition to the guns, but skilled attention and careful handling had kept these hardy Walers in the pink of condition in spite of all the work they had done.

A description of our poor first line wagon team of E sub-section will suffice to show the level to which our boasted teams had fallen. The wheelers were a worn out pair of bays, one a jibber and the other unsuited for anything heavier than a cab. There were no centre horses. The leaders were, on the off side a little black mule, willing enough but only about thirteen hands and handicapped by the scar of an old wound on the shoulder, the riding leader was a roan mare, nearly 16 hands, completely broken- winded. She was as willing as a horse could be, but her roaring was audible hundreds of yards away and her bellows were not equal to her courage.

Naturally the gallant efforts of the little black mule and the big broken-winded roan – the wheelers' contribution was negligible – were unequal to dragging a loaded ammunition wagon up a gradient of at least one in six. The lame duck wagon began to roll backwards. My groom and I scrambled off our horses and chocked up the hind wheels with stones out of the ditch. The wagon stopped, and, as the attendant gunner quickly put on the brake, rolled back no further. After a few minutes rest for the heaving flanks of the roan leader to settle down to tolerable movements, my little groom, the dismounted wheel driver, the gunner and I started to push behind, and foot by foot, using every ounce of strength we had, we worked our way up the long and stiff gradient. I have given a somewhat detailed account of this proceeding. Every march I must have spent hours on similar duties at this stage of the war. Most battery captains in those days could have qualified as world's champion shifters of under-horsed, overloaded wagons. But throughout the war our battery never had the gunners' crowning shame of a stuck gun team.

We had even developed the technique of taking the battery through a gate with stone gateposts considerably closer together than the width of an artillery vehicle. Most of the gates into Belgian farmyards being of this pattern, we had ample practice. The simple, but effective, method is this, No. 1 gun team increases its speed to trot or canter. The horses are drawn very close together so as to squeeze through the gap without injury, and the off wheel is directed straight at the offending gatepost. With a gun moving at speed behind a powerful gun team something has got to go. A field gun will stand any shock whatever, and, within limits, so will British Army harness. The post came out of the ground, or broke off, on every occasion, and the rest of the battery quietly marched through at its usual sedate walk, the wheels of each vehicle overrunning the fallen post without difficulty. In this way the obstacle is negotiated without even a check and without dismounting a driver, an important consideration when the enemy is engaged in shelling the area.

As we neared the top of the hill a staff car with a broken spur on the radiator shot past. Next to the driver was the major general commanding 74th Division. General 'G' waved his hand as he passed, an unusual greeting from a major general to a sweating gunner officer. Something was up! At last we overtook the rest of the battery. They were halted about a mile ahead, just outside a brewery. A battery on the march does not wait for a broken down ammunition wagon. I had not expected to see the others before the usual dinner halt at midday for water, and feed. In Bret Harte's immortal phrase, 'here was visions about'. As soon as I hove in sight the major trotted up on his horse labouring under obvious excitement. I heard at once that, as he passed the battery, the general had shouted from his car, 'No firing after eleven today; armistice.' We dismounted and walked inside the brewery where the hospitable brewer, Monsieur Du Brule, presented a cask of so-called beer to the men, and, for the officers, dug up bottles of forty-year-old double-brewed beer, which looked, and tasted, exactly like champagne.

Over our beer, which was quite as powerful as Rajah's peg (brandy and champagne, the champagne taking the place of the more prosaic soda, the whole constituting the world's finest corpse-reviver), one of the officers, 'H', celebrated in the mess for invariably producing the obvious comment, remarked, 'Well – we've fired our last round.' I'm afraid we all laughed. It sounded quite beyond belief. To my ears it seemed about as likely to be true as that some unheard of relation had died in Australia and left me a couple of million. I think all of us had forgotten utterly that we had ever done anything else but fire 35lb steel jam pot shaped canisters of high explosive at complete strangers.

We suddenly realised the truth, or, at least, I did, and it was that we were no more amateur gunners, but actually experienced hard-bitten soldiers with more experience of war as it is, among our little party, than was to be found in the entire British Army of pre-war days.

I finished my beer and went out, nominally to look at the horses and take charge of the midday feed, but, actually, to think quietly over the new situation. Although another member of the mess enjoyed, and, on the point of age and manner fully merited, the soubriquet of 'grandpa', I was a good deal older than most of the others, and probably realised more than my friends the terrific moral change that 'the end of the war' would bring to every man and officer of our amateur army. I would have liked the quiet of a church to find my bearings. But there was no church. To a horse lover, the long line of our trusty animals contentedly chewing in their nosebags presents an atmosphere of quiet peace not less perfect than that of a cathedral aisle, and I found in this contented munching just what I needed, exactly as I had found it a hundred times before when the beastliness of the war had got the better of me.

Part 2: Letters

CHAPTER 7

Letters from France

July 1916 to November 1916

30 July 1916

Dear Mama

Now I am at the wagon lines of our battery. Expect to ride up about noon to see the colonel in command. At this place there is a little village which is very pretty. Really nice country, farms and things, and streams and bridges.

Each battery has its own wagon lines and horses dotted about in the village and I had a hunt to find this one, with an ASC wagon wandering round after me with Thomas and our kits in it. Lovely weather, just as at home very hot in the sun and beautifully cool at night. Overhead are the usual aeroplanes buzzing about. I am supposed to censor my own letters so it seems.

I shall get two horses allotted soon and should be most comfortable. The men I have talked to said they'd much rather be up at the battery as it's more comfortable there. They are territorials from where I was born. The sergeant major is a regular from the horse artillery, and has been an instructor where I was at Larkhill. There are some other regular NCOs as well.

I don't know how much I can say or not so had better say very little this time. Am absolutely in the pink to use your favourite expression. The officers live here when they come to the wagon lines for a rest. The house is very nice kept by the village schoolmaster who has four little children and a nice wife. All the civilian inhabitants are here and go on just the same as usual.

Yours, Douglas

AMATEUR GUNNERS

2 August 1916

Dear Papa

I write this at the expense of sleep as I may not have another chance for days. My duties are varied and irregular but usually finish about 12.30 am and begin with a stand to at 3.45 am. Liability of course for any hour in between.

We get orders to 'strafe' trench mortars of the Hun at any hour of the twenty-four, and we strafe them thoroughly (strafe is now used officially in army orders for a bombardment). The officers are very good sorts and the CO, or battery commander, is a regular colonel with practically only one leg but with a brain like a razor and as keen as mustard. Really his surviving here is quite heroic. He is about ten months older than I am.

The communication trenches are glorious with poppies and cornflowers and scabrous with thistles. I will send you a squashed poppy as a souvenir. Our guns here are very well concealed and the Hun has much fewer than we and no big ones. There is firing all round nearly all day and night and heaps of shooting at aeroplanes. There have been no casualties in the battery and some small shells occasionally come over to us but they are not aimed as they don't know where any of us are and so never do any damage.

One of my jobs is to take charge of ammunition wagons when they come up at night, about thirty-five horses and men, and lead them along a track in the dark avoiding old shell holes. You bet I get them away as soon as possible as a few shells over would mean a horrible tangle and stampede of horses probably. I usually get rid of the teams in about half an hour but it is an anxious time as they are quite in the open and the Hun must hear them rattling about. I fancy we don't shell their wagons either; possibly it is a convention not to do so.

There are quite young lads as gunners but they do very well indeed. Later on, in a week or so, I shall start observing from the infantry lines. We have very cunning hidden posts down there. You do four days at a stretch there and see our shooting at close quarters. All say it is most interesting and nobody ever gets hurt.

Rats in thousands but quite harmless, and mosquitos in billions, thank goodness the rats don't bite like they do, The cuisine is admirable, quite as good as at home and colonel's servant who waits used to mix drinks at the Oldhall Club! We did a fine strafe today and blew a lot of German emplacements into the sky. We only fire high explosive.

PS. Please send me some packets of envelopes like this a hundred box of decent cigarettes.

Yours, Douglas

13 August 1916

Dear Papa

I go down tomorrow morning for a spell of four days with the infantry. I had some night last night, got back from synchronising watches with the other batteries at 10.30 pm. Slept from 11.00 pm till 1.20 am. Then 1.20 to 2.00 am preparing for action, 2.00 to 2.30 am rapid fire, 2.30 to 3.00 am cocoa, 3.00 to 3.30 am read letters, etc. and Weekly Times (which will be a great addition), 3.30 to 4.00 am fired again, 4.00 to 4.30 read Times, 4.30 to 5.30 am 'stand to' the detachment at guns, 5.30 to 7.30 am sleep. That is an exceptionally heavy night.

We have to be very careful on the telephone as both we and the Bosch can take off each other's messages, so we use all sorts of roundabout ways of saying things and a most absurd and clumsy code initiated by the brigade CO. All places are named by letters. People have nicknames, e.g. I am 'Fly-by-Night'.

Get Mama to buy and send me out another torch of the same pattern with the next lot of refills. I'm getting the hang of things a bit better, but it is not so easy to keep all the new things in your head at once.

Had heavy rain to make things more unpleasant last night. I see in *The Times* no less than three of my fellow cadets have been wounded. Only one of them a friend.

Yours truly, Douglas

19 August 1916

Dear Mama

I have already written nine notes tonight so if this letter is pretty stupid that's why. I am down at the wagon lines now, six miles or so in the rear with the horses, where I am in sole command.

I have no horse of my own as yet but am riding all the officer's horses in turn. I don't fancy the other officers are much of horsemen, except the colonel who was head of remounts at the War Office and now of course with one leg that is as straight and stiff as a gatepost his riding days are over except for ordinary things.

Pretty country here and there is a small town a mile off where you can buy most things. I enjoyed a two hour exercise ride today very much. I have my eye on a tall lean thoroughbred horse here that they want to get rid of. I'm going to try him tomorrow. If I get him for mine we'll be a pair of skinnies. He is a weaver but is said to be quite a good mount and very fast. About five of the officer's horses belong to the colonel. Some of them are very small thickset ones very steady goers. Others which he rides not so. The sergeant major has a perfect picture of a mare, which the colonel says is not up to weight! Utter rot. She looks to be worth quite 150-200 guineas and you bet he won't part with her. He is an old regular roughrider.

Last day with the infantry I performed my toilette down by the first aid post, very weird with three or four dead on stretchers with blankets within a yard or so. But it didn't worry me at all. Everybody is very cheerful and amusing and I enjoy the life quite well. The conditions hereabouts make enemy stuff pretty harmless except for bad luck which case you wouldn't know anything about it.

Mosquitos are fewer and rats more plentiful but quite harmless. The battery cat, a waif, has come back after a week's absence and has deposited three kittens in No. 2 gun pit. They don't mind explosions a bit, though I expect the kittens are bound to go deaf.

I stop here until Wednesday and then go on a gas course in the next village (which is very close) with a corporal and one man. I think the colonel is satisfied, at least he usually now calls me 'Long Un'.

Yours truly, Douglas

21 August 1916

Dear Papa

Much obliged for letters, cake, and fruit which arrived in tip top order. We have had the same wet here as you but it has cleared up again and has been most beautiful today and yesterday.

I had two and half hour ride with the exercising party round the beautiful country. Every little village has troops in it and the Indians all over the place make it extra picturesque. Churches round here have very beautiful spires of a solid type. Not so bulky as ours at home but similar. I am riding a weird blood horse in the afternoons. He is well disposed but quite unschooled and very hard to steer. I managed to teach him quite a bit today and am going to have a go with him in a bit of a field we have hired for grazing tomorrow morning. Most of the officer's horses are pretty tame mounts. I don't fancy that they can be great horsemen except the colonel. I rode a thoroughbred polo pony of his called Tuppeny this morning. He was very comfortable but quite uninteresting. The horse I shall probably get is the one I am trying to train. He's about 16 hands, kind of a chocolate-coloured chestnut, with raw jagged hipbones and a spine like a mountain ridge. He is skinnier than I am and very hard to get the bridle onto. I think he has been roughly or ignorantly handled and will respond to good treatment. He's got plenty of go in him which I like but has a curious habit of dashing off at right angles down side roads. He needs determination on the part of the rider.

There is a French lady photographer in this one-horse village, so I'll try and get her to take my photo tomorrow on the horse, it will be a historic picture entitled 'somewhere in France'.

Don't want any more envelopes just now as I have bought lots.

Yours, Douglas

25 August 1916

Dear Mama

Have been today in the gas school wearing helmets in chlorine and other gas chambers. If one was going in for mining or anything extra precarious these things would seem more – I wouldn't say natural – but more normal. But to think that every man has to know exactly what to do in case of gas attack and do it right in twenty seconds without warning, with the penalty of a certain and horrible death for the slightest mistake, and then consider all the fools and fatheads there must be out here in the army! That means casualties of course. If you lose or damage your helmet and there is gas

– well it's all up. We gassed a cat today slightly with German lachrymatory mixture and he didn't like it. He wept copiously but was all right again very quick.

I bet the Bosch is sorry he started gas now. The helmets are absolute protection if in proper order and used correctly. I expect after this course I shall be responsible for the safety of the battery against gas. Which is some responsibility.

Yours, Douglas

28 August 1916

Dear Nellie

A fine parcel of apples just arrived and they are delicious. The cardboard box got pretty battered but the fruit didn't suffer.

I am off again to the infantry tomorrow afternoon for three days. The trenches will be pretty muddy and slushy. But that we've all got used to now and scarcely notice.

We had an accident in the battery today which was serious enough but might have been much worse. A gun burst and three men got cut about with some bits, one, an infantry colonel, rather seriously. However, they might much more likely have been killed.

With the exception of a wild mallon, lavender blue, the flowers are nearly all gone now. But there are lovely swallowtail butterflies about and quite a lot of sparrow hawks and such like birds of prey. Hope your bee stings are quite recovered now.

Weather decidedly broken now but the rain is interspersed with very bright sunshine which makes it much better. Have just got the news about Romania joining in which is good. It means that Russia has been able to show very great strength on paper as Romania is taking no chances.

Yours, Douglas

30 August 1916

Dear Papa

Am down again doing forward observation officer and the rain has converted the trenches into lakes about six or eight inches deep. Otherwise it is very quiet and quite pleasant.

Please ask Mama to order me some more refills and keep sending them out at a rate of say one a week. One of the last three she sent me was not active. I shan't bother to return it but she might mention at the shop that it was quite useless. I think I had better have a reserve lamp, same pattern, in case mine goes wrong. See what you can buy at a reasonable price in the shape of a collapsible lantern to take a candle.

We assisted in a most successful small raid last night which resulted in the capture of eight Bosches. Generals all over congratulated the infantry colonel also the artillery who assisted them by encircling the part with a curtain of shells. I was supervising our telephone.

Yours, Douglas

1 September 1916

Dear Mama

Have finished my spell down at FOO again and am to be relieved at six this evening. I directed the fire of the battery yesterday and the colonel seemed pleased with the result. Our trenches are pretty close to the Bosch ones there so you have to shoot cautiously.

We were firing for only twenty minutes. Had a fine day again today so the going is much better than when I came down when it was very sloppy. Am keeping excellently fit, although I have got several thorough wettings during the last few days. Living out here it doesn't seem as if getting a good wetting makes any difference at all except causing a certain amount of discomfort.

I think the colonel seems fairly satisfied with my efforts at least he is very civil, I mean officially when I write a report of anything. At mess, etc., everything is quite informal and we don't have any particular rank on these occasions.

Since my gas course I have got the job of putting all the gas protection in order. They are very bad indeed and it's really an impossible job to get them right. The dugouts and things are not really adaptable being old and haphazard in shape. This job is of course extra to anything else I have to do.

Yours affectionately, Douglas

9 September 1916

Dear Nellie

Am writing this at our observation station at 7.00 am. There is such a thick mist that you can't observe anything so I may as well use the opportunity.

We have a few Bosch prisoners working at our wagon lines now building standings for the horses. Our men say they never saw men work like these Bosch do. I haven't seen them yet and hope they will be there when I go back again. We are doing a lot of firing these days and the Huns are getting fed up with it. They have odd shots back at our position but there are so many batteries about here that they have no exact idea of their whereabouts and so they only make holes among the weeds. They are not likely to hit anything except by a fluke.

We have lost the battery puppy which is sad. I expect someone has pinched him. The cat and her three kittens are still with us and the kittens look splendid. They don't mind the guns at all although the concussion of firing sometimes knocks them over.

This gas protection business is a perpetual worry. Of course the doorposts and things don't fit very well and the rats dig holes in the earth and none of the dugouts were made by the French with the idea of gas protection. We were firing at intervals all day yesterday from 6.30 am to 1.25 am this morning. Unless we had bad luck we ought to have put a good many Bosch in the casualty lists and we have certainly given them some extra digging to do.

We do tremendously well in the eating line. The colonel has about three huge parcels a day sent out with all sorts of things. He is temporarily leaving for a few days to look after something else, so we shall have more to do.

The Somme progress is not spectacular but it is increasing. I know something about our artillery there and the quantity of it is absolutely unheard of. Also no Bosch aeroplane comes within three miles of us down there and the Bosch live like hunted rats in a thunderstorm.

We are on top of them all right now.

Yours, Douglas

16 September 1916

Dear Papa

Thanks for any amount of yours and Mama's letters.

I have been unable to write the last few days as we have suddenly moved to a new position about two miles further north. The reason is that more people are coming in and we have to squeeze up.

We came to this particular spot as the shooting from our brigade has a very high reputation and that is the sort of artillery they needed. We have therefore left the most comfortable gun position in the division, and living there was very much like living in shanties along the edge of the top field at home. What we have got into is a dump heap of rubbish. The position is all over the place and ramshackle and groggy. Down below in the chalk 30ft or 40ft underground are our sleeping quarters. Very musty and mouldy and not at all nice. The down below part was originally built by French miners and is shell proof against everything imaginable. Please double or treble the supply of torch refills (tell Mama any kind of colour of socks will do).

We flitted from the old position by moonlight; it would have made a magnificent picture. We came the last two miles (of course we had to go round by the rear) on a light railway sitting on top of the guns on trolleys drawn by six mules harnessed tandem fashion. All our supplies come up that way. There are so many batteries piled up around here that everybody shoots over us, we are the front one, and the din is terrific. The Hun simply scatter a few shells about (he hasn't many to spare) the area and trusts to luck. He always manages to land them where nobody lives. We have our own wireless apparatus to shoot with aeroplanes, and did so today with excellent results.

We arrived here at 3.00 am and were up most of the night. At present I am digging a dugout for the colonel to live in. He can't stand the subterranean business with his useless right leg. I have got ten days to make it with two assistants and it has to be moderately shell proof and quite gas proof. The divisional gas inspector said that the latter was impossible. The next visit I hope will prove him wrong. By the way he visited an abandoned position and told me that my arrangements were 'practically perfect'.

The Hun is getting a hammering now all right. While our friends behind were shooting I saw a Bosch blown quite 150ft in the air through my glasses from our very remarkable observation point. We camouflage everything with painted canvas and grass and wire because all aeroplanes take photographs nowadays. We use aerial photos to show the Bosch positions and also the weak spots of our own. I want my camel hair waistcoat, if it is at home please send it out. It's pretty cold even now observing at night.

Yours, Douglas

PS. Still very fit and getting on well with everybody and all kinds of jobs.

18 September 1916

Dear Papa
I have suddenly been transferred to a new battery, D/302. Colonel Bate says he is extremely annoyed and upset about it and hopes to get me returned shortly. As known, the position of D/303 was simply appalling and is only said to be temporary. I hope I don't get transferred back again too soon.

But the position apart, it is most annoying to get shifted among new people after one had settled down and made friends and got to know the men. The new battery commander is a very different type. Much more civilian like and gentle in manner. The old one was very fierce at times but a regular regular if you understand. This one is a regular too but much milder and I should fancy rather too gentle.

This position is a muddy sort of place but then all the country is that after rain like we had today.

Yours, Douglas

23 September 1916

Dear Mama
I had a pleasant walk this morning to the nearest village, which is quite large and not very ruined, to get the battery pay. The weather the last two days has been lovely with bright sun and not too hot. I can hear the Somme

guns far away a dull rumble and so I fancy can most people in the north of France. Anyway I hear from a friend at Caen that they hear it there.

The official army intelligence that we get makes out that Bosch moral is very much worse. Ever since July, they have either been driven back or they have been making costly and futile counter-attacks. We have absolute mastery in the air and more guns and more shells. In one instance they had positions for eight guns in a wood. When we captured the wood we found forty smashed guns there, that is to say they had five lots of guns knocked out in the position one after another. I believe our heavy artillery there is indescribably powerful and keeps up an incessant show of shells day and night on every Bosch battery, trench and supply column.

My bunk here is quite delightful, light and airy and very cheery, as my man has covered the walls with pictures out of the *Sketch* and *Tatler*. I have a table and a chest of drawers, homemade.

Yours, Douglas

25 September 1916

Dear Nellie

Have had nothing from home for a day or two but I know they have stopped things at the base lately. We have had a gorgeous four days of Indian summer and it looks like continuing.

I do want stockings as one has to wear long boots up in the forward trenches and socks are awful, they work down in folds under the instep. With stockings some garters will be necessary.

My bunk here is really excellent, almost as comfortable as my room at home and we shall shortly have stores supplied. I am getting a British 'warmer' from the men's stores, quite good enough for falling about in the muddy trenches in. We have much more spare time and I sleep in the battery. I went over to my old position this morning about some ammunition and stole the colonel's basin which is a good one.

I am very fit. Dogs are now forbidden in the army but we have a very friendly cat in the battery. There are two regular sergeants which is all right. They look on me as being much more an officer than the others who are mostly territorials.

Yours, Douglas

29 September 1916

Dear Papa

I got your and Mama's letters all right. The collapsible lamp is A1 and as you say very rigorous.

We have had nearly a week of fine weather but it rained all today. Life is going to be hardish in the winter, but that is bound to be so. We shall be provided with plenty of stores. I had a fine hot bath last night down behind the wagon lines and a decent dinner with the veterinary officers and the French interpreter in a big estaminet where they are billeted. We had a five-franc bottle of so-called champagne.

Don't make out your letters are not worth reading, I am awfully glad to get them and everybody is very disappointed if nothing comes by post for them.

They say the courage of the Bosch remains wonderful, they have been slaughtered in thousands and thousands on the Somme, and a gunner from there told me that we now fire twenty shells to their one. They brought along one of their famous 17-inch down there and we put three of our big guns onto it. In three days they knocked it out and when we took its position there were only small bits of it left.

Your affectionate son, Douglas

30 September 1916

Dear Nellie

Have just finished drawing a trench map, most elaborate in three colours on the piece of linen in which the last parcel was stitched. The stuff came in very handy as anything of that sort is pretty hard to get hold of out here. I have just conducted a major general around our position. I can't tell you his name. Without one of him a belt wouldn't be any use at all.

My new battery is only about three miles south of where we were before and I often look across to the great landmark from which the king watched us strafing the Bosches, it stands just about one and half miles behind my friends. We had three aviators in to lunch yesterday.

I have had a slack time the last two days and the weather today is lovely so that everything is all right. My watch is going first class and this pen is also a great luxury and I hate writing in pencil. Altogether we don't live as strenuous a life in this battery as the other, except we get FOO more often and the front line is much more muddy and uncomfortable.

The Bosch prisoners who work around behind look very contented and well fed. They wear civilian clothes and caps, German army boots and have a big blue patch in the middle of their backs. The patch is circular and round about as big as their heads.

We had two German aeroplanes overhead today, and just before that two shells fired by the enemy anti-aircraft failed to explode in the air and fell and burst about 30yds down the road quite harmlessly. Captured Bosch letters on the Somme are full of sneers at their own airmen who sit in theatres covered in medals and never dare go up when any of our planes are about. I don't believe our Somme casualties amount to a quarter of the German losses from what I hear.

Your affectionate brother, Douglas

5 October 1916

Dear Papa

I got the parcels with cakes and stockings for which many thanks. That chocolate cake is my favourite and everybody else. The pears were delicious but the yellow ones wouldn't have kept another day. I don't know how long they were on the way.

The Bosch is knocking our trenches about with his trench mortars and we keep trying to knock them out without much success, I think the Huns run them about on rails. I have nearly finished the extension of our mess to double the size, having walled, floored and roofed in a dark cavern, put in shelves and a writing desk. I haven't quite finished the floor. I took a long time with odd scraps of wood full of nails and the chalk is very hard to pick out and the debris has to be carried up out into the open in small boxes or bags. I am hoping to get hold of some green canvas for wallpaper out of a friend in the engineers.

The weather is not so bad today, but it takes two or three days for the mud to dry up and it usually gets spoiled before its dry. When it is dry it is like cement. Had nothing from you today. I always miss the post as I am too busy with other things to write before the post goes.

Your affectionate son, Douglas

11 October 1916

Dear Mama

We have had decent weather the last two or three days.

Last night all sorts of stunts were on. I had to stop up until midnight. We fired off at 2.00 am until 3.00 am then again at 5.00 am. The Bosch tried to imitate us and do a raid, with disastrous results for the Bosch. According to the papers this region seems to be doing raids more than anybody and some of them must have given the Huns a fright. On one our men threw ten bombs down each of seven dugouts full of Bosch who wanted to surrender but would not come out. The main purposes of raids are various. They are to accustom our men to leave the trenches, to annoy the Hun and inflict casualties and, above all, to identify the divisions and find out where the various German brigades are.

I bought twenty bottles of white wine from an infantry colonel here which is a great improvement in the mess. The water is horrid, as if it is chlorinated by the sanitary people to prevent typhoid. It tastes awful and makes you get up in the night more than once. I believe the stuff is quite bad for the urinary arrangements.

It still keeps quite warm except at night. I have made some very nice friends among the infantry on this front. All our stuff now comes up on a new narrow-gauge railway on trucks drawn by mules. The system is all right except that these things are very vulnerable to shell fire. At present the Hun is hardly using any guns at all, and has not fired a single round at our position since I came here. I see the French have made another advance but Romania seems to have made a mess of it.

I dressed a horse's foot here last night with what I could get in the way of antiseptic and so on from an RAMC man. The horse had picked up a nail coming up and when I got it out the foot was bleeding. I did it in four thickness of sacking to keep the mud out, for fear of tetanus of which the soil is full.

We have three small graveyards in our position, mostly French, one Hun and three Scotchmen. Our men keep them tidy and free from weeds in their spare time. There is an army order which enjoins us to do so.

Everybody is rather dreading the winter's mud. It is very much like Kenley mud only the roads are not metalled so that except for the main roads it is simply ploughed fields and you can imagine what that gets like with heavy traffic.

Rats are all over the place and there is a mouse walking about on the table eating crumbs holding them in his forefeet like a monkey and nibbling away with one eye on me. He sits down only about six inches away.

Yours affectionately, Douglas

15 October 1916

Dear Papa

Got yours and Mama's letter today.

I have just come back from the front line to find that the newest joined officer has gone to the wagon lines instead of me. As we are now one short it will mean two days up the line and two days here which is a bit thick. However we may get another officer attached. I am rather fed up not going back to the horses. I have had one day or rather half a day back there in the last seven weeks.

It's gone jolly cold this afternoon, but I have plenty of warm things at present. Also have two torch batteries in reserve. The CO of the infantry asked me to dinner last night which was a pleasant change. Company headquarters where I live up there is about 20ft down and only lit with candles and it takes a fair amount of agility to get up the stairs. Coming back to the battery is like going to the country from the slums, and a day in a bust up village behind is like going to London. At the battery one lives very much like crofters on the moors. I really can't undertake to write home every day and if I did they certainly wouldn't arrive every day, as I can never catch the post but have to write when I can and let it go next day. Glad you got some apples anyway, I suppose mainly off the big tree down by the stable.

We get a good supply of tinned fruit out here which is very welcome. All sorts of things are sold in the infantry canteen up near the line. I actually saw one man buying tinned prawns there today and by the same token we had them for dinner at battalion headquarters last night. Considering that everything has to be carried up and the cooking facilities are a brazier with only a sloping passage up to a trench to let some of the smoke out, the diet is extraordinary. One gets usually porridge, tea, bacon and bread and jam or even toast, tinned butter and tinned milk. For lunch, cold beef, hot potatoes, tinned fruit, usually apricots and cheeses. Tea with jam and private cake, dinner, soup, hot meat and potatoes and issue beans, tinned fruit and sometimes even suet pudding(!) and coffee. It's just the good food that keeps one going as an FOO rarely gets three hours sleep up there, not that there's much to do but that you have to be out and about most of the twenty hours observing and trying to spot positions of enemy trench mortars and things.

At this battery we do about the same excepting porridge but the cooking is not so good which is absurd. It is largely a matter of management, and of course the infantry have more men and so are more likely to have cooks in the ranks whereas ours here just had a few lessons.

We had rain and hail this pm so the mud is with us again. Five minutes heavy rain makes a slimy quagmire in this soil.

Tales of six months ago of the French being finished looks rather ridiculous in the light of the Somme, but the strain must be simply terrific in all directions.

Your affectionate son, Douglas

20 October 1916

Dear Mama

Had a very quiet day today so I set to and built a staircase down to the officers' mess which is a great improvement and pleased the major greatly. I have just used the stair in moonlight or whatever light there is and it is an enormous improvement. It is steady and safe whereas the old one was sloped in the treads and of greasy smelly earth and clay. I think I have contrived too that the water won't run down them anymore. Next job is to enlarge and improve the officers' mess which is far too small and has nowhere to put anything.

The Bosch hardly fires any guns about here but goes in for trench mortars heavily. They of course don't affect us except when we are up in the front line. Fine weather still holds and we have been issued with rubber waders for wet weather. Really the government does provide awfully well for everybody out here.

Alexander Douglas Thorburn, 1882–1942.

Thorburn was commissioned as second lieutenant in 1915 and went on to attain the rank of captain during the war.

Thorburn's war took him from France to Salonika and then Palestine, where he fought against a determined enemy and the unforgiving desert conditions.

Thorburn and his fellow cadets at the Royal Artillery school at Topsham Barracks, Exeter.

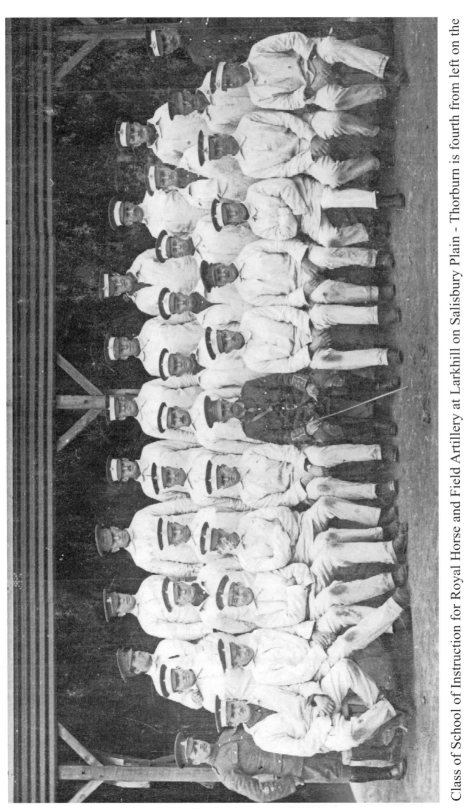

Class of School of Instruction for Royal Horse and Field Artillery at Larkhill on Salisbury Plain - Thorburn is fourth from left on the front row.

No. 1 gun of Thorburn's battery and its horses on the Western Front.

British 4.5-inch howitzer on the Western Front.

The SS *Manitou* that carried Thorburn and his battery from Marseille to Salonika in 1916.

British horse-drawn transport on the move through the Macedonian countryside.

Officers and other ranks after the order to not wash or shave for eight days prior to the Battle of Sheria to conserve precious water supplies.

Driver Macmeniman, a member of the battery and Thorburn's groom on active service in Palestine.

Thorburn's batman Driver Sidney Clements who was later killed near Beersheba in Palestine at the age of nineteen.

Water camels in the desert – a peculiar creature according to Thorburn, but capable of great endurance.

A knocked out British tank near Gaza in November 1917.

Archie and Arthur, two of General Allenby's 'White Mice' that proved so vital for carrying supplies in the Judean Hills.

Thorburn with his horse Baby at El Ferdan near the Suez Canal.

No. 4 Gun just fired by Gunner H.A. Springett during the battle for Jerusalem.

Captured Turkish guns and equipment following the Battle of Sheria.

Thorburn believed that, 'The gallantry and devotion of the animals of our various armies deserve a striking monument in the heart of London, but, alas, their services have not been recognised in that way.' In 2004, such a memorial was finally unveiled near Hyde Park, London.

What an absolute bore the censoring of letters is in this war. Some of the men write long epistles full of twaddle to about six girls on the same day.

Yours, Douglas

22 November 1916

Dear Nellie

One is allowed I believe to use paper headed like this, at least an officer of our battery asked and they said it was all right. If the censor objects he can tear the top off.

Nothing much to do here while we are waiting except when one is orderly officer. I went out for a ride this morning to exercise a few horses and bought some odd things in the town this pm. Our camp is in a very poor quarter of the town but the town itself is fine. The people are pretty-Spanish looking. Lots of French colonial troops about doing odd guard duties. It does look peculiar to see half a dozen Hun prisoners being marched off to work under a guard consisting of one Chinese trench soldier. I don't think the Huns mind a bit. The quantities of French soldiers are a perpetual surprise. I suppose they are all on leave; the variety is most picturesque, I don't suppose there is a single unit which is not represented: Africans, Arabs, Chinese, Indians of some sort, Turcos, Zouaves, and all the various regiments of the ordinary army. Except for our Indian troops our uniforms look very sombre and dull compared with theirs and are too much alike.

It's really quite odd being able to march over and buy anything you want in a shop. I bought a French automatic pistol today – my revolver got pinched at Havre on the way up and I didn't like the idea of having no weapon in the place we're bound for. I got an automatic as they are much lighter and go in one's pocket. Great change being able to get a real good dinner in the town. Also to be able to fill my pen.

The absence of mud is the most welcome feature of a change from the trenches.

Yours, Douglas

CHAPTER 8

Letters from Salonica

December 1916 to June 1917

6 December 1916

Dear Papa

We have been on board since 1 December and have so far had weather like midsummer on Lake Windermere. I have never seen so calm a sea.

We have seen all the islands, Corsica, Sardinia, Elba, Pantelleria and are now just off Malta. I saw a line of palm trees off the African coast with my glasses. We have a destroyer as an escort and one day a French destroyer came tearing up and reported a submarine 11 miles off, so we went 25 miles out of our course. We potter about a lot and sometimes sail up and down for five hours or so. The ship is a good one, eight thousand tons but slow. We are as comfortable as in first class quarters on any liner; in fact it is identical with that.

We had a concert yesterday and I wrote the words for a topical song which I and two other officers of our battery sang. Words were much admired and it is suggested we send them to the *Bystander* or some paper. The fine weather is of course fine for the horses and so far they have stood it very well. It is hard to keep the smell at a bearable strength as there is so little room to sweep out. We have had no news except some oddments by wireless, so when we get papers it will be quite funny.

Not much time as I am orderly officer and not much to say. Our major is commanding the ship.

Yours, Douglas

10 December 1916

Dear Mama

We have had a glorious trip and have arrived but not landed – most beautiful sunshine and as calm as a millpond all the way. I believe three ships were sunk by submarines close to us but they didn't get us luckily. One ship contained a general going home on leave and they took him on board as a prisoner. It is very pleasant to be in port and not to have a lifebelt on and to be able to have the light on after dark.

There were great boxing matches on the way. The port is most beautiful from the bay and is full of all sorts of ships and warships of four nationalities.

We had to work hard to keep our horses alive. Five have died on board, none of them ours, but they have suffered terribly from the heat and want of air and the crowding down below. We shall have to have at least a fortnight for the horses to recover and be fit for work. They have had to stand absolutely for ten days and some of them in the dark and others beside the engines. Fortunately it was so smooth or we might have lost a lot.

The war seems to be going pretty badly just now, the old Hun is not dead by a long way yet, in fact he seems quite as lively as we do.

This letter may arrive in time to wish you all a Happy Christmas, if it doesn't I can't help it. Glad my two horses have travelled very well. I also, I think, saved the sergeant major's pony which was very weak and wouldn't eat. I had fed him for two days.

There are gorgeous snow mountains in sight and sun on the minarets and things are like a coloured photograph.

There isn't much to say really. There are some pleasant officers on board – but one lot are fearful outsiders. We had a little mess by ourselves with the vet officers which was very nice.

I'm sorry to leave the ship.

Yours affectionately, Douglas

18 December 1916

Dear Mama

I have an opportunity at last of writing a letter.

We arrived here safely about a week ago. As usual nothing was arranged. No water, almost no food or forage, no candles and people turning up at all hours of the night without notice so that all supplies get less and less. Things are better now and we have some candles bought in Salonica. We are in a huge plain about ten miles south of Salonica and I suppose about forty or fifty miles from the firing line. The snow mountains in the distance are lovely and about twelve miles off south you see the sea. The plain is one mass of white tents and horse lines – there must be quite ten thousand horses and mules wandering about and in lines. Bullock carts come along the road in quantities and patriarchs riding on diminutive donkeys, women in baggy cotton trousers and small boys selling tangerines and figs and the *Balkan News* – quite a good little paper.

I have had two parcels from Fortnum and Mason, one containing steak and kidney pudding – very good – and the other a lovely roast chicken, etc. These are all most welcome only I should like to know who sent them. I wouldn't mind stopping here for months, the weather is good and we get lots of riding.

The sun is quite hot at midday and there is much mud. The town – we have been there twice – is muddier than a ploughed field, but no particular smells to notice.

Will write again soon, Douglas

26 December 1916

Dear Nellie

We have had the most lovely days for Christmas and today, just like those few hot days we get at Easter at home.

I have had some most delightful rides out to the hills that border the valley. The colours of the snow mountains in the distance are splendid. The people are picturesque, the women wear scarlet and various coloured trousers, and the men are like Father Abraham when old and the boys like little cherubs, they ride on diminutive donkeys on top of enormous packs of all sorts of goods and somehow the donkeys manage to get along. We saw a wedding reception in a village – which is said to be a dangerous place and where you are not allowed to go without a pistol. There was one of the small local pony carts filled up with the trousseau in front of

116

the door and a balcony up above with the bridesmaids with branches of evergreens stuck up on the balustrades. The trousseau seemed to consist mostly of scarlet blankets and bedding. There was a band of sorts of wooden trumpets etc. and altogether it was quite amusing.

Figs here are bought on strings about eight to ten a penny, from Serbian refugee hawker boys about twelve to sixteen. By the way send me a bee veil soon, as mosquitos are said to be very bad and malarious later on.

There is hardly a tree to be seen about in this valley but there are quantities of stones which will make splendid paths in a battery position

Yours, Douglas

31 December 1916

Dear Mama

I saw Colonel Bate today, he has just arrived here and looks only fairly well. Food, water and so on has got all right now here and I would like to stay where we are for months. However this is peace soldiering.

In the town you see, Greek, Italian, French, Russians, Serbian and English troops of all sorts and kinds, it is Babel in the extreme, but French is the best medium so I get on fine there. When I arrived at Bate's tent he said hullo, where did you pick that up referring to my pony. He is said to be about the best judge in the army, so I was rather pleased. As a matter of fact I can't ride him just now as his back is tender and he simply dances about all over the shop.

We have made a fine acetylene lamp for our mess tent which is splendid and we 'make' carbide for it off every motor lorry that is willing or careless. I do the catering for our mess and have arranged a fierce dinner for Hogmanay:

Soupe – Fin de l'Anne (old bones etc. stock)
Soles Frites (got in fish market at Salonica)
Poulet Roti (cold tinned from parcel)
Boeuf Roti (rations)
Pears (tinned)
Desert: Figs and dates
Coffee

Not so bad considering; we have got an excellent cook, who can do wonders on a fire consisting of charcoal in an old tin can and an oven made out of a bit of tin and clay. The wind is the most troublesome thing at present but the rain has kept away which is all I care about. I suppose we are kept here until the Greeks take some definitive steps.

Yours, Douglas

4 January 1917

Dear Mama

Not had much from you lately but I believe one or two mail steamers have got sunk on the way here. Letters take about fourteen days apparently to come out.

We are very comfortable here – tho' tents are not the best houses on a windy night. Still they are special double tents and very good ones.

There is really nothing to write about. We go on exercising horses, drilling and practicing use of packsaddles, as roads for wheeled traffic are extremely rare unless they have been specially built for the soldiers. The trouble is that there are deep gullies with steep sides running in all directions so steep that it is just possible to lead horses up and down, and you can imagine the job with heavy guns and ammunition wagons.

I went over to draw new mounts the day before yesterday: there were twenty-six hundred sick horses in the hospital, you cannot imagine the thousands and thousands of horses all over the plain. Our 130 in the battery look like nothing at all.

The rubbish published about riots and things in Salonica is very absurd. The town is about as riotous as Little Sutton or Raby Mere. Occasionally a Greek gets killed unloading a gun off a ship, but that doesn't worry anybody at all.

There is no doubt that mules are the most suitable beast for the army. They never get ill and they are so clever. There are loose mules wandering about all over the place. Somebody offered us an engine for making baths for the men if we'd find them a mule. So I went out with three grooms and rounded one up in half an hour. It took about one and half hours before I could get a head collar on him. But I managed it all right, and so men got a hot bath the next day.

I have been wearing my teddy bear coat today; it is long grey goatskin body with blackish brown sleeves of some softer fur. Some of the horses are frightened at it, but neither of mine express any objection.

Yours, Douglas

20 January 1917

Dear Papa

We had mounted sports arranged for today but rain has made them impossible. We have built a very fine jumping course which Howell and I designed and built with the assistance of the carpenter. A hurdle, a wooden stone wall, a two-bar jump, a three-bar jump side view, then a thick hedge in the middle of two small ditches and then a water jump consisting of a low row of rushes and about 9ft of water beyond it. We put up wings to all the jumps made of boards and white washed them, making the course quite a picture. The guests were to be nurses and doctors from the Serbian hospital which is about half a mile across Galiko River.

The country and way of life of the inhabitants is altogether biblical, you see Joseph going into Egypt with Mary on the ass, another ass conveying a huge wooden plough and with a little donkey trolling behind prehistoric ox carts and the earth is good ground, stony ground and thorns springing up and all the rest of it.

There is nothing to relate about our doings, because we are simply on a peace footing. I don't write very often as the mails are few and there is nothing doing at all out here.

Yours, Douglas

31 January 1917

Dear Nellie

I got a big post last night, five letters in all, two of them yours for which many thanks.

I don't know that there is really very much that I want out here and probably when we do get up the line – which will not be for a good while yet – it will take so long to let you know that when they arrive the climate will have changed completely. The summer here is said to be practically the same as India. You might try and get a couple of shirts of a tropical pattern e.g. with padded backs and finished off like a tunic with pockets etc., so as to be worn without a tunic. Also one plain of khaki duck 'shorts' shaped like football trousers.

We have got stuck here owing to infectious mange among the horses and have had terrible wind and rain for some days. The horses stand it wonderfully but of course if you imagine them toed on lines on top of Bidston Hill in a gale of wind and rain you get an idea of what they have to put up with and they have cut down their feeds to make it worse. One lies awake and listens to the rain pouring down and the wind howling and thinks of the poor beasts out in the open. The tents we live in are pretty good at keeping out the elements but sometimes when the wind is extra strong the water gets in under the sides.

Our notice to move up was cancelled next day and we may be here for weeks yet.

You would like the shepherds here with their large flocks which graze about the country. They all carry shepherds crooks of the authorised pattern.

We have great quartet hymn singing in the officers mess tent. The officers at the Serbian hospital over the river have made us honorary members of their mess but at present the floods have made the journey across too wet for going except mounted.

Yours, Douglas

17 February 1917

Dear Mama

Have been rather occupied lately and so not written anything. I am writing this in the Serbian hospital mess where I have been dining. Tomorrow we are – some of us – riding up the valley to see a boar hunt organised by the Serbian Crown Prince. This ought to be good fun. I am taking back in my pocket from here a medicine bottle of maraschino to make a fruit salad with – we are having two doctors to dinner tomorrow.

The weather has been lovely today – it is like living in another world when the wind stops blowing. We hear via the navy of great destruction of Hun submarines and that our new Mediterranean patrols are very effective against them.

Am still very well and generally all right.

Yours, Douglas

PS. With wind and sun we are pretty much beetroot colour.

7 March 1917

Dear Papa

Have just come back from Salonica where I have been buying things for the canteen.

One goes in by getting lifts on various motor wagons carrying anything from sides of beef to coils of barbed wire or Greek washerwomen, changing from one to another when they stop and get out much the same way only that they come a part of the way out in the evening so I have the horses meet me about five miles or so away.

I think I told you I had to send my big horse to hospital and they won't issue any more riding horses here at present so I'm badly off. The old white-stockinged pony is however in great form and this evening took a lot of riding. I jumped him over two small ditches full of water – which he loves doing and charges at them like a racehorse – and that excited him so I had fireworks for a quarter of an hour or so. Once he has a bit of a gallop he wants to go on and dances about and spins round like a mad thing. I have two bits on him now as once he bolted with me twice in one day. When he does get away he takes two huge jumps in the air and then tears away just like a dog after a rabbit. However I can stop him with the two bits in 40yds or 50yds and though his knees are funny looking he never makes a mistake however rough the ground is. He really is the best mount anyone could wish for and except when a bit excited a baby could ride him. Over a short distance I doubt if anything alive could catch him even now when he must be thirteen- or fourteen-years-old.

We are sure to move off very soon now which is good as we shall get up into the hills for the hot weather. I am awfully glad we came out here as the country is really most interesting. To my mind quite preferable to being cooped up in the trenches in France.

Yours, Douglas

15 March 1917

Dear Mama

It is sometime since I took my pen in my hand – which is a pencil – the reason being that we have marched for about a week. I really can't remember when we started, picking our way mainly at night over tracks across country – no walls or hedges and pitch dark

I got some parcels and letters before we started but in the confusion and all night and day marching I don't remember much about them.

The enemy has only one gun which fires at long enough range to reach our lines!

It is some job getting strings of guns and wagons about at night over ditches and fords and so on. However we get there in the end. I am to be in charge of wagon lines here – but there are no villages or houses or estaminets – in fact no inhabitants at all in the country. Though junior subaltern I really do a captain's jobs now.

Tropical kit will be wanted any time. Even now the sun at midday is quite noticeably hot. A hat is not a requirement and in a very few weeks it will be as hot as India

Yours, Douglas

25 March 1917

Dear Mama

First a grumble. You have done me pretty badly by not sending the tropical kit as and when asked you. It is now as hot as the hottest day in August at home. I have no thin things. I sent for them in plenty of time and got nothing but surely you are in a great hurry and that sort of thing. What I am going to do now Lord only knows. I don't care a button what quality or price or material – nor would you if you were here – only send them off at once. If not I will get heatstroke or something.

We are up in the line and I am in command of a detached section of guns all on my own. I fire from Greece into Serbia and it is great fun. It is lovely country, like Cumberland, there are crocuses, grape hyacinths, and other like flowers growing wild. I live in a little valley with a beck – a well – and a tree alongside. Close to us is a 60-pounder section and infantry battalion headquarters where I lunched today with the Colonel

Duputron who is very nice and hospitable. My section has the best position of all the batteries hereabouts – and I have disguised my guns with lots of local colour until I can hardly find them myself.

Choc cakes excellent. Send the tropical stuff quickly: one pair khaki shorts, one taffeta shirt, one oxford.

Must have spare pads.

Douglas

18 April 1917

Dear Mama

This is your birthday I remember, so many happy returns thereof. I expect you got news that the French had taken ten thousand prisoners on the Reims-Soissons front so that is the best of birthday presents.

The weather is absolutely perfect and will be until the great heat begins. Now and again it is extremely hot already but not uncomfortable probably owing to being in the mountains. I got complimented by the brigadier general about the protection I had made in our last position which had saved damage. The country is now a mass of flowers. Orchards all over the place. Mulberries – not for fruit but for silkworms – are the principal trees. For a perfect account of our life in France get the Pearson's Monthly for Feb '17, and read 'A Day of Peace' by Sapper. It is marvellously good.

We are living all together now by a lovely stream. I have had a very quiet day as there has been no firing. Some days ago we were at it carting stuff about all night for two nights, so that a bit of extra quiet is rather welcome. It hardly ever rains here, but so far the nights are cool to almost cold. We ought to get plenty of wild strawberries if we stay here long enough; the rations are extra good and very plentiful. I don't know if I acknowledged the last parcel or not. I never know the day of the week and day and night get mixed up so hopelessly that one simply goes on and the weeks slip by.

One day we shoot, another we get shot at and the next you forget all about both. I can quite see the fascination of a gypsy's life which is just about what ours is only without any shops near.

Yours affectionately, Douglas

28 April 1916

Dear Mama

I have this morning had a slight scratch from a bit of anti-aircraft which came out of the sky and scraped my neck. I got a scratch no more and had it dressed at the hospital; it doesn't amount to anything, in fact I have had worse knocks playing hockey.

We had two days heavy rain which were trying as my section has been all over the country; up to now we have been in five positions. We got shelled out of two of them, fortunately without casualties. Today is lovely weather again, hot and sunny. I am on my way to the wagon lines for a few days so that I can get this scratch dressed. My neck is more bruised than anything.

I should be grateful for an occasional parcel of biscuits in tins, chocolate, or anything of that sort. The rations are wonderfully good, but of course they can't manage vegetables.

The wild flowers get more and more beautiful every day – all sorts that you only see 'in the best rockeries at home'. The *Weekly Times* is quite a boon, please have it kept up for me.

Yours, Douglas

6 May 1917

Dear Papa

My 'wound' is now a thing of the past – it was only a scratch but they inoculate you for tetanus and return you in the casualties in case of blood poisoning as otherwise you would be negligible for compensation pensions and things in case of anything going wrong.

Our OC has been made an acting-major and I have become an acting-captain and second-in-command of the battery. That is not so bad considering there are piles of officers senior to me all over the shop, and all the other officers in the battery are also senior.

Now however you only get acting rank while 'in command' of a unit and that sort of thing, so that if you get sick or get transferred to another unit you revert to your 'permanent rank' – Major Miles would then become a second lieutenant automatically again which is absurd. Such is the extraordinary arrangement. Still I have nothing to grumble at as I never expected to be going about with three stars on me.

Weather is still lovely, flowers are simply extraordinary. I have got the bit of shell that hit me in the neck with the date and place stamped on it. Rather a good souvenir.

Your affectionate son, Douglas

PS. Many happy returns of your birthday, a bit late but no matter.

10 May 1917

Dear Mama

I am writing this at 4.30 am, as I am on duty at present.

We are now sitting up two hours each through the night and firing off and on; there have been several 'shows' here lately and the stuff has to go off without delay when wanted. Aeroplanes are the curse of this war. Everything has to be done at night in the way of changing positions, and if you fire at all with an enemy plane up you get spotted and shelled. It is rather trying but you get accustomed to it that I can now usually 'spot' an enemy aeroplane by the sound of the engine from inside a dugout. That sounds a tall story but I saved one position of ours twice in that way. The planes fly along at a great height, far above the clouds, then when they get over our lines they shut off their engine and glide down quite low without being heard. In one position I was in we were much haunted by these nuisances and for two days had to stand literally perfectly still and do nothing and practically do without meals as the least movement gives away a position.

It is now compulsory for all troops to wear pith helmets from 8.00 am to 6.00 pm. As yet it is only really hot from about 10.30 pm to 4.00 pm and quite cool at night.

I am just beginning to get used to being called captain, tho' I am only acting-captain, i.e. I am entitled to wear the badges and draw the pay while second-in-command of this battery. Otherwise I should only be second lieutenant. The pay and allowances come to about nineteen shillings a day.

Yours, Douglas

PS. My 'wound' is all finished with.

11 May 1917

Dear Nellie

If my last letter arrives safely you will see that I am now addressed as captain, a pretty quick rise from gunner last June.

Pay and allowance amount to nineteen shillings and sixpence a day when you have three stars on your sleeve in the RFA, which is quite good. I probably owe promotion to the battery commander Miles who put in many good words for me; the rank is only 'acting' there being no permanent promotions now so that if I go sick or away from the unit for a fortnight or get transferred or wounded or anything I go back to second lieutenant as also does Miles who is acting-major. It seems most unfair but there it is and of course I have been very lucky to get promoted at all as I was junior in the battery.

One of us having to be by the telephone at night now so I get time to write letters. It breaks the nights up rather badly being on two to four, and four to six as well as the days labours. We have shot a lot lately as there has been plenty doing round about here.

Send me out some thin vests like I always wear. You remember the rags I started out with some of them are still going but not much is left of them. It is hard to get anything done up the line, boots wear out quickly and there is no leather for repairs. Watches go bust and stay bust as the only local population is snakes and frogs and tortoises and green lizards. We have got hold of a good gramophone which is a great pleasure. I have an excellent dugout and the mess is very comfortable. My servant called Clements whom I have had ever since I joined this battery in September is really a wonderfully good boy. He looks after me like anything and is quite devoted. When I got hit by a bit of anti-aircraft shell I was at an observation place on top of a mountain. He ran all the way up, over a mile of steep going to give me assistance.

We are in country just like the hill behind Currsey house. Trees are lovely and in the valley are vineyards and mulberry orchards. We have a stream handy about the size of Currsey Beck. The frogs in it make an infernal row. We keep one of the mules called 'Clarence' up with the guns for odd jobs, he is a regular pet and as well-mannered as any horse. Doesn't mind shellfire or gun fire or anything

Yours, Douglas

21 May 1917

Dear Mama

We shall probably move again a bit shortly but not far. They do fairly keep us jogging about here. We are all extremely fit so far. Lots of changes among our officers, but I am probably a fixture. I hope so as if I got moved I would revert to second lieutenant. They dated me back to 19 March so I've scored quite well in the pay line.

Tropical kit not arrived yet. I managed to buy a pair of shorts for four shillings and sixpence in the canteen though. It is quite impossible to get anything here now. The canteen are sold out in half an hour and cigarettes are becoming unknown. Even woodbines are looked on as treasures. Ask Papa to get Rycroft to pick me out two good two shilling, six to three shillings, six pipes without silver mountings and square them out.

We have knocked the men off work from 11.00 am to 4.30 pm now as the sun is pretty hot. My present job as captain is really much less strenuous than before because I was really doing it as well as section commander. We've had a good rest the last fortnight and done a few jobs, built roof and made a good bridge over a river. Those tunics my tailor made have been simply wonderful. I have only had the second one on about a dozen times and the other one I have worn daily and quite often slept in it and it is still quite smart. Of course it now has leather patches on the elbows and leather binding round the cuffs but that is rather fashionable than otherwise. The *Weekly Times* is greatly valued by all of us out here, the *Balkan News*, our local army paper, comes irregularly and we pick up the missed bits about three weeks later.

The country is now full of magenta, white scabeous, blue canterbury bells that flower in a circle on the end of the stalk; large pink wild roses; the mulberries and vines are just beginning to flower. Scarlet poppies all over the place great ranks of thyme and all sorts of huge purple thistles as big as peonies. There are no inhabitants of course anywhere. Most of the reports in the paper about this front are absolute fiction. They gave an account of the 'battle' that took place very near here. Nobody in the firing line there knew of any battle except what the papers invented.

The war correspondents probably live in Jamaica or Fleet Street or somewhere equally near the scene of the action and are consequently compelled to use their imagination.

Yours, Douglas

CHAPTER 9

Letters from Palestine

July 1917 to April 1918

27 July 1917

Dear Mama

I started a letter several days ago, I have no idea when. I also lost it some days ago.

We had a trip in open trucks on the railways, with a bit of wooden section built on them to keep the sun off. Then we got here on so-called cultivated land which really means fine dust about four inches deep. No shelters from the sun are provided except what we can make for ourselves out of blankets, bits of tarpaulin and wagon-poles. Water is strictly limited to one gallon a day per man for all purposes including washing clothes and the horses have to go three miles for a drink, and now and again we bathe them in the sea about four and half miles off. We rode this morning to the first place Abraham built a well. We could just not see Beersheba and only the height that commands Sampson's scene of temple demolition.

Camels all over the place, they are good beasts and not a bit smelly. Their drivers are natives with blue shirts on. You know my address is D/268 now. You also know I never wanted to go to the Holy Land. If the rest of it is like this I don't want to see any more. By the way I have at last got a tooth mended which gave way last November. It was a dickens of a job and four different dentists had to have a go at it in different hospitals as I ran across them. However I got it done at last at the place the Turks first attacked the Suez Canal at.

We get a wind blowing almost every day about midday which covers everything with fine dust, then about 2.00 pm the wind drops and the flies swarm. They never leave you once they start. You brush them off and they come back again and again.

Then late on, say 1.00 am or 2.00 am or a bit after, there is a colossal fall of dew which soaks everything.

Yours affectionately, Douglas

16 August 1917

Dear Mama

We are doing ferocious training and losing pints of perspiration a day. I may be a little thinner than usual probably am, but that is natural, every time you go out to do anything you come in soaked with perspiration right through shirt, breeches and tunic and even a matchbox in tunic pocket is far too wet to strike matches on. As for Aunt Ella's questions about heat in the shade – well if there was any shade anywhere I might be able to answer it. The only trees are small fig bushes which grow in the sand here and there, houses there are none and tents get saturated with sun that they are hotter than outside. I rode by the place where Abraham started well-digging, this morning. He must have been some sort of Arab or he'd never have bothered. It rains here I believe in October, otherwise never at all. The plague of the country is septic sores, due I believe to sweat sores and dirty desert dust.

There are no poisonous insects I have met yet – but sandfly fever is not uncommon. You would probably find it pretty tropical looking at home, but everybody is all shades of brown and black out here so you don't notice it.

My long war views from the very beginning have been justified haven't they. Thanks very much for the peas, beans and fruit which arrived after all.

Yours, Douglas

2 September 1917

Dear Mama

The flies are getting more annoying every day probably because the quantities of horses round about.

Have just come back from some practice shooting where we did very well with the general looking on, our new general is a most delightful man. He is not a strafer or an interferer but I should say a first class man. Our late colonel is now brigadier general in our old division.

This country abounds with small green frogs just like those on that pumice stone I once bought in Paris if you remember; also large earwigs, grasshoppers (large size) flies (some like pins heads) sand flies (which cause sandfly fever) and ticks of which I had one in my hair and with its head buried in my face this morning. There are also lizards, countless chameleons – apparently no snakes or tortoises. Some of the men have gone as brown as cascars but I don't really get sunburnt. In peacetime this is great barley country and supplies two of the big scotch whiskey firms almost entirely, but now it is nothing but bare dusty plains. When the rainy season comes it will be a sea of mud. There is a distinct autumn feel in the air and more wind than there was.

Yours, Douglas

19 September 1917

Dear Papa

You've probably got my last about being in hospital with sandfly fever. It doesn't amount to much, high temperature for a couple of days, and then a week or so convalescing. There are no after effects and nobody knows much about it.

Apparently it only comes on for a few weeks in the year. I ought to get a week or so in a convalescent home which will practically amount to a week's leave. No use addressing anything here as I shall be long gone before anything of yours could arrive.

I travelled down in a palatial hospital train given by the Sultan, most gorgeous and comfortable, with red crescent instead of red cross. Everything painted white outside and in. Dates are rife in Egypt now but not in Palestine. Coming down the Nile the cotton is just beginning to be picked, sweet potatoes are being gathered.

I haven't anything particularly interesting to say.

Yours affectionately, Douglas

7 November 1917

Dear Mama

The Turks are retiring fast before us. We have captured all sorts of places. I have not had my boots off for a week and except last night had only slept two hours in any twenty-four. Last night I slept for six hours though with interruptions about every hour. I am sorry to say that my batman Clements was killed as were all the officers' servants except one, and he was wounded. Please insert in *The Times* a notice 'Died of wounds rec'd in action Nov 4th Gr. S.A. Clements, soldier-steward of Lt A.D. Thorburn RFA; faithful unto death.'

We have not been allowed to shave or wash for some time to save water. The dust is terrific and the food dry biscuits, bully beef, cocoa and occasional date. I manage to light a fire for a few minutes every other day. I have at least four days beard and am as filthy as a tramp. Quite well though and never been in any danger so far.

Yours, Douglas

13 November 1917

Dear Papa

I wrote you a line just after the Battle of Beersheba and just before the Battle of Sheria in both of which we took part. As a result of the operations as you know the Turks have retired hastily northwards. Our brigade of artillery received congratulations and thanks from the infantry brigadier general – the general commanding the division and the corps commander who is the next man here under Allenby. We did not have many casualties but on our battery commander Miles lost his brother who was with him at brigade headquarters. It was an old-fashioned kind of fighting in the open.

131

At present we have gone into rest a long way back but I expect we'll soon advance again as the railway goes up. The whole question out here is supplies which depend on water for animals and you can only go where the water is. The day of the Battle of Sheria they brought the water right alongside of us. Just imagine the job, water for all the horses and men of an army carried up in tanks on camels. Next day I took our horses to water and it took over four hours there and back. On the way – which was all over dead men and horses with their concomitant smells and flies – I picked up a souvenir or two, a spur a part of a saddle and a sword. I also inspected some captured guns, ox-teams, drivers and all. We then sent out teams and brought in more captured guns and things. Miles took a photo of me, hadn't washed or shaved or undressed for five days, and as I had had my head clipped all over I looked beautiful. I shall have my hair cut only clopped right off in this country. It is too dusty to have any hair on top. I hope to send the spur home to you.

The flies are almost intolerable. We've got near the canteen now and so get lots of good things to eat and drink – before that for over a week we lived on biscuits and a bottle of water a day with an occasional date, bully beef now and then and some cocoa when we could light a fire. Now we've got eggs and bacon, tinned fruit, peas, lobster, sardines, fresh onions and bread. Wonderful!

We have also plenty of water as we are close to the Great Wadi. These big wadies are really rivers waiting for the rainy season to fill up. The biggest have some pools in them all the year round.

We had great superiority in this offensive especially in guns so that everything went pretty smoothly.

Yours, Douglas

21 November 1917

Dear Papa

No post has reached us for some time. We have been out of action for a bit and still are. Lots to do however making up deficiencies in equipment, etc. Our horses stuck it out splendidly really, very hard work and very little water and only bare feed, I told you that out of seventy-two hours on one occasion I rode my horse sixty hours. I hardly ever walk a yard now – always ride.

Railways and water are the determining factors in this country. The keeping up of supplies is difficult – we use railways, light railways, wagons, camels, donkeys, packhorses, motor lorries, and caterpillar tractors. But the camels are most noticeable there are countless herds of them.

The country where our advanced troops have got to is reported to be very different and it looks pretty lumpy on the maps. Some of the wadies are very hard to cross with wheels, fortunately for us our four gun teams are comprised of absolutely first class animals and can get up an ascent of about one in thirty even when the wheels are eight or ten inches deep in sand. Considering that the vehicles weigh about two and half tons that is saying a good deal. My job on the march however consists in getting the tail end over these places, the weak teams, and so on and the baggage wagons. One of the latter is a small Turkish cart we captured drawn by two white donkeys – also picked up on the road. The donkey wagon looks fine going along.

The general saw the horses today and was very complimentary. In this sort of show horsemanship is half the battle. And keeping the horses fit is really done either by getting around the supply officer if he is friendly or round his supply dump on the quiet if he is not. Unless there is a shortage there is always a surplus and the thing is to get some of that. We do very well indeed that way. We are living like fighting cocks just now regardless of expense. Dinner today: soup, lobster, stewed steak and onions, tinned apricots and coffee. We have no tents, only bivouac shelters and it is jolly cold at night. And when it rains too it is rather cheerless.

However we are all fit and well. I am just getting rid of a septic sore on my hand. In this country the least scratch or graze is apt to fester probably owing to the flies. Everybody gets these sores now and again.

Yours, Douglas

3 December 1917

Dear Mama

I could walk to Jerusalem from here if it wasn't for the Turks in between. Not a bad country but there are too many of us here for the water. We get lots of oranges now and again, not quite ripe but very welcome change from tinned beef and biscuits.

Today is the first letters I've had for ages. None of the cigarettes have arrived yet. I am as well as it is possible to be, rather dirty and smelly but very healthy.

You will know from my letter before that we assisted in the capture of Beersheba. There is a good bit of water there but then we had to go forward. Then we went up and round by 'Sampsonville' and then round here. We shall not be in touch with civilisation for a long time I expect. I swapped a pint of water for a chicken two days ago. My new servant is called Cockerill. Quite a nice man who makes pianos in peacetime.

No time for more, post is going

Douglas

6 December 1917

Dear Papa

I take this opportunity of writing a short bit. Probably won't get another for a while.

As you know from the papers we are fairly near Jerusalem; the few inhabitants left are a mangy lot of vagabonds with most unsanitary habits. There is a big monastery here. I called there and had a glass of wine and figs with the superior – an Austrian. We had a pleasant conversation in French. Mostly about Latin authors. Rations are pretty bad at present. Biscuits, bully, jam, tea and dates for all meals. These are not improved by three days trip on camels. Sometimes we get one-third bread and two-thirds biscuits instead of all biscuits. High up in the mountains as we are now it is cold at night and we feel it coming up from the plains.

I suppose we shall take Jerusalem sooner or later. The monks are glad to see us. There is no entry in their visitors' book since the war began until our troops got here. Great famine of them at the moment.

Yours, Douglas

12 December 1917

Dear Nellie

We are up in the mountains 2,000ft above sea level rather like the valley of Glencoe. We are quite close to Emmaus and in easy sight of Jerusalem – captured one or two days ago. It is mighty cold up here at night with only bivouac sheets as covering and when it rains in torrents with a gale blowing as it did two nights ago and all the next day things are a bit thick. A bivouac is a tent composed of two sticks like walking sticks and two sheets of canvas about 4ft square.

We are not allowed to go to Jerusalem – in fact troops that take places seldom go near them. Staff officers of course immediately drive into these towns in motors and put up in houses with hot baths and so on. I have not had my clothes off me for over ten days and as for a bath the last I had was in the sea weeks ago. There is no water to wash in except a little muddy stuff as thick as soap. I can fancy the Manchester and London Jews coming back to this country. You can grow olives and grapes here and there and keep a few sheep and that's all. There is nothing but stony hills like the roughest part of the Welsh mountains. Hardly a tree except olives. Handing over to the Jews is the biggest joke I ever heard.

We found a few wild narcissus and some small white crocuses today while shooting at a Turkish battery. The few village Syrians dress in rags and live in filth. Food is not too plentiful either, as mountaineering is hard on the camels.

Am very fit indeed.

Yours, Douglas

15 December 1917

Dear Mama

I took a ride into Jerusalem yesterday. It was unfortunately the Sabbath and most things were shut but I managed to buy a sack of decent brown bread, cabbages, carrots, figs and a few tinned things which made a welcome change after bully and biscuits. I also bought a fourth watch (my other three being hors de combat owing to sand dust and rain). It cost me thirty-seven piasters, i.e. seven shillings and sixpence, and is a first class full hunter. A marvellous bargain.

135

Had fine weather the last few days but we have been warned to expect 30 inches of rain in a fortnight any time now. Bread fried in olive oil is my usual breakfast these days. Quite good too.

People in Jerusalem talk French, German or English quite a lot. I find my German most useful. Of course I have my little dictionary and can buy and bargain in Syrian all right. Our division is referred to in reports as dismounted yeomanry. The number of it is twice my age and four more or to give another way six times our number in Lorne Road plus two. The Bedouin still wander about, quite a lot of dead in the village near wanting to be buried. Dead horses, camels, mules and donkeys all along the roads.

Yours, Douglas

28 December 1917

Dear Mama

Our infantry are making an advance and I am waiting for orders to open fire. I have got such a stiff neck today that I can't move my head at all which is very awkward and painful.

The wretched horses are getting so little to eat that they look like greyhounds. It is almost impossible to get stuff along after the rain. We have had two fine days and got our blankets and things dry now. I found beautiful cyclamen wild on the hills this morning, there will be carpet of them soon as the plants are all over the place. The rain always comes from the sea – which we can see from here far away.

There is not much of the modern atrocity form of warfare out here – the enemy hasn't much artillery and so far we have met no gas. When the rains are over it should be fairly pleasant. But it rains about 30 inches in a month or so. I bought a fine sheepskin coat in Jerusalem for less than thirty shillings. It is a splendid coat for cold weather with the woolly side in. In rainy weather you wear them wool outwards and it keeps all the rain out. They are not heavy except when sopping wet and are wonderfully warm. We have had no mail for some days now and the newsletters have not been plentiful. They are just a slip of paper with the official communications printed in small type. Three or four months seem to be the time for parcels to get out if they ever arrive.

The Turkish prisoners captured vary a good deal regards conditions. Some of them look and are very underfed, and others look all right but their uniforms consist of anything at all and an Austrian or German overcoat. They are brave fighters – and of course we have had the advantage all ways ever since this show started. I should judge things will settle down to a standstill before long.

Everybody must want refitting pretty badly. The monasteries round about are used as hospitals and ambulance places. The Turks don't shoot at them much, in fact they seem a decent lot of people. Our Christmas Day was the limit. Everybody was soaked through all day. It was impossible to light a fire to cook. Fortunately I had been into Jerusalem the day before and bought a primus stove, a leg of mutton (one pound), a mincing machine, five eggs at sixpence, raisins, figs, and various other odds and sods. We cooked and ate most of the day with rain dripping down our necks through the tarpaulin and went to bed soaking wet into wet beds, I don't want another Christmas of that sort

Yours, Douglas

13 January 1918

Dear Mama

We are in rest now in a village. There are too many livestock at night to sleep in the houses unless it is very wet. Our landlord lives in the same yard. In his hut are two wives, six or eight children, relations, about twenty sheep, fifteen or so goats, four cows, and a donkey and himself all in one room. The houses are built of stone stuck together with a mixture of mud, manure and straw. Two of the houses in the yard are only about 5ft high and 10ft across with a hole to go in at about 2ft high. Whole families live in these hovels and grind grain and bake bread therein.

We have a jolly little black Turk puppy called Abdul which was found in enemy trenches near Jerusalem. He is a nice little companion. I bought the hindquarters of a scraggy sheep today for forty piastres, i.e. eight shillings and fourpence – not bad at all. Also three dozen eggs at two and a half shillings each. Fortunately I bought a pocket dictionary last time I was in Egypt it comes in very handy now, as the natives of course know nothing but Syrian.

We shall be glad when the rains are over. Of course the flies will begin again but theses torrents of rain are bad to contend with. We captured a Turkish field kitchen at a place called Ramallah which is a great benefit to the men as we can get a hot drink ready for them while marching. Only infantry have travelling kitchens in the British Army.

Yours affectionately, Douglas

28 February 1918

Dear Mama

I came down through Jerusalem yesterday from the gun line to collect horses and harnesses and stores which are all over Palestine. It is the dickens of a job. I came from where Jacob went to sleep and saw the ladder. The weather is extraordinarily wet and cold still up in the mountains, but another three or four weeks will see the end of it.

The country is getting covered with scarlet anemones and cyclamen all over. When the rain stops it will be fine I fancy. Rations have been pretty good lately, the cheese rather especially which is delicious.

There isn't anything to write about except mud and rain and scrambling over rocks with heavy wagons with ten horse or mules, and sometimes sixteen or twenty in the soft bottoms of the wadies.

Three days ago I bought figs and almonds from a Bedouin with bare feet and turban and rugs all complete – he spoke American and had three gold teeth in the front of his mouth! And occasionally you will find one who has worked as a lascar on an English ship and speaks Hindustani. I shall go off up again in a couple of days and what with the harness and horses lent in every direction and borrowed too the confusion will be terrible.

What a fuss there is in the papers about food rations. The people ought to have tea, milk, sugar, bully and biscuits for three weeks on end like soldiers do and march and fight on it and they would know when they are well off. Of course we usually eat twice what we need in peacetime and that's why they make such a fuss now.

News is rare now – only the *Weekly Times*.

Yours, Douglas

10 March 1918

Dear Papa

It has long become sheer platitude to say this is an extraordinary war. Yesterday morning I was part of a small battle and spent the very small hours getting guns and wagons and unloading ammunition along a so-called road which had been made 'possible for wheels' the night before. 'Possible for wheels' means really almost impossible and I had to deal with a gun jammed on two big rocks with two wheels off the ground and another wagon jammed between it and a stone wall.

I always come along with the last vehicles and when I found this jammed in the pitch-dark and blocking the only way along it was rather serious. We worked away and the Turks were firing small shells all around us. Luckily out of the column blocked behind and all my lot of men and horses we only had one horse wounded. Well out of the middle of this show I am sent on a 'course of instruction' near Cairo and am at present writing this in bed in a good hotel in Jerusalem on a Sunday morning. You have to bring rations to the hotel or else you live on bits of things. Bread is not allowed to be sold and various other things do not exist. I am going to go to church at 9.30 with my servant and then later on by motor lorry down the Jaffa Road to Ludd.

March weather here is variable according to records – fine or hail and thunderstorms. So far it has been lovely. This sudden move of mine will mean no letters for some weeks as they will go up the line and down again.

I am extremely fit except for a few bruises and cuts falling over rocks in the dark.

Yours, Douglas

20 March 1918

Dear Papa

Today is a half-day at the gunnery school so I came in here for a bath and dinner. The climate is quite excellent now in Egypt tho' pretty hot in the middle of the day except in houses.

We have sort of wooden huts at the school which is out near Heliopolis – only twenty minutes tram drive from the town. These huts are neither

139

wind, dust nor rain proof so that we get a bit of all weathers inside. A refresher course as it is called is quite a nice change but most of the stuff taught technically magnificent and practically quite absurdly useless. It is not worth wasting much brain energy to get a good mark in the examinations. As I said the training hasn't much value and the army has definitely decided to kill all desire for promotion, and all ambition by making all promotion purely according to seniority irrespective of merit. Consequently one simply jogs along in the ordinary way without worrying at all. It will take about another ten years of the war for me to get back to captain again. However I don't care a tinker's cuss one way or another. After getting praise from all kinds of generals for what our brigade did in the show there are no decorations or mention of this.

Kind regards to anybody you meet.

Yours, Douglas

CHAPTER 10

Letters from France Again

August 1918 to November 1918

6 August 1918

Dear Mama

I have been pretty busy for some days and so have not written. Thank you very much for biscuits and cake they were excellent. We got fresh tomatoes in the rations today so don't bother to send them out, better sell them and use the cash.

There are simply millions of wasps about here now but they are pretty good-tempered ones. My mosquito curtain has ensured me uninterrupted sleep ever since it came.

Bosch planes are buzzing about all over the place tonight but a good way off from here, far enough away not to cause us any worry. I have just got the roof onto a new dugout for the major it has been rather difficult work but I like that sort of a job as well as anything I get to do.

We have had rumours of Turkey chucking up the sponge but I don't believe it. At least I see no reason to.

We have had quite a lovely evening with our new excellent gramophone record – especially a series of 'Egyptian ballets' by somebody or other which are really beautiful.

We do a lot of setting houses on fire nowadays – in fact we run a competition with another battery in setting alight places where the Bosch live. He certainly is inclined to take things lying down hereabouts and we must give him a pretty rotten time.

I am really sleepy to write any more.

Yours, Douglas

AMATEUR GUNNERS

10 August 1918

Dear Papa

We have advanced our line hereabouts the last few days – not an attack
or anything of that sort but the Bosch decided to go back a bit. He was in
a considerable salient here and I think our perpetual firing got a bit on his
nerves. At present I am sitting at ease with part of the battery that didn't
move forward – so I'm having a very quiet and peaceful if solitary time.
I have got a considerable boil or carbuncle on the side of my neck which
is rather a nuisance as it is just where my shirt collar comes and my tunic
collar too. It looks as if it would finish soon though. We have had no rain
for four or five days and that makes things much more comfortable. I am
living in a decent little cottage, extremely comfortable. You might please
send me out a cake of toilet soap.

We got vague rumours of another considerable success on the Western
Front yesterday but I have heard nothing definitive yet except a news wire
'many prisoners – some guns – cavalry in action!' I have just heard some
more details but not official. Anyway our troops have 'got their tails up'
all along the line and I think Foch's command is going to be a great
improvement. By the way I am told Foch is pronounced to rhyme with
Bosche.

Nothing more to say.

Yours affectionately, Douglas

16 September 1918

Dear Papa

Having managed to make a shelter which keeps the light in I can write at
night, we can't have lights after dark owing to aeroplanes who would
probably bomb and machine gun us if they saw a light. I have got the
horses in a fine place, along a cutting made for a road and their heads are
mostly below ground level – being on a slight slope there is also draining.
The men and I are in holes cut into the banks roofed over with old bits of
corrugated iron the Bosch left lying about.

Our quarters are therefore quite good and we have had no rain for two
days. Before that, being on the move one just had to lie down anywhere

– that being only for an hour or two. On long halts one could normally get under a wagon cover or something. Fortunately the wet held off until we stopped and could get a bit of cover. Probably the cause of the stop was the rain, so that we were bound to get time to make some shelters.

Aeroplanes were brought down near us the other night when over trying to bomb. It was an extraordinary sight. I hear one of them had a crew of six. There was only one survivor out of the three planes – a corporal who managed to get safely to earth in a parachute.

I saw a yesterday's *Daily Mail* today – a great treat – as one gets absolutely no news of the war here.

Yours, Douglas

6 October 1918

Dear Mama

Have pulled out for a day or two at most and have just had my first bath for over seven weeks. As I have not had my clothes off more than twice during that period you can imagine I needed a bath.

I got Nellie's cakes today. If the box had been a bit stronger they would have arrived perfectly but they got rather squashed. However they were quite eatable and a very great luxury to all of us. As you would see in the papers we have got the Hindenburg Line in our sector – 70ft dugouts and all. Present tactics simply make these deep places traps to get caught in. One opposite here exploded, it was three stories deep and then below again was a tunnel large enough to hold whole regiments of infantry. On one occasion our battery caught the Hun in the open making a counter-attack and killed simply hundreds and hundreds. Our division had just been described by the army commander as equal in gallantry and courage and devotion to the best in the whole British Army. Such praise from anyone higher than army corps commander is rare – and I should say that the whole document is most exceptional.

I enclose an endorsed cheque for two pounds. Please buy me a pair of fur motoring gloves with all or part of it – I don't care much what they cost so long as they keep my hands warm and are long and big enough to go right over the wrists of my British warm. There is a sort with fur outside and jaeger wool inside – these are splendid. Perhaps the leather gauntlets I have already if you can find them would be better, in fact I'm sure they would on second thoughts, so send me them out instead, if you can find them and a couple of pairs of knotted gloves to wear inside. If you can't find them (they should be in the hall drawer) get another similar pair with jaeger lining if possible. Buy me an Orilux lamp and three refills and a set of Phillip's military soles and heels for boot size nine. You can probably get these things out of the two pounds enclosed – I think you will find my gauntlets all right and you needn't get the fur motor gloves in that case.

Douglas

30 October 1918

Dear Papa

Moving every day about ten to fifteen miles and having to arrange for people all over the place to find you at the next halt is no simple matter. Of course the gilded ones who live in chateaux, drive in motors and compete in boot polish with one another do not move a finger to assist in any way. Perhaps it is as well, as what little they do attempt results in complete and perfect chaos.

I have just read an account of the German offensive in March – it reads like a fairy tale. In fact it is quite an interesting account of what a series of battles look like to those who direct them. Of course commanders-in-chief never hear any details except isolated cases of gallantry. The whole defence reads like a well ordered and conducted scheme perfectly carried out and coordinated. I have met dozens who took part in the fighting and what their feelings must be when reading that account I cannot imagine.

What actually happened in March on the Somme was this: after the first great Hun push in the fog nobody got any orders from anywhere in the sector concerned, communication was only possible by runners who usually didn't arrive because their destination had moved ten or fifteen miles in the meantime. Some units held out to the last and others didn't and in the inevitable pauses for breathing space most people managed to find out for themselves what was going on next door and whether they'd better run for it or not. One thing is certain the Australians – our best shock troops – saved Amiens, and the motor traction of the 6-inch batteries that saved the whole show. Probably those in chief command don't think so but I have no doubt of it.

The difference between various divisions (in all armies) in fighting qualities is one of the most surprising features of these big shows. We had a good chance to judge as we supported six different ones. It depends on heaps of things, the chief of which is the character of the colonels and GOCs of divisions. Some divisions still spend all their energies polishing brass and painting wood to please people who inspect them when in a quiet area. The old army can say what they like about that sort of thing but our experience is that we don't want them in front of us in a big battle, or on either flank either.

Great rumours today about Austria, all unofficial of course until they prove to be otherwise. Why they can't let the troops know how the war goes on I can't imagine. The reason is indifference. We are 'the troops'. We don't matter – they are the brains. But they forget that we fight and they don't. Also that we live sometimes as well as tramps other times like fowl of the air or rabbits in their burrows while they live much better than any ordinary civilian.

Yours affectionately Douglas

PS. Gloves a great success. No need for long stockings I have plenty.

Part 3: Observations

I

Horses, Mules and Camels

A cavalryman friend once said to me, 'Yes, most of the war was utterly foul, but, at any rate, we did go to war like gentlemen, on horses.'

I am afraid that the gunners of the future will go to war like motor mechanics.

From very early childhood days I have cherished, for any kind of horse, that sort of affectionate regard which seems sheer nonsense to those who have not felt it. My greatest treat as a very little boy in London was 'to go and look at the horses in the park'.

In war, or perhaps in war as it was, the part played by these animals has always been of the first importance. The victories of Alexander the Great were largely due to his employment of heavy cavalry as the decisive weapon. It is thought that the first horsemen were the original invaders of ancient Egypt, Genghis Khan conquered the world from Romania to Peking by means of the hordes of Tartar horsemen who followed his banner. The 'Great Horse' of the Norman chivalry was the means of victory for the knight in heavy armour, and examples of the importance of the horse in war, from Biblical days right up to the present mechanical age, will occur to the memory of every reader.

In the Great War the services of the horses and other animals such as mules, donkeys, camels, etc., were as conspicuous as their sufferings, and, to a lover of animals, as I am, it seemed, at times, as if the efforts we had to ask of them were more than I could bring myself to demand.

Their patient sufferings were terrible to think of. I have never seen any figures of the animal casualties in the Great War but they must have been colossal. I have seen rows and rows of horses and mules killed by shellfire in France, I have ridden my horse up mountain tracks in Palestine which were lined for miles with the dead bodies of Allenby's 'white mice' (the

147

army name for the white Egyptian donkeys which kept us supplied with such rations and forage as could be provided in the Judean hills. The mud and steep mountain goat-tracks had defeated the baggage camels).

The gallantry and devotion of the animals of our various armies deserve a striking monument in the heart of London, but, alas, their services have not been recognised in that way.

In our battery we all, except some of the drivers, were lovers of horses. Our horses were our chief interest and greatest pleasure. Although we knew perfectly well that mules are tougher and can produce more effort for the food available, we always chose horses in preference and left the mules for those who fancied them. At times, for all that, we had quite a stud of mules and they were, without a single exception, magnificent workers.

There are certain differences between horses and mules which are worth recording. The average mule has far more brains than the average horse. For example, if the leaders of a team of four are not doing their fair share of the work, you would always see the wheelers pulling the whole load in the case of a horse team in the bands of ill- trained drivers (probably infantry or Royal Army Medical Corps [RAMC] transport), whereas, in a mule team, if the leaders are not pulling their share, the wheelers do nothing whatever, and the careless drivers soon find themselves standing still. On the lines, if horses start kicking they quickly lame one another unless separated, while mules will kick at each other for hours without ill consequences; they evidently enjoy boxing matches, and land each other heavy blows in the ribs which make resounding thuds and do no damage whatever.

I believe that the reputation of the army mule for vice is quite undeserved. Most animals are only vicious when they are, or have been, frightened. Mules are naturally very timid creatures; it is enough to show a good mule the whip to increase his speed materially, there is no need to touch him with it. All good mules, and by 'good mules' I mean well-treated mules, work better for the regular driver whom they know and trust than for a stranger, but a good horse will work as well for one good driver as for another.

Many legends about horses upon which I had been brought up proved utterly fallacious. For instance, I had been told that a horse would refuse to drink unwholesome water, and that a man could safely drink water which his horse had approved. It is not true. Horses which are really thirsty, as they are in the desert, will drink water with green slime floating on it; water so full of mud that it has the colour and consistency of strong cocoa; water with dead men and dead camels lying in it (very dead in many cases), even water of such a poisonous smell that a man who had not had his boots off for a week would hesitate to wash his feet in it. Our horses drank greedily, on several occasions, of all these kinds of water and took no harm.

Mules, on the other hand, although they will eat and thrive on fodder so mouldy and unwholesome that no horse would touch it, must have good water. They will not drink bad water, however thirsty they may be.

Another example of behaviour in the horse lines shows well the superior intelligence of the mule. If a horse gets his leg over a rope or chain, he will struggle and kick until he has lamed himself unless a picket hurries up and disentangles him at once. Your mule, however, stands perfectly still until a picket, in passing, notices his trouble and puts the chain in place, and does himself no harm whatever if left entangled.

In our battery the horses all had names. The mares were usually known by the Christian name of their driver's best girl, geldings by some remarkable Christian name that struck the men's fancy. The numbers branded on their hooves were, of course, duly recorded in the horse book, but in discussions between section commanders, and even regular NCOs, such as the sergeant major, the claims of Queenie and Floss to promotion to the gun team would be gravely debated, and one would order Clarence or Horace to be saddled for some purpose without a smile. Clarence was a mule we 'adopted' one dark night, distinguished both for his amiable disposition and for the wound stripe which decorated his head collar. Jimmy, a grey, was the mount of the farrier QMS; one afternoon in France he bit five drivers in the neck in less than five minutes. I believe I could still name every team horse and its position in each team in the column on every important march; in the course of our long travels, we must have handled more than five hundred horses and mules.

Most of my waking thoughts, after I was promoted captain, revolved round matters connected with these most lovable friends and servants of the guns. How could I save them a little work? How was I to get them a

149

trifle more shelter, a bit more forage, a little better cover from enemy fire? If the proverb, 'That the horse grows fat under the master's eye' is true, then our horses should have been excessively stout. And their usually excellent condition, under conditions of almost Arctic cold in the Vardar Valley, under tropical heat in the desert, in the wet and mud and cold of a Flanders winter, was due to the careful attention they always enjoyed, and the trustworthiness of the corporal who presided over the forage issue from beginning to end, the tireless work at the chaff-cutter of diminutive Driver 'B', and the devotion of the veterinary sergeant.

Here I must interpolate an astonishing episode concerning a mule. On the coast near Gaza, a so-called driver joined our battery. So-called because, although his army designation was Driver 'D', he had never been instructed in any of the duties of a driver, could neither ride, drive, groom a horse, or clean a set of harness. Learning that in private life he was a solicitor's clerk, and as he had white hair and wore spectacles, the major kindly made him battery clerk to give him a job he could easily manage. But he proved to be no better as a clerk than as a driver. So, after a while, he was given the dud driver's job, the rather rusty spare wheel harness to look after, and various odd duties such as picket at night, chaff cutting, and fatigues in connection with the forage.

After Beersheba, we found a stray Turk army mule branded with the iron cross on the near hind quarter. I suspect some Turk unit had turned him loose in the dark, for he was the most dangerous outlaw that ever went on four legs.

Being a magnificently proportioned animal, fat as a pig and strong as a bullock, we kept him chained to an ammunition wagon handrail. If anyone approached him with a nosebag at any time, he would rear up and try to beat the man's brains out with his forefeet, like a fighting stallion. To take him to water his chain would be slipped through the head collar of another mule, and so both were allowed to follow the horses at will. In a waterless country, animals do not need leading to water. One morning, on asking the corporal in charge of the picket for anything he had to report, he replied 'nothing except that Driver 'D' had disentangled 'Iron Cross' from his chain during the night.'

No competent driver would have gone within 10ft of Iron Cross at night for all the tea in China. Driver 'D', however, seemed quite unaware that he had done anything remarkable, and when I explained that Iron Cross was an unpopular animal for obvious reasons, the little white-haired bespectacled driver astounded me by asking, as a favour, if he might look after and ride this mule in a team instead of the odd jobs he had to do.

As the loss of Driver 'D's services, for all time, would not have been a serious matter to anyone but the man himself, I fell in, at once, with his suggestion. From that day onwards, until the Armistice in Belgium, Driver 'D' groomed, fed, and rode Iron Cross without the slightest difficulty. The outlaw mule and the perfectly useless middle-aged driver struck up a friendship. The mule remained dangerous if handled by anyone else. In the forge he was a perfect gentleman so long as Driver 'D' held the foot on which the shoeing smith was working. Unless his friend was there, Iron Cross was unmanageable, and, after kicking most of the forge all over the scenery, would put the entire farrier party to flight without delay. After the Armistice, when Driver 'D' got his discharge, Iron Cross was still with us in Belgium. The outlaw mule relapsed to his original wickedness, and, without his driver friend, nothing could be done with him. The only solution to the problem was a bullet, and, meat being very scarce in Belgium at the time, a local butcher was glad to buy the carcase at a good figure.

So ended our buckshee Turk outlaw mule, and the most remarkable friendship between a harmless little man and a big, wicked, man-killing terror of an animal, the worst we ever had on our horse lines.

An episode illustrating the intelligence, and strength, of mules should be recorded. On one occasion, I rode back from the Jerusalem area to Latron (the pleasant neighbourhood of the monastery built in memory of the two crucified thieves) to bring up six horses supplied by remounts, and a GS wagonload of stores. The fine 16 hand horses were in magnificent condition, but, being newly out from France, had not learned to pass camels without becoming unmanageable. Horses that are unused to camels invariably find them alarming in the extreme. Most horses become accustomed to camels in a few days, but some never quite lose their fear of these ungainly creatures.

It was the rainy season, and unfortunately, just before I started with my heavily loaded wagon, a sharp shower changed the dry earth beside the road, on which the already loaded wagon was standing, into a greasy and slippery place, on which my powerful but unseasoned six-horse team failed to get enough foothold to start the wagon. A miserable looking pair of skinny mules had come down from the hills with me to bring the necessary drivers and their kits in the limbered wagon which belonged to brigade headquarters and was popularly known by the contemptuous name of the 'pip-squeak'.

To help the six big horses to get a start on the treacherous mud I had the pair of scarecrow mules harnessed in front of the six horses, and, although these undersized mules cannot have been more than half the weight of any pair of the six horses behind them, the loaded wagon moved off steadily towing the limbered wagon behind.

As I was making good progress up the long hill towards Jerusalem, I decided to leave my curious-looking vehicle and team alone, although to a critical eye a team consisting of two undersized and shabby mules followed by six 16 hand horses in gorgeous condition hauling a loaded baggage wagon and trailing behind an empty limbered wagon was certainly a peculiar equipage to be led along the road by an officer of the RFA. As it turned out, it was providential that I had left the mules in the lead of this team and had brought down Driver 'M' to handle the long reins of the wheelers from the box seat, for, on rounding the corner where the road winds up past Lifta and there is a sheer drop of quite 40ft into a glen planted with olive trees beside the road, a camel convoy, belonging to the RAMC, hove in sight. Sick and wounded from the Jerusalem area were evacuated in camel-borne stretchers. The sight of a column of two hundred camels marching along a narrow road in pairs, the white sun awnings over the stretchers flapping steadily up and down like huge wings attached to the camels' backs 10ft or 11ft from the ground, was likely to drive the six horses, newly out from France, into something like frenzy. There being no way of turning off the road, and no room on the road to turn round (the ill-designed GS wagon of the British Army has only a quarter lock, and needs nearly 35ft of space to reverse in) I yelled to Driver 'M' to jam the brake hard on, and to the driver of the mules to keep the traces tight until the camels had passed.

The time occupied by a hundred pairs of camels travelling at something under two miles an hour, with intervals between the pairs varying from 2ft to 20yds, could be calculated in minutes, no doubt, by the mathematically minded. To me the time seemed quite half an hour, although it probably only was about ten minutes, but, in those few minutes, each of the six horses performed every antic familiar to the rodeo ring, and made determined efforts to jump over the precipice and get further away from the nightmare column of white winged camels. But for the incredible strength of the two little toast racks of mules and the weight of the wagon, which between them kept the team anchored, fore and aft, between traces as rigid as iron rails, the whole six horses would have been lying dead in the bottom of the glen beside the road, before half of the camel column had swayed its leisurely course past us. The wise little mules dug their toes in, and pulled for dear life. A pair of horses will not pull continuously at a load which does not shift, but mules will, and these did, and held the whole plunging six tons of mad, sweating, terror-stricken horses on the road, until the last pair of camels had gone past. Mules in hard condition are capable of feats of strength that have to be seen to be believed. This little pair had probably had nothing better to eat for months than mouldy peas and rotten barley, and yet they had the strength and determination to hold the whole crazy outfit on the road, and so saved the lives of probably all six horses and four drivers, to say nothing of their own. After this remarkable feat, they calmly continued their journey as if nothing whatever had happened worth mentioning, flopping their long ears at every stride, like any other pair of shabby, hard-working hybrids.

However, I saw to it that these gallant little scarecrows fed on the best we had, for once, as, on reaching our destination, they revelled in a double feed of the sounder peas and barley usually reserved for the horses' more delicate stomachs.

Camels (Baggage)

The camel is a most peculiar creature. He, the baggage camel, is a sour-visaged, vicious beast. His kick, delivered sideways, may be counted upon to break a leg, or a rib, if it reaches the target. His bite is often poisonous. His neck is, apparently, as elastic in range as a pair of dog-tongs and, consequently, a wise man never stands talking with his back towards a camel.

Camel Transport Companies (CTCs) were, invariably, in our days composed of bull camels exclusively. A legend of how one experimental cow camel company had to park itself out of sight and smell of all the other camels on the Palestine front owing to the unwelcome attentions of strays from other units may have been based upon rumour, but the fact that in the breeding season bull camels go 'maknoon' and have to be muzzled is undeniable, the procedure being to stun the maknoon bull by beating it on the head with long poles until senseless, when a rope muzzle is put over his jaws. During this period the bull camel foams at the mouth continuously, and the muzzle is never removed, except at feeding time, until the foaming at the mouth period is over.

On the other hand, I know of no other beast of burden which, in return for his comparatively small ration of food and water, carries so heavy a burden. The army load for a packhorse is 250lbs, for a camel 450lbs. The food and water ration is the same for both.

Camels and dromedaries are two names in different languages for the same animal, the former Arabic and the latter Greek. The idea, popularised in inaccurate schoolbooks, that the dromedary is a camel with two humps is totally fallacious, the two-humped variety being merely the Bactrian breed.

The camel seems to be a survival from a prehistoric epoch. There are said to be no wild camels in existence. The camel of today is the product of hundreds of years of domestication, and is, comparatively, a new arrival in Africa.

The habits of camels are unlike those of any other creature. They always look pictures of misery; when in low condition they develop mange without having to wait for extraneous infection. They are bad tempered, sullen, and quite untrustworthy. They cannot jump even the smallest ditch, and they remain upright on the march purely by balance. When loaded, a strong push will capsize a camel into a nearby ditch or drain, and in a very short while he will die, unless relieved of his load and helped right side up.

It must be clearly understood that these remarks apply to baggage camels, whose value in 1914 was about seven pounds and ten shillings a head, and have no reference to the Bishareen or Mebari riding camel, which resembles the beast of burden no more than a racehorse resembles a country farmer's cob.

The camel is fed twice, at dawn and at dusk. His food in the Army was millet mixed with chaff of straw (tibn).

His ten gallons of water a day are given him in the heat of the day at noon. A camel is watered every day when being conditioned for a hard journey; on the march in a waterless country, he is watered every third day when he fills his tanks with, roughly, thirty gallons in one, often interrupted, drink. On long stretches where no water is to be found, he can easily carry on for a week from his tank supply. But no man knoweth how the camel realises that there will be no water on the third day and so contents himself with five gallons daily. When pumping water from his tank to his stomach, the camel hangs his tongue out at the side and makes a noise like the cistern of a WC which is in a bad state of repair.

Should a camel not get water on the seventh day he will probably be all right at midday on the eighth day. But, if allowed to go waterless for nine days, he will usually refuse to drink at all, and die of want of water.

Probably through living in countries where water is only to be enjoyed at the end of the march – camel-using peoples always travel from one water supply to another – no camel ever gives in until he is actually dying. I know of no other common and cheap animal whose courage can compare with that of the camel. He is, in his way, quite heroic.

Camels are picketed by tying the lead rope tightly round the knee, reducing their four legs to three. So picketed they cannot stray far, or move as fast as a lame man can walk.

The loading of a baggage camel is an art, but not one difficult to learn. The camel's head is swayed up and down, the driver at the same time making a noise like clearing his throat, and, in about a minute, the beast lowers himself to the ground on to his deep chest, which is equipped with a tough, horny sole to rest on, and then, swaying from side to side, he works his legs partly under him, and wedges his body firmly in position. The beautifully made packsaddle of wood and linen pads stuffed with wool is lifted on to his hump, the hand woven linen girths are not fastened until the camel is on his feet. The camel being so tall can carry the most extraordinary articles on top of his load. The usual load will be sacks and bundles of grain, or bales of goods which are dumped into a large square of rope netting anyhow, and balanced accurately on the packsaddle. On top of the usual load I have seen such things as large tables, legs upwards,

155

quite long ladders, tent poles, ploughs, or baggage of the largest size. Nothing is too awkward to travel 10ft up on top of a camel's hump.

A camel marches with all four feet in a line, he does not need to have a leg at each corner like an ox or a horse, and, should his master foolishly pack the saddle with a heavier load than the camel can manage for a day's march, the curiously wise beast refuses to stand up until his load has been reduced in weight to what he considers reasonable. An overloaded camel will certainly die on a long march, so he is rightly the final court to decide what constitutes a reasonable load.

We had in our battery camel column, of eight beasts and four drivers, a gigantic white Sudanese camel of such an amiable and friendly nature that his driver never had to drag him along by his rope, as the other drivers dragged theirs, sometimes for twenty hours out of the twenty-four. This camel's driver was known to give the animal dates with his mouth, not the kind of thing many men would care to risk, and once when I tested this big white beast to see what load he could carry at a pinch he got up off the ground and walked off willingly with 1,150lbs of barley on his back. But this camel was, in every way, exceptional.

Camels under shellfire are a perfect nuisance. The fact that shells are bursting among them and killing their fellows does not seem to interest them. A long line of baggage camels is an easy target for a gunner, they are so big and move so slowly. When observed and shelled the camels usually strolled about looking for something to eat, the drivers having wisely taken cover or fled for their lives. No amount of casualties among the camels seemed to disturb those engaged in searching for the scanty bits of thorn or scrub they browsed on, and unpleasant risks had to be taken before the surviving camels could he driven or dragged to a place of safety.

The endurance of the baggage camel was only matched by that of the camel drivers. These men, recruited in Egypt, are really professional experts devoted to the duties of their profession, and athletes of amazing muscular development and stamina. The camel drivers were plucky, willing and cheerful fellows, most ready to do anything we asked them in our fragmentary Arabic in return for their morning mug of tea – a luxury they much appreciated. When detached for service with a battery, or company of infantry, they got a drink of hot tea when our men had it –

in their own camel company a small loaf of dry bread, water and a double handful of lentils was all they could expect for the day's ration – from our standpoint a poor and monotonous diet, but, from theirs, equally monotonous but quite sufficient.

I owed my life to the youngest of our camel men, a boy of about sixteen. One dark night I was asleep, colonial fashion, with the inside of my saddle for a pillow, and my horse's reins round my ankles, spurs rammed into the ground to prevent the reins slipping off; an admirable device, for your horse will throw his head up and wake you at the slightest unfamiliar noise. Suddenly in the pitch darkness a hand seized mine, I grabbed the reins, and the boy Hassan led me out into nowhere at a fast run, shouting, 'Gemel maknoon', from which I understood that one of our camels had gone crazy in the usual manner and was liable to mangle anyone until stunned with the heavy pole carried by camel men for just such occasions. Hassan, the boy, died of a slight cold in the head, or something equally trifling, somewhere along the Jaffa-Jerusalem road. These people, while physically magnificent and of extraordinary endurance of fatigue, have no power of resistance to any illness and die of ailments that would not even make a white man ask to see a doctor. The usual explanation was that they were fatalists, but I suspect the real reason is that the food they live on is not good enough to give them any powers of resistance to illness.

Our division was ordered to France in the early summer of 1918, and we were, therefore, not present as spectators when the famous race for baggage camels took place after the Armistice.

I give the account of it at second hand, as related to me by an onlooker. The course was one of about a mile, the starting line was marked with flags fluttering on long poles imbedded in the ground, far enough apart to allow the competing camels, over three hundred in number, to line up side by side. The drivers, who usually lead their camels by a head-rope, were mounted for the race, and, at the starting signal, a revolver shot, the whole line of camels surged forward in a fog of dust, speed being obtained by vigorous application of sticks and by the yells of 1,500 or a thousand wallahs, every one of whom would be certain to have made bets on some camel of his own particular company. Every man would certainly have staked his entire capital consisting of one piastre (two and a half pence) or even so reckless an amount as five piastres (one shilling) to back his fancy.

Through the clouds of dust at last appeared a gigantic camel with a crushing lead of about 200yds, travelling at the limit of its speed, and fleeing in terror from the clamour in the rear. The driver, who must have been suffering the tortures of the Inquisition, managed to keep his clumsy steed straight enough to pass between the winning posts, and won in a common canter, so to speak (camels do not really canter), by roughly a quarter of a mile. But there was no stopping the frantic animal when the race was finished. On it careered, clean through the walls of a hut belonging to the YMCA, which stood directly behind the winning posts, on the far side of which it emerged, carrying window frames and various fragments of the building hanging round its neck, until it disappeared over the skyline of a low range of hills, still in full career.

Mounted officers pursued the winner and brought it back, complete with its rider, who, marvellous to relate, was still alive, unhurt, and, in his own estimation, as great a personage for the moment as the King of Egypt. It is related that bets were finally settled after several hours of altercation which led to serious fighting. And so the camel men had their own little festival to celebrate the end of the war, a festival which will be talked of in camel men's circles long after most of us are forgotten.

II

Discipline

Discipline has been defined as 'instant and willing obedience to an order'. The discipline of an artillery unit must be of a very high order. In such a unit as the RHA, where driving drill is carried out at the trot and gallop, it is obvious that, even in peacetime, orders must be obeyed instantly, and exactly, or collisions and accidents involving loss of life will be inevitable. A collision between two vehicles, weighing about two tons, and moving at a gallop behind six powerful horses, is bound to have very serious consequences, both to drivers and horses. In action a trifling error will often cause loss of life, either to the infantry over whom the battery is firing, or to those manning the guns. The order 'stand fast', designed to avoid calamities of this kind, is, therefore, obeyed literally and instantaneously.

Discipline whose motive force is fear of punishment for disobedience is of an inferior order. Without discipline soldiers are merely an armed mob of no military value, and subject to the same onslaughts of panic, unreason and brutality as any civilian crowd at a football match. The herd instinct, one of the strongest instincts of a population concentrated in towns and cities, must be eradicated as far as possible in the process of converting civilians into soldiers, and that is the reason why the countryman is more quickly converted into a soldier than the townsman. The countryman's wits may be less keen, but he is accustomed to think for himself, and act by himself, instead of blindly following the crowd.

Discipline cannot be obtained by any universal system, nor is there any absolute standard to be aimed at. The system which proved successful in the German Army would have proved disastrous in the French Army; that of the British Army, neither so rigid as that of the Germans, nor so elastic as that of the French, would have been unsuited to French or

German regiments. Any attempt to introduce the discipline of the British Army among colonial regiments, such as the admirable Australian Light Horse, would have resulted in utter chaos. Even in the British Army, units recruited from Lancashire mining towns had disciplinary arrangements totally different from those of regiments such as the Wiltshires or the Norfolks. The fact is that every army or regiment needs to have a system of discipline in accordance with the educational, social or national characteristics of the men who form the troops. The discipline of the Australian Light Horseman was not of an inferior kind because he habitually addressed his own officers by their Christian names, and British officers as 'Boss'. He meant no offence, and none was taken except by the insular and narrow-minded.

French soldiers, who addressed their company – or battery – commander as 'Mon Capitaine', and were usually addressed in reply as 'mes enfants', were only emphasising the semi-paternal attitude of the French officer towards his command. (To French and Belgian soldiers, the British regulation of one hotel or restaurant for the men and another for the officers is utterly barbaric, not to say Bochian.)

Discipline is a two-sided business. It consists not only of instant and willing obedience to orders on the part of subordinates, but it depends at least as much upon those issuing the orders having a full understanding of, and sympathy with, those men who will have the duty of carrying their orders out. Such orders will not be carried out willingly and instantly unless those who receive them have absolute confidence in their superiors' ability and consideration. One or two ill-considered, or ambiguous, orders from higher authorities will weaken the discipline of the best unit. Orders repeatedly cancelled, or altered, lead to sullen and perfunctory execution of orders in the future.

As Napoleon tersely puts it, 'Order, counter-order, disorder.'

Military discipline is intended to teach the habit of obedience to an order. In war, many orders must seem unreasonable to those who receive them, and must often result in heavy casualties as the result of obedience, but a well-disciplined unit will carry out orders however apparently unreasonable, and in the face of evident peril to themselves, only if they are inspired by complete trust and confidence in the ability and sympathy of their superiors.

DISCIPLINE

Soldiers, that is good soldiers, are not, and should not be, mere machines. A good disciplinarian never forgets that the troops are men of like passions and aspirations as his own. Only the insular and ignorant consider that every system of military discipline, whether French, German, colonial, Turkish or American, which differs from our own, is inferior to the British system; and in stating this definitely as an observed fact, the writer can refer to his, possibly, unparalleled opportunities of studying the troops, allied and enemy, of the following nations: Australians, Arabs, Belgians, Bulgars, Bengal Lancers, Canadians, Cossacks, Chinese (Labour Corps and French Tonkin Muleteers), Deccan Horse, Dogras, Egyptian (Labour Corps and camel drivers), French, Germans, Greek Venizelists, Highlanders (Scotch, Greek and North-west Frontier Indian), Irish, Italians, Jamaicans, Japanese Navy, Moroccan cavalry, New Zealanders, Portuguese, Queenslanders (Australian Light Horse), Russians, Serbs, Sikhs, Senegalese, South Africans, Turks, United States and Welsh.

It will be noted that the above list exhausts almost the complete alphabet, and that the observations offered on the subject of discipline are the fruit of experience and not of theory.

III

Map Reading

An officer who can't read a map should stay
on the barrack square.

The organisation responsible for the supply and production of maps must have been the most astonishingly efficient of all the departments of the whole war machine.

No one can hope to be a first class officer or NCO in any branch of any army without thorough training in the art of map reading. In the Great War this was not adequately recognised, except in the artillery, engineers, and cavalry. It was absolutely pathetic to find, as I often did, officers of infantry, ASC, RAMC, machine gunners, and other branches of the army wandering about in the dark, utterly lost, and unable to take the first elementary steps to find their way, even in the required direction.

Apart from their inevitable inability to be at the place and time ordered for the carrying out of whatever duties were required of them, the unnecessary hours of the labour of marching inflicted by these inadequately trained officers upon their men and animals were nothing short of scandalous, and led to justifiable discontent and loss of confidence among the troops, and serious and unnecessary exhaustion among the horses and mules allotted to them.

This is no exaggeration, as the following two examples will show. On one occasion in Palestine on a reconnaissance ride, when the map gave almost no detail, Colonel 'R' enquired of an infantry captain in a semi-permanent camp what his exact map reference was, and was given a position over thirty miles away, the exact location of our last night's halt.

MAP READING

On another occasion, also in Palestine, a machine gun officer, leading a column with many heavily laden pack mules and eighty or a hundred men, awoke me at midnight to enquire his way. His destination was a railway station, and I explained to him that all he had to do was to follow the wadi he was then in until it ended, incline right until he struck the railway, and follow it until he came to the station. He thanked me, and marched off. One would have thought that a child of ten-years-old could not have failed to follow such simple instructions, but at 4.00 am I was woken up again to find the same officer with the same trouble, in the same place as he had been four hours before. The language of the men he led when they recognised me again in the moonlight was lurid, and who can blame them. The mules were exhausted, and hanging their heads. This four hours useless marching in choking dust, and the consequent decline in the discipline of the troops and condition of the animals, was entirely due to the authority responsible for turning out a leader of a column on a night march who was totally unable either to read a map or use a compass.

A gunner who cannot read a map perfectly, and identify his position exactly in daylight or darkness, is a public menace who will, eventually, inevitably inflict serious casualties on the infantry for whose protection he is intended to provide, and probably also on the unfortunate artillerymen who are unlucky enough to be under his command.

There seems no possible explanation for responsible persons, whether officers or NCOs of infantry, artillery, or even medical services, being sent on active service untrained in the simple art of reading a map, and of the art of finding a way from A to B in daylight or in darkness.

For the instruction of officers in the art of finding a given point with map and compass, there is no exercise equal to the following. After dark, officers are ordered to report mounted to headquarters. A map reference is then given them, where a man has been posted during daylight with messages in writing. The officers ride off at intervals of ten minutes, and their times of departure are recorded. The officer who returns with the message in the shortest time has, obviously, proved himself the winner of the competition.

In the 268th Brigade this exercise was frequently undertaken in desert and trackless country. By various ingenious means the speed gradually rose to that of a horse at a hand-gallop. (For active service, for mounted

163

units, the compass should be oil-floating instead of the commoner needle-balanced pattern, as time is wasted waiting for the compass disc to settle with the needle pattern.)

With accurate maps such as are provided in war, fire can be and should be, unhesitatingly, directed upon an invisible target in the dark from a gun position occupied also in the darkness by a battery commander capable, as all should be, of locating exactly the position of his guns upon the map.

An example of this was our shelling a fortified Palestine village from a position at Ain Yebrid occupied in the dark, and relying on the accurate one inch to one mile map composed in 1878 by Lord Kitchener, when a lieutenant in the Royal Engineers. Using more modern and larger scale maps we regularly performed this simple feat of gunnery. Success, or the avoidance of disaster, depends, of course, entirely on the accurate recognition on the map of the position of the battery on the ground.

Occasionally, as in Salonica, accurate maps were not to be obtained, and copies of faulty maps were issued, no better being available. By shooting in daylight, however, a gunner who knows his job soon discovers mistakes in a map, and the guns soon showed us that the map-maker had forgotten to allow for the magnetic variation of 4 degrees for over three miles across the middle of our zone. But errors of this kind in maps were most unusual; in fact I believe that this was our only experience of faulty map construction on any of the three fronts on which the battery served.

All normal animals and savages can see in the dark. A small proportion of civilised human beings have preserved this gift of night vision. An experienced officer will endeavour to discover, as early as possible, any men in his command who are gifted with night vision, and will always place such men at the head of the column for night marches over broken, or shell holed, or wire entangled, or otherwise dangerous country. Units which possess no men with night vision will be wise to move in dangerous country at night with their transport animals at the head of the column, and avoid disaster by relying on the ability of horse and mule to see danger before his human driver. The drivers should be warned, in these cases, that their animals are to be given discretion in such matters. In a country like Salonica, where swamps, ravines (called dere), and precipices are always met with, a night march without some such provision is nothing short of a nightmare.

Experienced captains of the RFA, and officers who had duties of the same kind to perform in other branches of the army, under difficult circumstances, found out these devices for themselves. As far as I know, no instruction of any kind was officially imparted in any part of the British Army in such matters; and this, undoubtedly, accounted for the variation in condition of the horses and mules of different units campaigning under identical conditions.

IV

Portrait of a Battery
Sergeant Major

There is no more lordly spectacle on earth than a
man who understands his job supremely well.

Battery Sergeant Major (BSM) 'G' was our battery sergeant major for
over three years. A professional soldier of rather below medium height
he had twenty-two years' service to his credit. As a sergeant major he was
invaluable; a pattern to all the battery in smartness and efficiency, his
knowledge of the details of his profession and his sense of discipline
spoke volumes for the excellence of the training of our small pre-war
regular army. The discipline among the NCOs and other ranks of a battery
depends almost entirely on the character of the battery sergeant major.
No matter how keen and efficient major, captain, and subalterns may be,
a slack or slipshod BSM connotes a second rate battery.

Some of us amateur officers must have struck the professional BSM
as very odd, and some of our unprofessional methods must have made
his close-cropped hair stand on end. But our BSM's favourite boast was
that, 'he never had and never would let an officer down,' and he was a
big enough man to admit that all knowledge and brain were not the
exclusive possession of the regular army, and that, even when purely
military problems had to be dealt with, the regulation method of solving
them was neither the sole method nor the speediest.

He had all the good qualities and most of the weaknesses of the
professional NCO. He had no aptitude for tackling any difficulty except

as laid down in the training manuals and with the authorised tools (for example, no other way of cutting barbed wire had ever entered his head beyond the use of the regulation wire cutters. He thought my habit of never carrying wire cutters little short of lunacy until I showed him how every farm labourer cuts wire with one blow of a stone against the edge of a spade. He could scarcely believe his eyes and thereafter considered me as a person of remarkable intelligence).

In his own province, however, he was the complete master of his trade. Without reference to Army Form G1098 he could give the number of bits, stirrup leathers, short cheek pieces, or shoe cases on the establishment of a battery. He could, on inspection of 'small stores', remember, without the help of any book, the particular compartment of the eighty odd trays in the vehicles wherein any missing part or spanner should be found, any wretched screw of advanced age looked like a horse as soon as he had mounted it; he was an expert signaller and telephonist. Beyond all this he was a very human character. On parade the picture of unapproachable dignity, I have seen him behind a shed on hands and knees demonstrating to an inexperienced driver the proper way to scrub a dirty set of harness.

At a review by an inspecting general BSM 'G' dressed, except for the gold crown on his sleeve, in exactly the same clothing as the least of the drivers, made the BSMs of the other batteries look like a comic opera party, with their officer's caps, fancy tunics and breeches, and goose-necked spurs. He was always the neatest and smartest soldier of the brigade on every inspection, every article of his turnout from chin strap to spurs was perfectly regimental and regimentally perfect. He was an example to everyone in his loyalty to his battery, and his smart turnout was a daily demonstration to everyone of what a soldier should look like. With the exception of two sergeants we were all amateurs trying to be real soldiers, and here we had before us every day a real professional, a master of his simple trade, 'that most lordly spectacle on earth, the man who understands his job supremely well.'

In spite of the failings common to most NCOs of the pre-war professional army, failings known beyond any shadow of a doubt to all the sergeants' mess, he had the respectful admiration of every sergeant under him. As a testimonial that of a regular sergeant who joined us at Kantara, on the way home to France, shows the estimation in which he was held by his subordinates. This Sergeant 'W', in charge of D sub-section, could do nothing right according to the BSM. I was, temporarily, in command of the new centre section and, fearing this apparently very excellent sergeant would become discouraged, I tried to encourage him by saying that I didn't know, and didn't want to know, what was the trouble between him and the BSM, but, as his section commander, I was entitled to say that I was personally quite satisfied with his work in charge of D sub-section.

Sergeant 'W' thanked me, and then gave the BSM the finest testimonial I ever heard one man give another. He said, 'Yes, sir, he's giving me the worst gruelling I've ever had in my life, but by God, I have to say that he's the finest soldier I ever ran across.' To this surprising remark I could only reply, 'We all know that.'

The BSM was right as usual about Sergeant 'W', there was something queer about him. He went on leave when we reached France, and never came back to the battery. You could trust one regular senior NCO to hear anything unusual about another from the sergeant major of the last unit, provided both BSMs were 'serving soldiers'. The old regular army was a trades union, the members of which were loyal to one another, but in which a black sheep had little chance of recovering from the consequences of a serious false step.

BSM 'G' went home before the end of the war. Our loss was irreparable. The various sergeants who tried to take his place were nothing more than feeble imitations. But by the time he left us his work had helped to make the battery a machine that almost ran itself, and so these feeble imitations, who stepped into the shoes of our senior NCO, served their purpose, and kept things going on the lines he had so well established.

He was a great little soldier.

V

Portrait of a Subaltern

Les hommes sont rares.

French wit has produced this remarkably true estimate of our nation: 'The English are a remarkable people.

'They consider themselves superior to all other peoples, but the Scotch consider themselves superior to the English.'

'B' joined us at El Ferdan on the Suez Canal. He had come out from England and, having been ordered to report at 268th Brigade Headquarters, was posted by the CO, Colonel 'R', to C Battery.

As he walked into the woven grass hut in which the battery had its mess at El Ferdan, the first impression we formed of him was very favourable. He was very big, very Scotch, and obviously very modest, probably very efficient. Our recent acquisitions in the subaltern line had been none of these things.

It has been my experience that while a bad Scotchman is very bad indeed, a good Scotchman, what they themselves call a 'guid mon', is the earth's finest product, but modesty is not usually a characteristic of the first class Scot, whereas painstaking efficiency is.

In our battery a new subaltern was given every chance of finding his feet comfortably. He was immediately made to feel himself one of the party and at liberty to disclose whatever of his earlier history he felt disposed to reveal to his new associates.

'B' promptly informed us that, in civil life, he was a ship's engineer, that he came from Aberdeen, and that he had served in the Scots Greys with the rank of sergeant. (We were not in action at El

169

Ferdan but were engaged in acclimatising ourselves and the horses to desert conditions.)

'B' at once gave evidence that he was more than an ordinarily capable horseman. His handling of one of our more awkward riding horses led to enquiries which elicited the information that he had held the rank of rough-rider sergeant in the famous cavalry regiment in which he had served.

It was generally known about the time 'B' joined us that important offensive operations were soon to take place.

Rumours of this kind start, probably, at the base hospitals where drastic clearances must take place to make room for the inevitable casualty arrivals. (It is quite a mistake to suppose that the most valuable spy work has to be done in, or near, the front line. In war, front line people know very little of what is going on outside their own small sector, and nothing whatever of future operations. The ease with which strangers can gain admission to base headquarters, whether in Cairo, Alexandria, army headquarters in France and Salonica, was always a source of wonder to us front line amateur soldiers.)

As soon as these rumours became evidently based on something definite 'B' had an accident, and went to hospital with a broken collar bone, the consequence of his horse putting its foot in a hole in the sand and falling with him at full gallop. While in hospital his one anxiety was that he should get back to the battery before the show started. He was simply terrified, to judge from his pathetic letters, lest, on his discharge from hospital, he should be sent to the ammunition column instead of to our battery. (The ammunition columns on active service, besides supplying the fighting units with ammunition, are used as reservoirs of officers and men for the batteries to draw upon in case of need to replace casualties. As they are also used as a dumping ground for officers and NCOs who are regarded as of little use in a battery – every battery officer and NCO regards 'duty with the column' as the equivalent of what is euphemistically known among the higher command as a 'Bowler Hat'.

Major 'M', being most unwilling to lose the services of 'B', sent me to ask Colonel 'R' to apply for his immediate return to our battery on discharge from hospital. As this request was granted at once, I had the pleasant duty of visiting 'B' in hospital at Ismailia, and instructing him to get mended up quickly as we wanted him back in the battery as soon as possible. That, I think, was the beginning of a friendship between 'B' and myself which has lasted until today, and I trust will go on indefinitely.

Like most competent marine engineers 'B' was full of contrivances and ingenious devices. On one occasion, on the hills near Jerusalem, a careless sergeant ordered his No. 3 to fire before the layer had 'engaged the plungers'. The effect of this carelessness is always that, when the howitzer is fired, the muzzle flies up to extreme elevation, bending the thick steel rod between the elevating pinions to such an extent that the gun remains at extreme elevation, and is out of action.

In the circumstances it seemed certain that the gun would be out of action until such time as a horseman could ride nearly 40 miles to the ordnance depot with the bent elevating arc, exchange it for a new one, or wait while the bent arc was straightened and ride back 40 miles to the guns. 'B', however, with the assistance of the fitter and no better tool than a hammer from the forge and the rocks off the hillside, succeeded in bending the elevating gear straight enough to restore the gun to action in about two hours. Considering that the task was to straighten a steel rod roughly two inches thick, a hammer and some rocks being the only available tools, 'B's bit of Heath Robinson engineering was remarkable. But at sea, in the engine room, such things have to be done, and are done, by every second engineer on most voyages.

In the neck-breaking climbs up the goat tracks on the hills of Palestine, where our guns had to be dragged in the dark up rocky slopes with so precarious a foothold that on one occasion no less than twenty-eight horses had to be harnessed to our No. 1 gun in place of the usual six, and a daylight view of the way we had come convinced each one of us that no driver's nerve would have been equal to an attempt had he been able to see the crazy precipices on both sides of our track, 'B's exceptional strength and ready resource often contrived, out of a rope and spare draught pole, some primitive tackle to help a vehicle round, or over, a lump of rock the size of a dining room table. At other times, when another subaltern, clean for the first time for weeks and hoping for a decent meal and a sleep in comparative comfort, found himself on turn for the duty of laying out a telephone line in torrents of rain up and down precipitous rocks in pitch darkness, 'B', although he had had a similar duty the night before, would often volunteer to 'come along and lend a hand as soon as I've had a mouthful or two.' Shamefacedly we usually accepted his offer. Company on a job like that is worth 'all the tea in China', and 'B's assistance was like having a squad of experts along with you. Everyone was always ready to do his damndest, but 'B' was ready always to do a shade more than his share, and be a bit more unselfish than the best of us.

He had the proud nickname, among our infantry, of 'the big Scotch gunner that didn't mind shells', and that title was earned. 'B's broad back and, when he turned round, his broader grin, often put a bit of extra heart into a man who had had all the shellfire he could stand.

Of course we all valued him, but, like most of the good things that fortune sends along for us, we did not appreciate him to the full until we had lost him. The story of our parting with 'B' is worth telling.

It was on the Somme in September, 1918. The battery was in position in a quarry west of Ronssoy. We had no dugouts of any kind, and the whole of the guns of the brigade were in the valley in line, covered from enemy observation by the rising ground in front, but with no protection whatever against enemy shellfire. Our mess and battery headquarters was a bell tent, there had been no time for a more secure battery position to be organised.

I received word from the major that a move forward was ordered for our battery, and came up from the wagon lines, which was three miles or so in rear of the gun position to make arrangements for the move. I had dinner with the others in the tent, after sending off my groom and horses to avoid the risk of them being wounded by shell splinters of which enough were flying about. The others pressed me to stay for a game of cards, and, at midnight, I set off to walk back to the horses. It was a difficult task to find one's way out of the valley in the dark; shell holes and barbed wire were on all sides. 'B', as usual, came along to 'lend me a hand'. On our way out of the valley we found an infantry limbered wagon with a pair of mules capsized in a shell hole. When we had assisted the driver to turn his vehicle and team right side up, quite an impossible task for one man in pitch darkness, I found he had no idea of his way home, and offered to guide him in return for a lift in the wagon. As his destination was less than half a mile beyond my own horse lines this plan suited me admirably.

We had only left the valley a few minutes when the enemy artillery put down a first class gas bombardment on the valley. My infantry driver and I looked back and saw the flashes of bursting shells all over the valley we had just climbed out of. The driver remarked that we were in luck. I agreed, but suggested that we should have been in the middle of it but for the help of my friend 'B' in righting his team. The driver agreed, with the words, 'And I 'opes he don't cop out with a bit o' that lot.' I hoped so, too.

Next morning when I came up with the teams to move the guns I heard how he had 'copped out' and gone to hospital. The gas had caught the gunners asleep by their guns in the valley. The officers had gone to bed half way up the hill. 'B', in his pyjamas and slippers, spent most of the night carrying collapsed gunners up onto the hill out of the poisonous valley which gradually became full of the fumes of the 'mustard gas'. Before long 'B' was nothing but a blister, and was forcibly removed to hospital.

In some of our earlier wars that kind of conduct would have been recognised by the award of a medal, and of an extremely rare medal. In the Great War such acts were seldom recognised by anything of an official nature. They were, however, not forgotten by the men who had benefited by them, and were gratefully remembered by the friends who missed their best subaltern so sorely. 'B' was unable to take any further part in the war, but official recognition of his conduct went so far as the bestowal of…a wound stripe.

VI

Horace the Hen and
Abdul the Pi-dog

Our humblest servants.

A writer of exceptional powers of vivid phrase-making has described active service in France as 'long periods of boredom punctuated with intervals of terror.'

In a battery such as we tried to make ours, this description would only be true of us in our weakest periods. Boredom we were usually far too busy to experience, terror is a phenomenon that afflicts the undisciplined and neurotic, and we were neither of those things.

The old saying that 'all work and no play makes Jack a dull boy' is equally true in peace and in war. No unit that is either dull or bored can hope to be a first class fighting machine, and therefore commanding officers who know their job will endeavour to prevent both officers and men from becoming dull, bored, or stupid.

A battery of field artillery was practically continuously in action. The only experiences we had to compare with the regular periods of infantry 'out of the line' were when we were moving from one front to another, or undergoing refitting, or recuperation, after unusual efforts.

Such recreations as football were impossible for gunners engaged in serving guns in the line; drivers whose life was an eternal round of harness cleaning, stables, and ammunition transport had little leisure or energy left for organised athletics. The only occasions when such activities as football, tug-of-war (mounted), paper chases (mounted), or wrestling on horseback were possible, or even desirable, were those rare times when the battery was out of the line, and the gunners, having no gunnery or ammunition humping to work at, could relieve the overworked little drivers of part of the endless labour which the care of a 150 or more horses entails.

In action the most satisfactory form of amusement for officers and men was the keeping of pets. These took many forms, and varied from a family of kittens born in a gun pit near Arras, tortoises which swarmed all over Macedonia, a magnificent Macedonian sheepdog puppy rescued when its mother, which had gone wild and which sometimes attacked the sentry at night, had to be shot in the hills behind Cidemli, chameleons caught on the fig trees on the Palestine coast, and various dogs, including a well-bred greyhound, Bint, a pointer bought in Marseilles with a tin of cigarettes, and an Irish terrier, also several nondescripts of the well-known Heinz breed, and finally Horace the Hen and Abdul.

Horace the Hen happened in this way. One day, near the Suez Canal, I met a wallah who wanted to sell me two Egyptian chickens. The price he asked, khanisi piastre, one shilling each, was so low that I bought them, although they were evidently stolen goods. On reaching the camp with the live chickens still struggling in the nose-bag tied to my saddle, I examined my purchase and found that the birds were so skinny as to be useless for the kitchen.

In desert life all animals, hens, dogs, goats, sheep, etc., can safely be left running about loose. There is nowhere to go in the desert, so no animals stray away, food and water being where their owners live, and nowhere else. This gives even the smallest desert camp a patriarchal appearance, and a charm of its own. In true desert fashion I turned my chickens loose, and they soon found stray grains of corn dropped by the horses, ants in the loose sand, and other nourishing pasture round the men's cook-house.

The Egyptian hen is not used to regular rations; it lives, exactly as the sparrows, on what happens to come its way. As our two chickens, which we quickly decided were cockerels, were going to live under conditions of incredible luxury, from the point of view of an Egyptian fowl, we looked for a dish of roast chicken before very long. But it was not to be. One of them died; the other, a pink and yellow speckled bird, which we called Horace, took to roosting in the woven grass shed where we had the officers' mess, and one day laid an egg in an empty case which had once contained whisky.

175

After that, Horace was officially taken on to the strength and took his place in the horse book, being correctly described in horse parlance as: Hen, roan, saddlemarks both sides, near hind partly, age undetermined.

After being taken on the strength Horace carried out the duties of a hen with commendable precision, and laid an egg daily until such time as the desert trek to Beersheba necessitated ruthless reduction of baggage, and compelled us to transfer our Horace to the cooking pot with many regrets.

Abdul the pi-dog had a short life also. His only duties were to be a willing playfellow for anybody who wanted to play with him, and that meant every officer, NCO or man who happened to meet with him.

Abdul was, roughly speaking, a smooth-coated coal-black Aberdeen dachshund, with a snow-white tip to his tail, and the front half of each of his forepaws white. We found him in an abandoned Turk trench at Beersheba. As his youth and the shortness of his legs made travelling under his own steam beyond his powers, when the battery was on the march he travelled in style in a little Turkish cart drawn by two white Egyptian donkeys, which marched in rear of our column. The little cart, in which we carried our portable forge and coal, was a capture from the Turks, the donkeys, Archie and Arthur, had been won one dark night near Sheria, and the harness for our unauthorised pair of little entire donkeys was ingeniously made by our master-craftsman, Saddler 'K', out of pieces of broken reins.

Whenever we met our CRA, General 'H', on the march, he always enquired politely after the health of our donkeys.

Abdul came to a sad end. Somebody transferred him, for extra safety, from the donkey wagon in which he had travelled in perfect safety for at least a hundred miles, into another captured vehicle which was 'attached' to our brigade headquarters. As his lead was far too long, a yard and a half instead of the proper six inches, the first time the conveyance bounced over one of the big rocks which litter the foothills in Southern Palestine, Abdul shot over the side and broke his neck, as the long lead, which the idiot who had transferred him without orders had fastened him by, hanged him as neatly and effectively as possible. So, through the stupidity of some unknown admirer, Abdul died a felon's death while in a state of comparative innocence, owing solely to his extreme youth, and we lost a valuable playmate.

176

VII

Some Tips for Gunners

A pound of practice is worth a ton of theory.

1. 'Near enough is no use.' This relates to ranging. An observer, when registering on a target, must never assume that a round which appears to be quite near the target is really close to it on the ground. What appears to be quite near from one OP may easily be 50yds away. A target is only registered when actually hit.
2. 'Fools rely on one round; wise men take an average of five.' This also relates to ranging. One round may be exceptional, and an average of five rounds is essential to establish the true MPI (mean point of impact).
3. 'When asked to fire at anything, fire at something.' Infantry often select impossible targets for gunners to engage, impossible to hit at the range, owing to size. Aeroplanes and balloons report moving targets miles out of range of the battery notified. An experienced gunner will, invariably, fire when requested. It encourages the infantry to have their request attended to, and the more promptly you fire the more confidence the infantry feel in their artillery. It has happened that an aeroplane observer has reported 'target' on the first round fired in the direction of a target indicated at a map reference eight miles outside extreme range of the battery notified. A battery earns a fine reputation by observing this tip. Confidence in their artillery support is of paramount importance to the infantry. The target selected may have been one of no importance, but knowledge that the gunners in support will fire day or night thirty seconds after fire is asked for means a confident battalion.

4. 'A good farrier doubles your teams.' The foot of a horse is the most delicate and complicated of mechanical devices. In a horse-drawn unit every officer should have passed a shoeing course. If a battery cannot arrive at its allotted position at the required hour it might as well have stayed at the base. Cold shoeing is an abomination, and a shoe lost on the march is nothing short of a disgrace to the regiment.

5. 'Guns are like women. They do unaccountable things without any apparent reason.' This means that occasionally a round will not fall where accurate laying, correct orders, range line and wind corrections should have directed it; variations in manufacture both of shell and charge, atmospheric changes, either separately or in combination, can account for enormous discrepancies. I have known the range of two successive shells vary by 500yds in a range of 4,200yds, and have seen a shell burst on the target fired from a gun that burst at the breech when the trigger was pulled.

6. 'A good shoot calls for a word of praise to the layer.' Often at the termination of a successful piece of shooting, one is apt to think that the success is due to one's brilliant corrections. It probably was. But without the accurate work of the layer nothing would have saved you from a complete failure. A good officer makes a habit of asking for the layer's name after each successful shoot. The laying of the battery improves as a result of it.

7. 'The gun with the burnished breech is probably dirty.' The 'eyewash' unit is not always the most efficient. There is plenty of work for a limber gunner on active service without his using a burnisher. Some batteries have been known to resemble the battalion which had flashing buttons and rusty bayonets.

8. 'Double observation is four times single.' For accurate shooting on a target of supreme importance forward observation from both flanks simultaneously with the observers connected by telephone gives absolute certainty of effective fire. This expedient, though extremely simple, is seldom used. Batteries in the line could, and should, cooperate in this way as a matter of routine.

9. 'Cooperation, observation, communication.' Without these three, success in war is impossible.

10. 'Order, counter-order, disorder.' This maxim, one of Napoleon's, is

self-explanatory. The expectation in the minds of subordinates that orders will be countermanded frequently leads inevitably to slow and half-hearted execution of every order. In a first class battery in a high state of discipline every order is carried out at the double and with eagerness.

11. 'Remember the tail of the column.' March discipline for the CO. It is easy to forget that when the head of the column, where you are, is over the top of the hill, the tail is still toiling up it. A thoughtful leader of a battery or brigade on the march will refrain from increasing his pace after a hill is climbed until the last – and usually the weakest – team in the column has had time to reach the easier going. Concertina marching, as it is called, is a terrible strain on the tail of a column, and indicates a thoughtless leader.

VIII

Manslaughter

And they smote them with the edge of the sword.

Among Western peoples of modern times there is general agreement that the taking of human life is the foulest of all crimes. The soldier's art is the killing of his fellowmen, his training is directed solely towards making him an expert man killer, there is no other purpose in his training or trade.

At the same time the profession of arms is, with the exception of China, esteemed an honourable profession among all nations. It is, therefore, obvious that man slaying in war is to the general conscience something quite different from man slaying at any other time.

An efficient soldier, in the exercise of the trade he has learned, that is, the art of war, is an expert killer of armed men. All his other activities are subordinate and contributory to this one object.

Disarmament conferences have attempted to draw a distinction between offensive and defensive weapons. The absurdity of attempting to draw such a distinction is evident to anyone who has taken even a humble part in actual War. Every weapon, from a battleship to a knuckle-duster, is capable of being employed for offence as well as defence. In fact the defensive value of any weapon whatever, from 15-inch guns, through tanks, machine guns to Mills Bombs, rifles, bayonets, down to trench daggers and knobkerries, is no more and no less than its offensive value.

Attack is the chief tactic of defence. Consequently, without the employment of offensive weapons, defence is impossible, and to pretend that any nation should be adequately armed for defence without being

180

equipped with offensive weapons is to put forward a proposition which is so evidently absurd that one is forced to doubt if it is made with any other intention but to befool the public.

Probably no man ever went to war with a greater dislike of killing anybody or anything than the writer. I never cared for shooting or hunting for the one reason that killing is distasteful to me. And yet, in the Great War, employing every means at my disposal, and every scrap of intelligence that I could command, I contributed every German, Turk and Bulgar to the list of enemy killed and wounded that I could possibly manage; in some cases the effort involved considerable risk to my own safety – in shooting a battery from a sap the amount of risk taken by a FOO of the field artillery is a matter for his own decision on each occasion – in every case the infliction of casualties upon the enemy was a matter for self-congratulation, without the slightest feeling of having committed any act deserving of reproach from anyone.

How did it come about that countless people of most un-murderous instincts like myself could feel the utmost satisfaction in inflicting hideous wounds, and often instantaneous death, upon fellow men in time of war?

The simple, and I am certain quite untrue, explanation of the pacifist is the term 'brutal soldiery'. To the convinced pacifist every soldier is a brute, or a potential brute. But, as every single normal officer or man who has served in actual war knows, the British soldier is anything but brutal. He is, on the other hand, in the great majority of cases a kindly, soft-hearted creature, ready to give his last cigarette to a wounded soldier either in allied or enemy uniform, and to treat a prisoner just as he would treat a friend in misfortune. I never met a brutal officer in the Allied armies; we never had an officer in either of the batteries in which I served to whom the term brutal could possibly have been applied by anybody, and yet, to every one of them, the killing or maiming of troops with high explosive or gas shelling ranked as a most laudable and satisfactory job of work.

I believe the explanation to be, first: familiarity with the idea of death, and second: the primitive instinct of the watchdog.

When a man has for weeks, months, and years got up from his bed with the knowledge that each day will possibly, or even probably, be his last, the idea of death ceases to be an idea of something far off in the dim

181

future. Death becomes then an accident that may happen to anyone at any minute of the day or night, and the almost daily sight of bodies of dead soldiers awaiting burial leads the mind to the idea of death as something familiar and likely, instead of the improbable far off tragedy that death appears to us as civilians in time of peace.

The primitive instincts are those most deeply rooted in the human race, or, indeed, in the animal kingdom. The most remarkable and striking is the instinct of race-preservation. This, and not self-preservation, is the 'first law of nature', as is clearly shown by the maternal instinct common to both men and animals to try to defend their young even against the most hopeless odds. Most of the primitive instincts seem to be laudable in their intention and unselfish in character. They are probably the inherited race-memory of those impulses which alone ensured the survival of the species when life was a precarious adventure and existence itself was only possible where obedience to custom was unquestioned.

One of the strongest of these primitive instincts must have been that of the watchdog. In time of attack every man able to fight bore his part in safeguarding the people. Except in the cowardly, worthless and despicable such an instinct still persists. There is nothing so certain to unite a quarrelling nation, class, profession, or family as the threat of attack from outside. Propagandists and warmongers play upon this instinct, and easily arouse war fever among peaceable peoples by picturing imaginary dangers of foreign attacks. But the crafty abuse of this universal instinct of the best and most unselfish of the human species does not make the instinct other than altogether praiseworthy, and necessary if the race is to survive.

In this connection there is the knowledge that the other side is striving no less eagerly to kill and maim you and your fellows. War is big game hunting on the grand scale – with this difference, that both sides are the hunted as well as the hunters. The classic description of foxhunting as 'war with fifty per cent of the danger,' would be true enough if packs of foxes pursued the unsuccessful master of foxhounds to the limit of his horse's endurance, or perhaps beyond that.

IX

Wangling, Scrounging, Winning and Theft

There are more ways of killing a dog than
choking it with butter.

No attempt to describe the Great War would be complete if it did not include some account of the processes whose names I have chosen for the title of this chapter.

Wangling was the name given to the various methods of acquiring, by what the law terms 'subtle devices', those things of which we found ourselves to be in urgent need. It must not be supposed that these were usually luxuries.

In the Royal Artillery the establishment of a battery is set out in a printed list known as Army Form G1098. This has probably been added to and amended from time to time as circumstances rendered advisable.

As the officer responsible for the equipment of the battery in which I was serving I can state, without fear of contradiction, that under most conditions of actual warfare the establishment of a battery is pitifully inadequate.

The officers' horses, for example, are ten in number, and each officer has a groom who acts as horse holder. How either officer or groom can possibly perform his duties when they have only one saddle between them passes comprehension. No officer could possibly deprive a mounted man of his saddle and transfer it to the groom, nor could he perform his duties at such a pace that the groom could follow him on foot leading the second horse or riding it bareback.

Again, no battery can be one hundred per cent efficient with the official establishment of telephones and telephone wire. In one position we had to use continuously five times the total establishment of telephone wire and double the official number of telephones.

When we were marching about the desert each battery was allotted ten water 'fanatis', zinc tanks each containing fifteen gallons of water, which are carried two on each baggage camel. This supply apparently allowed for one gallon a day for each man with no margin for accidents. From the first it was plainly obvious that I, as the person responsible for the water, could not leave matters in this precarious state. In the desert no one gives water away. One bullet, a leaky tap, a shell-splinter, a collapsed camel and we should be short of water with no means of making our loss good.

We did have leaky tanks given to us, we had at least two shell-splinters through our water fanatis, we had a camel die 'on us' and yet we never went short of water because we carried four extra fanatis full of water on the guns.

We did not stretch our telephone wire to five times its original length, we did not manufacture extra telephones, our officers did not share their one saddle with their grooms. None of these things was necessary because we were adepts in the art of wangling.

On active service a man with his wits about him can wangle anything. At various times we wangled nine telephones, one water cart, five officers' saddles, twelve miles of telephone wire, hundreds of nosebags and hay nets, a day's forage for 150 horses, a wagon load of sleepers (needed for gun platforms in soft ground) from the RE, extra packsaddles in Salonica, and other essential articles of equipment too numerous to mention.

As I became more experienced it became clear to me that the official equipment of a field battery had been laid down either for conditions of warfare quite different from those obtaining in the Great War, or for reasons of paper economy for the purpose of Army Estimates.

True economy in war must be to shorten the war by every possible means. The only possible means we had of helping to shorten the war was to ensure that our battery should be always adequately equipped so as to be ready to exert its maximum power on every possible occasion.

This was achieved by wangling.

Wangling is not stealing. It is rather a battle of wits between the fighting soldier and those curious people who, both in army and navy, apparently believed that wars are won by careful office work and filling in official forms in triplicate.

Among the colonial divisions and corps it was sufficient to give evidence that certain stores were urgently needed to be given them at once, if they were available. But in the British Army it was not realised that the enemy are unlikely to wait until the usual requisition forms have been filled in in triplicate, filed for reference, entered in several ledgers, submitted for approval to the hierarchy of red tape and red tabs from Woolwich to corps HQ and consequently, if good men's lives were not to be sacrificed while pompous non-combatants were busily inscribing forms of various colours with the formulae, 'passed to you, please, for sanction and approval,' or, 'for information and attention,' wangling was the one sure and rapid method of getting what was needed and it proved successful one hundred times out of every hundred carefully planned attempts.

Everybody worth his salt wangled his way through the war for the immediate benefit of his unit, and, I am certain, for the ultimate benefit of his country.

Scrounging and winning. These have a different implication from wangling. To scrounge or to win a thing is to annex an article which has been left lying about.

In a well-run unit nothing is left lying about. If people on active service leave government property all over the place it is certain to pass into the possession of others who will be more careful to look after it.

Many things of value fell off the vehicles of badly run units on a night march.

One night I deliberately followed a notoriously inefficient battery with our cook's cart. This battery was marching in the dark to entrain at a French railway station. Long before they reached the station I had turned back as my cart was full to the canvas roof with spades, dandy brushes, brooms, hay-nets full of hay, surcingles complete with pads, mackintosh sheets and blankets and all kinds of valuable equipment.

At four o'clock one morning on the Palestine coast I won the finest hurricane lamp we ever owned, a brass one of an unknown make, which I believe must have been dropped from a transport vehicle of some Indian cavalry.

Now and then we won unusual things; on the Judean Hills, for instance, I found a large case of food and drink of the most luxurious description, odd sacks of millet for the camels, and once in starvation times a case of bully beef.

In France I once won a major's horse complete with saddle and saddlebags, but the groom, finding that the horse had strayed, applied to know if we had found it and so, of course, it was handed over at once.

Scrounging and winning are not stealing. Anything scrounged was returned at once if application was made promptly by the owner. But such claimants had to apply exceedingly quickly in most cases.

Theft. In our battery theft was treated as a serious crime. The only kind of theft permitted was retaliatory and this only with permission or even under instructions from myself.

Retaliatory theft was not a thing to be ashamed of. It was just and salutary, as will be seen from the two following examples.

On the Latron-Jerusalem road it fell to me to lead the battery single handed to the neighbourhood of Kiryat El Enab. The other four officers had gone on foot by a shorter route, impassable for vehicles, to take over a new position further east than the one from which they had been shooting.

When I arrived with the battery at El Enab the brigade major of the division leaving the area instructed me to take the battery down the hill and arrange the horse lines on an abandoned vineyard in the valley.

I arrived there about 11.00 pm in pitch darkness and torrents of rain to find, to my dismay, that half the place was already occupied by the battery which we were relieving, who had been ordered to march out at 4.00 am.

To facilitate transport I had had two nosebags filled with corn fastened to each saddle (or surcingle in the case of the hand horses), and when we came to feed the horses and mules two nosebags had been stolen from one of the saddles in the dark.

As soon as the loss was reported I went straight to the tent of the major commanding the other battery, where the following conversation took place:

Major: What do you want?

Me: To report that in ten minutes after our arrival your men have stolen two of my nosebags. What are you going to do about it?

Major: Who are you talking to?

Me: I don't know and I don't care. What are you going to do about it?

Major: Nothing whatever.

Me: Good evening.

I returned to my sopping quarters, sent for the sergeant major and ordered him to turn loose the looting squad.

When I awoke next morning our 40lbs of stolen corn, had been replaced by four sacks (400lbs) and a very fair horse. As we were in a Biblical area – Kiryat El Enab is the modern name of Kirjath Jearim – I felt moved to describe our reprisal as 'good measure, pressed down, shaken together and running over.'

The other case of theft occurred in France near Villers-Faucon. In this position the enemy shelling was continuous and heavy, and it was impossible to select horse lines of reasonable safety nearer the guns than a distance of several miles. In such cases I used to leave at the gun line our most worthless riding horse and Shoeing-Smith 'M' to act as a quick means of communication between guns and wagon line. Incidentally Shoeing-Smith 'M' had an uncanny sense of direction and could find his way across country in the dark without fail. An abandoned gun pit to the right of the gun position gave our old chestnut a reasonable chance of survival as the empty gun pit gave him fair protection from flying shell splinters. After the first night, however, the major sent me word that he wanted another horse as the chestnut had vanished, probably stolen by an Australian battery which was in action on his right.

That very evening an Australian horse strayed into our horse lines. We caught it, hogged its mane close – the Australians left about two inches of mane on their horses – shortened its tail, dyed one white foot brown with permanganate, and altered the number branded on its hooves. In the morning an Australian sergeant major arrived with two men and asked permission to look for a stray horse. I, of course, gave him permission at once. All our horses being Australians we had brought back to France

187

from the Suez Canal Remount Depot at Kantara, the stamp of horse did not betray our foundling, and although the three Australians inspected their own horse quite suspiciously they finally decided against claiming it and went off after thanking me quite politely. I think part of the success was due to my allowing them to wander all over our horse lines without anyone belonging to our battery accompanying them. I had little fear of their recognising the animal. We had been horse-copers by then for several years, and the men in charge of this particular job were not novices.

Provided the owners of the lost horse were also guilty of having removed our chestnut, which seemed probable, in this case also justice was done. But I could not ask them the question, as that would have been the quickest way of arousing their suspicion. In any case we replaced our old chestnut with a better animal.

X

Rations and Forage

'Feed the brute'.

If 'an army travels on its stomach,' still more does, or did, the Royal Artillery travel on its horses' stomachs. There is no quartermaster in the RFA. Brigade headquarters issues orders of a tactical nature to batteries and circulates information to them as to where rations, forage, ammunition, etc., may be obtained, but the actual process of obtaining them is left to each individual battery. Ammunition is brought by the ammunition column and transferred from the wagons of the column to the ammunition wagons of each battery at the wagon lines, to be delivered at the guns by the battery's own personnel in the ammunition wagons, where possible, or by means of pack transport, where mountainous country, or absence of roads, or the danger of shell fire, makes wagon transport impracticable, as was the case in Salonica and the Judean Hills, and on the shell blasted roads in the Somme area and the Ypres Salient. (The quickest and handiest method of moving 4.5-inch howitzer ammunition on packsaddle is to draw the ammunition boxed, as the rope beckets of each box, which contains two shells and the charges for them, can be slipped over the hooks on either side of the regulation packsaddle and travel securely without lashing and with no risk of galling the horse or mule carrying them.)

Rations and forage are the chief responsibility of the QMS, who, in a well-organised battery, is given the assistance of a thoroughly trustworthy gunner to take charge of the ASC wagons attached for the purpose of drawing rations and forage. The QMS in practice draws the rations and forage personally, the battery captain being always ready to smooth over any difficulties and make things easy in case of any trouble with the supply officer of the ASC. A good QMS is worth his weight in gold to any battery, and ours was very good.

Rations and forage are the fuel that keep the engines going in both men and horses. In moving warfare, inevitably, when extra efforts have to be demanded from both, rations are usually less plentiful, and forage is automatically reduced from the usual allowance of 10lbs corn and 10lbs hay per animal to the mobile ration of 10lbs corn and 2lbs hay per day. In moving warfare we found that the hours of work – very hard work for horses and men – tended to average from sixteen to eighteen out of the twenty-four, and this on a smaller allowance of food than the ration when the hours of work were only half as many. This is a problem due entirely to transport difficulties. It is obviously most undesirable that, in time of extra effort, food for both man and beast should be scantier than when less effort is required, especially as, when night work has to be undertaken in addition to the labours of the day, an extra meal is essential both for men and animals. The solution is plain. For moving warfare the transport must be largely increased above what is sufficient for stationary conditions.

In the probable absence of any provision of this nature the following are remedies which we found of the greatest value. For the men – the battery canteen should be kept well-stocked. In Salonica I was able to provide a pack mule which carried the canteen stores on the march, and, at each halt, my servant led the mule, called Clarence by the drivers, along the column selling sardines, chocolate, biscuits and cakes to any who had the wherewithal to buy them. On rare occasions, when my canteen was very prosperous and the need was severe, I was able to make gratis distributions. The arrival of Clarence was, on all occasions, greeted with a cheer.

For the animals, we carried on the baggage wagon a large trough like a dugout canoe, with ends of wood and a hull of metal. This trough was laid over a hole dug in the ground at each camp. A fire was lit in the hole, and the trough filled half full of water. Every particle of refuse, except tea leaves from the men's cookhouse, was cooked in this trough and all the hay seed, to save which all hay bales were opened either in the wagon or over a tarpaulin, the seed being carefully shaken out before the hay was chaffed for the animals to eat. In this way each animal got one to two pounds extra food at each feed time, and, as we carried a chaff cutter with us and chaffed every bit of hay, our animals did somewhat better than those of the units which simply fed the standard mobile ration of 10lbs of corn and two of hay.

For emergencies, and in moving warfare emergencies are to be looked for every day, we carried on the wagons an iron ration of 400lbs of corn for each sub-section. This corn was saved when rations were plentiful and was a godsend when, as sometimes happened, forage did not arrive.

As extra food for horses, both of the following are useful. About thirty per cent, of horses will eat bully beef. One of my own chargers used to eat half a tin of beef each midday, so that I could save her corn for a double feed at night.

In a country with shallow rivers, if a bit of bank is broken down into the river bed, the stream will wash away the earth and leave a mass of roots of weeds and grass. If these roots are washed and chopped in the chaff cutter a valuable addition of bulk food is obtained for the nosebags.

In moving warfare no horse, whether officer's charger, signaller's mount, or other outrider, should ever leave the horse lines without, at least, one day's forage in the nosebag. This should be a matter of routine and a responsibility of the NCO in charge of the forage barn.

Watering animals. The officer in charge should attend every watering order. Some animals are very slow drinkers and should be left at water until they have drunk all they can hold. Every slow drinker should be known and carefully watched by the officer, otherwise he will go short of water. One excellent, if hideous, horse of the cayuse breed we had in Salonica, a very heavy drinker, would play about with the water for fifteen minutes before plunging his nose well under and then drinking greedily. In charge of a thoughtless driver, with a perfunctory NCO superintending watering order, this most valuable draught horse would have never had a full drink and would have mysteriously fallen away in consequence.

XI

Camouflage

Camouflage protects a gun pit
better than concrete.

Camouflage, the art of concealing a battery in action from enemy observation, is one of the most important duties of the officer in charge at the gun line.

In our experience the best method of ensuring adequate camouflage was to appoint one of the officers OC camouflage and give him the services of an intelligent bombardier as his permanent assistant. This junior NCO must be permanently on duty at the gun line and responsible that every device for concealment of the gun position is definitely in place before daybreak.

The principles of camouflage are extremely simple. They were not understood until the latter part of the Great War.

As soon as the necessity for concealment from hostile observation was realised oceans of paint were used to daub guns and wagons all the colours of the rainbow. The vehicles of the artillery were repainted yellow, on top of which broad streaks of brown, green, blue and red were imposed to give a modern-art effect of cubism. The idea was to break up large surfaces into small ones. The system was adopted all over the front without proper appreciation of the situation. Guns, under modern conditions, never come into action except in what is known as a 'covered position', that is with something such as a wood or a hill between the battery and the enemy to hide the gun flashes from enemy observation. Any battery that failed to find a covered position soon ceased to take any active part in hostilities owing to enemy shellfire. A howitzer battery of high-angle fire guns needs no less than 16ft of flash cover, or the enemy will see the flashes when the guns are fired. It follows that paint camouflage as a concealment from ground observation is unnecessary. There remains observation from the air. Any sportsman knows that the eye of an observer trying to spot game is attracted by movement. It is movement that gives away the position either of game in peace or of soldiers in war. The observer of an aeroplane searching for the position of a hostile battery has his attention drawn by movement.

The approach, of a hostile aeroplane is notified by the aeroplane scout whom every battery in action must keep on the gun position, a specially selected man, with the sharpest of wits, eyes, and ears, and armed with a whistle and field glasses. The aeroplane scouts should be exceptionally able to stare into bright sunlight, be acquainted with the designs as well as distinguishing marks of enemy aeroplanes, and be relieved every hour. On the scout blowing his whistle the order 'stand fast' is given and obeyed instantly. (The old instructor's 'detail' of the meaning of 'stand fast' is unbeatable: 'On the order "stand fast" nobody don't do nothing.')

When an aeroplane observer sees suspicious movements he immediately takes a photograph. After development of the exposure, provided those studying the print know their business, the presence or otherwise of a battery at the place where the movement was seen can be readily determined unless the battery camouflage has been cleverly designed and the camouflage party has carried out its duties in a thorough and conscientious manner.

All well-run batteries keep in friendly touch with the airmen. A friendly photograph from the air will usually be taken on request, and in most cases the battery commander will be astounded to find that his carefully concealed position is as obvious as any ostrich which has hidden his head in the sand and forgotten that his body and legs are exposed to view from every angle.

No battery commander should be satisfied with the concealment of his battery-position until he has carefully studied an aeroplane photograph of the actual position. And the telltale features of an aeroplane photograph are one thing to a novice and quite another thing to an expert.

The guiding principle of camouflage from aerial observation should be this. It is useless to attempt to hide anything, but not difficult to disguise anything so that it will look like something different and harmless. For example, four or six guns at 20yds interval are obviously a battery. Fill up the spaces between the guns and spread netting or leaves over the top and from the air you have apparently a row of trees, a thick hedge, or even a big hog of swedes or beetroots. But all the men must stand absolutely rigid. The slightest movement anywhere is enough to ruin your attempt at disguise when an enemy airman is scouting overhead. The penalty for movement will be possibly smashed guns, probably dead and wounded gunners, almost certainly a move to a new position and all your work to be done again.

Wagon lines are different. It is quite impossible to camouflage lines of 160 horses from observation. The principle I adopted – of course with the knowledge and consent of the major – was to keep away from everybody, avoid all roads, railways and buildings and hope that others would provide more attractive targets for long-range guns and aeroplane bombs. So successful was this plan that our horse lines were never once bombarded even on the Somme in 1918. The only case of casualties in the horse lines was due to the folly of a battery of 6-inch Mark XIX guns whose commander came into action on the skyline, 100yds in front of our horses, and drew fire from the enemy counter-batteries before I could move far away from my most unwelcome neighbour. This was behind the ruined village of Villers-Faucon, and the stupid selection of this heavy gun position, which would not have been there had I been at my horse lines when the heavies arrived, cost me two first class horses I could not do without. I retired with the rest of my magnificent horses nearly a mile down the hill and found a retired spot in a sunken road exactly where the commander of the 6-inch battery could have placed his guns with perfect safety to himself and everyone else.

Observation from German kite-balloons or 'sausages' as we called them was mysterious. From one gun position you could see several of these observation balloons staring down the muzzles of our guns. And yet we fired continuously for many days without any attention from enemy counter-batteries. Either the balloons were dummies, which was most improbable, or the observers in them were entirely incompetent.

CAMOUFLAGE

Note on the study of aeroplane photographs

Compare photographs of enemy trenches, which you cannot know on the ground, with those of the portions of our own trenches with which you are familiar. In this way you will avoid mistaking cookhouses for gun positions and latrines for machine gun posts. Notice any shadows which seem abnormal, a certain sign of camouflage; in an occupied farmyard or garden the tracks show up white, so be careful to cover all paths in the one you occupy with grass and leaves so that the enemy may leave you in peace.

XII

Palestine Contrasts

The mixture of the very old and the quite modern in Palestine was striking. I lunched daily for over a week on Biblical fare – bread, wine, olive oil and figs – with the Abbot of Enab Monastery, an entirely pro-British, or rather anti-Turk Austrian, who had converted his monastery chapel into an operating theatre for the RAMC and whose monks buried our dead from the hospital under the trees lining the path to the chapel.

The wretched village of Kiryat El Enab is close by. Kiryat preserves the name of the Biblical Kirjath Jearim.

I watered my horses at the well in the valley Aijalon where Joshua bade the moon stand still. The village there is now called Yalu, easily recognised as the Aijalon of the Bible, all the Biblical J's properly representing a Y sound (as, for example, Jehovah is the Hebrew Yahweh).

At Biddu I found confirmation of the accuracy of the Biblical story of Joseph in the pit. The account is careful to say, 'The pit was dry, there was no water in it.' This is not merely an embellishment of the story. The people of Palestine, harried throughout their history by marauders, have always used holes in the ground to hide their valuables. On the hills near Jerusalem, where boulders are strewn about in all directions, natural caves have been hollowed out to store grain safely. The mouth of the cellar is closed by a large boulder, not distinguishable to any but local inhabitants from the thousands which litter the hillsides.

We chanced to find one of the water caves near Biddu where there was a welcome supply of thousands of gallons of sweet water which spared our footsore camels and weary horses a ten mile trudge to water down the rocky valley.

Obviously the Bible account of Joseph conveys that the pit was a place for grain and not for water storage.

PALESTINE CONTRASTS

At Belah, not a mile from the aerodrome with its up-to-date monoplanes, lived a personage who probably corresponded in every respect with the 'King of Belah' known to Abraham. Aeroplanes flew over the Jordan near Jericho and over the Dead Sea at the 'elevation' of 1,200ft below sea level.

One day I bought a dozen bottles of excellent Palestine wine of all varieties in the small township where Richard Coeur de Lion had had his general HQ in Crusading times.

Our battery came into action on the slope in front of Bethel, famous for Jacob's Ladder, and now called Beitin. Behind the village was a kite-balloon for observation, to the east of it the ruins of Ai which Joshua captured by a stratagem.

The association of field telephones and wireless, aeroplanes and primus stoves with these very old things was utterly incongruous, especially as the Syrian natives still live under purely Biblical conditions leading their flocks of sheep and goats to pasture, not muzzling the ox that treadeth out the corn with his little wooden sledge on the threshing floor, and ploughing often with a donkey and camel yoked in double harness.

The manger is still the safest place to put an infant as it was in Bethlehem; the little cattle spend the night with their owners in every house, sharing the only room with them and the sheep, goats and hens. The mangers are built as part of the walls and being shaped like half a pea-pod and kept only half-filled with chaff, the baby cannot fall out of his comfortable cradle while his mother is busy.

I was reminded many times of Jael and Sisera when a village headman, or one of his wives, courteously offered me milk instead of the water I asked for, in my case not to be followed by exploits with a murderous tent peg. The contrast was striking when a smile from the omdeh or headman revealed a mouthful of gold-crowned teeth and he bade me farewell in nasal Bostonian. (This sounds unlikely, but actually happened to me on the hillside south of Bethel.)

We did the most extraordinary things, bathed and scrubbed our camels in the sea at Jaffa, exchanged half a bar of chocolate and woodbine cigarettes for cups of sheep's milk with a native woman, found a villager to act as interpreter because, like one of our sergeants, he could speak

Hindustani as he had been a lascar on an India-going ship. We had a ceremonial lunch under the fig trees in the garden of a wealthy landowner. He invited all the officers to a lunch at which our host ate nothing, but walked round to see that all his guests had enough. We were not likely to leave hungry, as his daughters, who watched us eating through the lattices of the harem, had cooked eleven meat dishes including a lamb roasted whole and a kid stewed in milk.

I am afraid the subsequent football match, which we played against the sergeants to entertain our host, suffered somewhat as a spectacle from the lavishness of Muhammed's entertainment.

Examples could be multiplied of the incongruous contrasts in the Holy Land. Ford's tin lizzies ploughed through the sandhills and raced along the coast tracks where Pharaoh's war-chariots had travelled, a derelict tank lay in no-man's-land within rifle shot of where Samson's primitive weapon of the jawbone of an ass had proved more deadly.

And, most surprising of all, the townsman of twentieth century England stood the heat, the flies, the lack of water and the countless hardships of out of door life in such a country without suffering any more from sickness than those who called Palestine their home. Men who at home were accustomed to consider a damp sheet an alarming, if not a certain, risk of pneumonia, slept for weeks in the rainy season in snowy mountains on blankets so wet that water squeezed out of them with the weight of the sleeper, and not a man 'went sick'.

XIII

Shooting

'Near enough' is not 'target'.

Good shooting is naturally the object of any battery's existence. Good and accurate shooting was attained by field artillery batteries in the immobile trench warfare period in France by the adoption of methods belonging to the Royal Garrison Artillery (RGA) or heavy artillery. Targets were registered and written down in books for permanent use, guns were calibrated at ordnance depots with scientific accuracy, wind reports were received at regular intervals from the experts of the air, charges were carefully sorted out by their manufacturers' lot numbers, and everything possible was done to transform field artillery gunnery into an exact science.

The old-fashioned field gunner did not believe in this conversion of his battery into garrison gunners, and when moving warfare became at last a reality in France the old-fashioned field gunner came into his own.

Those batteries whose war experience had been confined to immobile trench warfare were completely at a loss without all the garrison gunner's fallals upon which they had learned to rely, whereas a divisional artillery such as ours of the 74th (Yeomanry) Division, with experience of the open warfare of the Palestine campaign, proved over and over again that the old-fashioned methods had become right up to date in the final stage of the general offensive in France.

For eighteen months in Salonica and Palestine our battery commanders and subalterns on duty as FOO had been accustomed to carry on with vague small-scale maps, hastily glanced at and bare of artillery detail, had obtained their wind corrections by holding up a wet finger, had sorted ammunition on the broad and simple principle of 'wet and dry', and had learned in the school of experience that the finest of all range-finders is the gun itself.

They had learned to make a reasonably close estimate of a range or a switch, and, without the help of any map, could usually be counted upon to burst their fifth or sixth round within effective distance of any target within range provided that they could see it from their forward OP.

This, the art of the field gunner, the trench gunners of France had never had the chance to learn. They were experts at close shooting, and, when properly equipped with all the complicated paraphernalia of the garrison gunner, they could undertake an accurate creeping or defensive barrage at any time, and there, for the most part, their practical experience finished. The gun pits they were accustomed to were beautifully floored with sleepers or bricks – every gun had had a circular trail-arc with permanent sandbag cushions to support the spade, telephone lines had been laid according to regulation on the sheltered side of deep trenches, labelled every 20yds or so with the sign-manual of the unit they belonged to, ammunition had been kept in almost hermetically-sealed lockers. A gunner's life had been orderly and scientific, and marvellous accuracy had been aimed at and achieved. But, once a general advance began, everything was different. Heath Robinson contrivances became the order of the day. Speed, not perfection, was the first consideration. The best battery was that which could drop a round quickest on, or near, a fleeting target; any bit of solid ground was a gun pit, overhead cover was dispensed with, telephone wires laid anywhere that looked unlikely to be used as a road. Any hole in the ground, or even a tent, was in a few minutes the battery headquarters. The old triple motto of that most experienced campaigner, our Colonel 'R', came true again as it had so often in the Palestine days, 'Cooperation – Observation – Communication', as the road to success in face of the enemy.

Extraordinary targets presented themselves (enemy batteries limbering up, whole battalions in mass preparing for a counter-attack). All a competent gunner needed was an enterprising battery commander, a quick eye, one or two first class telephonists, and a capacity for doing without sleep or proper meals for forty-eight hours at a stretch.

The truth is that field artillery were not really suitable for immobile trench warfare, either in training or weapons.

Trench mortars and heavy howitzers were in every respect better suited. The lighter equipment of the field artillery is designed for mobility and rapidity of manoeuvre. Any other employment is foreign to the proper constitution, equipment and training of the field artillery.

Indirect fire, the only modern method of shooting except in a catastrophe, enables the guns to be placed out of sight of the enemy. Observation of fire is carried out from some advanced point connected with the guns by field telephone.

I always found in shooting our howitzers that the best OP was one dead in line with the target. In ranging, a round off the line can easily be heard passing overhead to the left or right, and the observer therefore knows beforehand whether to look for his burst to the right or left of the target.

In passing, the most scientific method of ranging on the line OT from an OP to a flank is a purely garrison gunnery method far too slow and complicated for use in the field artillery, where quickness in finding the target should far outweigh in importance the expenditure of a few extra rounds of ammunition.

The experienced field gunner, in ranging from an OP to a flank, has only to form a mental picture of himself in such a position at O that the angle TOB is a right angle, and he will find his corrections automatically adjusting themselves to what is necessary. This hint was given to me when a subaltern by, possibly, the most expert field gunner in existence at that time, and I never found it to fail me.

Cooperation with aeroplane observation is interesting, but a poor substitute for Forward Ground Observation (FGO) for the RFA; in very flat country, such as that between Aire and Merville, aeroplane and kite-balloon observation cannot be dispensed with. But even in such country such work is more suited to RGA equipments.

I have said that gunnery is not an exact science. The reasons for this are legion. There is inevitable variation in range due to wear of the gun, variation in length, diameter and weight of the shell (all shells being manufactured to gauge between high and low variation limits), personal factor due to layer's errors, variation in the propelling power of the charge,

201

wind uncertainties (no wind blows continuously with the same force or even in the same direction at different altitudes). Field gunnery, and in fact most other artillery work, is at best of the 'hit or miss' variety, and direct hits are extremely rare, as any gunner knows who has had the opportunity to inspect a position abandoned by the enemy after a most effective bombardment.

Everyone who served in the army will remember occasions beyond number when German gunners fired round after round continuously at a safe distance away from the target. German gunners were too accurate and lacked the imagination to realise it. How many times did we sit in our battery position and watch the 5.9s land at regular intervals, too far away to be anything more than an interesting spectacle, every round so accurately aimed at what the observer believed to be his target. The French gunner, a more imaginative individual, would devote 100 rounds of the 150 allotted for a shoot to what he believed to be his target, and the remaining 50 he would use up in 'sweeping and searching' round about 'pour les spectateurs'. The Frenchman realised that, in an age of camouflage, no target was likely to be situated exactly where it appeared to be from the observer's side of no-man's-land. Statistics are unobtainable upon the point, but, in the absence of any figures to the contrary, I am prepared to wager a considerable sum that the rounds allotted to the audience were the rounds that did the damage.

Napoleon, himself of course a gunner, taught that success in military operations flowed mainly from the ability of a commander to imagine what the other side was doing, or likely to do. The 'spectateur' theory above instanced is a humble example of this great military principle.

A remarkable phenomenon in gunnery happened to me in Salonica when shooting a detached section of our battery. It was the almost universal practice of artillerymen on both sides to leave recognised enemy OPs undisturbed in the routine shooting which took place from day to day. At the beginning of a major operation – such as an infantry attack – the batteries best situated for the purpose would be given the special task of destroying the enemy OPs which overlooked the area of operations. This task had to be completed and reported as satisfactorily carried out before the attack actually began.

When the terribly unsuccessful operation known as the Jumeau Ravine attack was undertaken, our division had the unenviable duty of making a demonstration upon the Makukovo salient in full daylight. Preliminary to the demonstration-attack I had the duty of destroying an enemy OP situated near the top of a rocky hill opposite us.

As the distance of the target, a very small one, was within 50yds of our extreme range, 7,200yds with an unworn howitzer, our newest gun was to be used, our oldest and best shooting gun, No. 3, was impossible, as by then wear had reduced its maximum range by at least 600yds. My section contained Bombardier 'Y', our best gun layer, so he was transferred from his own gun, No. 3, to the new one, and everything was ready for the next morning.

When the next morning dawned, imagine my dismay to find a strong wind blowing directly from the target to my forward section. A wind-testing round established the fact that full range on my new gun would be roughly 350yds short of the enemy OP, I telephoned my orders to the guns, instructing the officer in charge to elevate the gun to 45 degrees with the field clinometer (really a spirit level) which would, theoretically, be the maximum range. I fired one round and found, as I expected, that the burst was considerably short of my target.

It is self-evident that, theoretically, the range of a high elevation gun – such as a howitzer is – will increase up to 45 degrees elevation. An elevation above 45 degrees will only direct the projectile upward at a steeper angle and to a greater height, but the distance travelled by the shell will, necessarily, be shorter and at a steeper angle of descent. The major was at the guns on this occasion, and after a short consultation on the telephone we decided, without any hope of success, to try 46 degrees elevation. Theoretically and reasonably the only result should have been that the increased elevation landed the next round further away from the target. Actually it landed considerably nearer to the target I decided to carry on the experiment, and finally at 47 degrees 15' elevation I succeeded in getting my full range and my fourth or fifth shell burst right inside the cave-like opening of the OP and as soon as the smoke cleared away I had the satisfaction of seeing through my Zeiss glasses long, heavy timber, beams and planks, rolling down the hill side.

I discussed this remarkable example of the triumph of experiment over common sense with many experts. The only possible explanation of this extraordinary phenomenon must be that the shells travelling upwards at a steeper angle got through the region of contrary wind more quickly, and had a longer period of travel in a windless area, and so did not lose the range they normally would have.

No other explanation seems to fit the facts, and I commend the problem to gunners of today, with the caution that in practice the theoretically impossible sometimes happens, but the thoughtful experimenter can usually find an explanation to account for the mysterious and incredible.

My elation at having dealt with this enemy OP so satisfactorily was naturally fully shared by Major 'M'. We were always a lucky battery, and the major's attitude to all insoluble problems was the very simple and effective one of 'Try everything you can think of and then think of something else, and try that.' Eventually most difficulties yield to this treatment, or we found they did, and it was not from silly sentiment that I caused to be engraved on the christening cup I sent to the first son to call that same major by the name of father, the brave motto 'A coeur vaillant rien d'impossible'."

Major 'M' and I did many other impossible things together during the war – as of course almost everyone learned to do – but I doubt if anyone ever carried through a more incredible piece of shooting than ours on the Bulgar OP on the hillside near Piton des Ronces.

My lesson was learned for the duration of the war, that a man who never throws the towel into the ring is a very hard man to beat.

XIV

Useful Hints for Visits to Remounts

*Was it a horse, Dave? It must have been, 'cause it
sartinly warn't nothin' else. David Hurum*

General: You will usually do better in the hands of the remount sergeant major. Remount depots, like dealers, want to part with the bad 'uns, and keep the good 'uns.

Choosing a mule: For pack mules and draught mules select those that look like large donkeys. The nearer the mule is to the donkey the stronger, tougher and hardier he will prove. This tip was given me by a professional mule owner from the colonies. It has no exceptions. For riding purposes – and some mules are excellent mounts – we found the long-legged, long-eared black Spanish type by far the best.

Draught horses: While a somewhat hollow-backed horse is the most comfortable mount for the indifferent rider, the roach-backed horse – that is one with a convex back and protruding spine – is the more powerful for draught work. The ideal draught horse has a straight shoulder (not sloping as in a riding horse), a short back, strikingly bent hind legs and extremely broad hindquarters. Unless otherwise very desirable, avoid a draught horse which has an overlarge head and neck. A great point in a draught horse is that the hocks should be close together. Wide-open hocks invariably spell want of power. A thin horse may often be chosen, provided he is fairly muscled. A horse is often thin in remounts because he is a willing worker. If, as you should, you have taken your AVC sergeant with you, he will tell you if sharp teeth are the cause of thinness in any horse, and if so, don't hesitate to take the thin animal whose teeth need filing.

For draught work courage and strength come first, and, curiously, bad temper and courage often are found together in horses.

To detect a stumbler lead a horse at a quick walk over rough ground. If he does not stumble at a fast walk over a rough surface he is not likely to stumble at the trot. To detect tenderness in the feet trot a horse fast on a metalled road. Examine closely for shelly feet, dropped sole and thrush (by smell). These are common faults in army horses, especially in remount depots where shoeing is often neglected. Dropped sole is the after effect of laminitis, which recurs almost invariably.

Always ride the best looking and handiest horse you can borrow when visiting remounts, and you will be credited with considerable knowledge of horseflesh, provided you don't talk too horsey.

Never take a horse however attractive that exhibits the vices of wind-sucking, crib-biting, weaving, or foul-feeding. These habits are all incurable and are copied by other horses.

XV

Popular Fallacies Exploded

As the native said when he saw the giraffe,
'I don't believe it'.

A volunteer is equal to two pressed men.
On active service I found the conscripted members of the British Army
identical in value with the 1914/1915 Volunteers.

A horse will not drink bad water.
I have seen thirsty horses drinking from a pool in the Wadi Saba which
was covered with green slime and which contained a camel that had
evidently been dead for more than a week.

The screams of wounded horses.
Horses and mules make no sound whatever when wounded or killed. A
writer who, in describing a battle, introduces the screaming of wounded
horses has obviously never seen one hit. I had to shoot over a score and
saw hundreds killed and wounded and none of them made a sound on any
occasion.

Horses are terrified by the smell of blood and the sight of dead animals.
They do not take the slightest notice of either. I once led a column of
twelve wagons with six-horse teams into an ammunition dump on the
Somme where the entrance was fetlock deep in blood in which were lying
the bodies of eight or ten horses killed by shellfire. Not one horse in all
my long column, which included four somewhat skittish outriders,

hesitated to wade through the pool of blood or took the slightest notice of the dead horses.

The army mule is a vicious beast.
I found mules as docile as but more timid than horses. The only difference is that the mule needs more expert handling. In the hands of a novice most horses work satisfactorily, but mules will only do their best for an intelligent driver who understands them. The proportion of vicious mules was, in my experience, not greater than that of vicious horses.

That the people of any country or race are braver than the people of any other.
The courage of most of the troops engaged in the Great War was astonishing, whether they were German, French, British, Turk, Bulgar, Serb, or other uniforms. Some peoples are, of course, degenerate but there are no super nations.

That a man can be wounded by a bullet or shell-splinter without being aware of it.
Every story of an unfelt bullet wound is untrue. The sensation of being hit is identical with that of being 'clouted' with a cricket bat.

That the soldier on active service is invariably guilty of sexual immorality.
We had only two cases of venereal disease in three years' active service which included such opportunities for the vicious as are afforded in Alexandria, Cairo, Marseilles and Salonica. It is simply a matter of discipline, difficult to obtain but nevertheless obtainable.

That British troops are impressed in any way by an officer who exposes himself unnecessarily to enemy fire.
Such an officer is regarded by his men as 'a blooming idiot'. Experienced senior officers have confirmed me in this opinion.

La fortune est toujours tour les grands bataillons.
This utterly trite and banal remark is popularly attributed to Napoleon. It was actually said by Madame de Sevigny and Napoleon denied the truth

of it. His version was the valuable tactical principle that 'fortune is on the side of the last reserves'.

A bit of shrapnel.
There is no such thing. A shrapnel shell consists of sixty or more round bullets enclosed in a cast steel container. The bullets are expelled from the shell when the time fuse operates and the shell itself falls intact. There are no splinters or bits of any kind.

XVI

Courage Under Fire

'Il n'est si poitron sur la terre qui ne puisse
trouver un plus poliron que soi.'

Probably no soldier, amateur or professional, has ever gone on active
service for the first time without some misgivings as to how he will
behave under fire. Probably also few civilians went to war less naturally
gifted in this direction than myself.

Physical courage can be learned like most other things; courage under
fire, an essential part of the equipment of the trustworthy fighting soldier,
I found to be more common than I had expected.

Modern weapons demand a different kind of courage from the old and
shorter-range varieties. High explosive, whether in bombs or shells
projected from light, medium or heavy artillery, or dropped from
aeroplanes, has in it something utterly distressing to the human organism.
The mere noise of bursting high explosive has a demoralising effect and
suggests dreadful consequences to any mind equipped with the least
imagination.

This, I believe, is the true explanation of what is known as shell shock.
Those possessed of strong nerves did not become shell-shocked even
when hurled many yards by the detonation of a large projectile in close
proximity. (As this happened to me on two occasions I can speak from
personal experience.) On the other hand, neurotic subjects suffered from
various degrees of so-called shell shock when an explosion took place at
a distance and no apparent concussion-effect was evident. Some men
totally devoid of imagination, and hitherto apparently fearless of death or

wounds, collapsed altogether and exhibited all the symptoms of acute shell shock when they saw a friend or acquaintance blown to pieces nearby by so small a missile as a rifle grenade, and on one occasion in my experience the demoralisation was so complete that it led to deliberate suicide on the part of the uninjured soldier.

I am grateful to be able to state that, although under fire almost continuously for two and a half years, I never as far as I know allowed my naturally nervous and timid nature to interfere with my determination to do my duty by my country, my battery commander and the men who looked to me for guidance and possibly example.

An officer of the field artillery, whether in the more perilous position of FOO or engaged in other duties in action, has usually to decide for himself the question of how far his duty necessitates taking various avoidable risks. Most of his more alarming duties are carried out alone, or with one or two signallers for company. It is easy for him to shirk any job he finds too dangerous.

Being the kind of person that I am I had to consider these questions very thoughtfully.

I came to the conclusion, which I still hold, that, with very few exceptions, the men of today are far more courageous in face of death in its most hideous forms than one would have expected. Ordinary men, in private life errand boys, shop assistants, bus drivers, miners, lawyers, merchants, schoolmasters and actors, faced the imminent prospect of being cut into slices by a stream of bullets from traversing machine guns, blown into fragments by high explosive shells, or strangled alive by lethal gases, with stoical matter of fact-ness. Uncourageous though I naturally thought myself, I found myself doing the same and treating such unaccustomed risks as all in the day's work.

I hold the opinion that the great majority of my fellows of whatever rank were, like myself, quite alarmed at the thought of a horrible, and possibly painful, death, unable to dismiss the idea of it entirely from their thoughts, and yet strong-minded enough to carry on with the dangerous jobs that fell to their lot.

The few who were entirely fearless I believed to be stupid people and devoid of imagination.

It comes down to this, I think, that true courage is not the absence of fear, but determination not to be deterred by fear of death or horrible mutilation from performing a dangerous job of work. One thought no worse of a fellow soldier for feeling alarmed in alarming circumstances. But one felt contempt and personal dislike for any officer or man who allowed his feelings to interfere with the proper performance of his duty.

The worst fear is the fear of being afraid. This most dreadful terror of all does not assail the naturally timid. But it did sometimes attack the fearless, and the experience was so terrifying in its novelty that in some cases – I knew of two definitely – the fearless soldiers committed suicide rather than face the struggle to overcome their dread of cowardice.

A remarkable compensation for the responsibility of the officer for setting an example of courage to his men (who are in many cases less inclined to be alarmed than himself) lies in the fact that responsibility for the lives of others does help one to forget to be afraid for one's own safety. An incident that happened to me in the Arras sector illustrates this fact extremely well.

I was making my way alone along a deep communication trench and came to a part which had been shelled that morning until the entire trench had been filled with earth churned into the consistency of soap suds, into which I sank knee deep at every step. My progress, in full view of the German trenches, slowed down to a crawl and in a few minutes further 5.9-inch shells detonated in front and behind me. So holding was the muddy scum of blown up earth that my impulse to run like the proverbial rabbit was entirely frustrated. I was not engaged in any particular duty, and seeing the entrance to a dugout near me I scrambled down the ruined stairway in a condition as near to complete panic as I ever was in my life, or ever expect to be.

Reaching the dugout at the bottom of the stairway, I found a small party of infantry belonging to a kilted regiment who had already taken refuge there and whose knees were knocking together as they saw the structure of the dugout steadily collapsing as the shells burst up above. Fear had dispelled the reasoning powers of these good fellows (they belonged to a first class battalion) or they would have seen that the danger of our being buried alive below was far greater than the risk of a direct hit from one of the shells bursting up above. They looked at me, obviously in mute appeal to an officer to do something about it. This feeling of others depending on one's powers of leadership finished my own panicky feeling, and I, in the most nonchalant manner, told the infantrymen to collect their belongings and follow me. I led them up the stairway and down the ruins of the communication trench as if there had been nothing to alarm me in the whole incident. This was not play-acting on my part. The responsibility actually worked like a moral tonic and the panicky feeling left me at once without any conscious effort on my part.

The question of exposing oneself was forcibly and, I am sure, correctly put to his subalterns by my first battery commander Colonel 'B'. His neat comment was 'You're not paid to stick your head up above the parapet and get it bust with a bullet to show your silly recklessness. But when there's something serious going on and you can't see to shoot from the duckboards I expect you to stand on the parapet.' Incidentally in trench warfare in a 'general strafe' most shells fall in the support line where the opposing front line trenches are close together. As these instructions of Colonel 'B' related to the Roclincourt sector north of Arras where the width of no-man's-land varied from 80yds to 110yds, the parapet of a front line trench in a general strafe was a more alarming, but actually much safer, locality than the duckboards of the support trenches.

XVII

The Base Wallah and the Spirit of the Firing Line

The Base Wallahs

If I were fierce and bald and short of breath
I'd live with scarlet majors at the Base,
Guzzling and gulping in the best hotel,
And when the war is done and youth stone dead
I'd toddle safely home and die—in bed.

From The War Poems of Siegfried Sassoon

'Let George do it'. 'All for each and each for all'.

Base wallah was the name given by fighting soldiers to those non-combatants in uniform of all ranks who littered the world from Whitehall to positions behind the firing lines of all the British fronts from Belgium to Mesopotamia.

Obviously war cannot be conducted on the modern scale without an enormous number of men engaged in purely administrative duties. What the fighting man found intolerable was the idea that non-combatant wearers of His Majesty's uniform should usually be given precedence in pay, promotion, decorations, leave, and all the other amenities of military service in war over the men who did the actual fighting. The fighting man's home was a muddy hole in the ground, the base wallah lived in a comfortable house. In the dugout light was a candle in the neck of a disused bottle; at divisional headquarters there was electric light generated by a motor lorry. The base wallah being nearer the source of supply had the preference in choice of horses, if entitled to a horse; drew the full ration of food of the more desirable sorts, even at times when the

214

combatants had to go short, kept office hours when the real fighting troops were toiling twenty-four hours a day.

All these inequalities were inevitable, but what we amateurs could not understand was why the combatant should always be treated as a person of inferior status. After all, in war the whole object of an army is to fight, and the non-combatant soldier is merely the ancient camp-follower in a fancy uniform and masquerading as a military man.

A list of base wallahs' jobs in the Great War would be nearly as long as a modern Army List. There were War Office officials, training camp permanent staff in England, AMLOs (Assistant Marine Landing Officers) on both sides of the Channel, base camp permanent staff in France, Line of Communications staff, Area Commandants, Town Majors, Railway Transport Officers and countless other refuges for the faint-hearted and often incompetent, discarded from the combatant units, most of whose duties could well have been performed by men unfit for combatant service, with the rank and pay of second lieutenant in the case of officers, or by civilians.

Some of the jobs created were tragically ludicrous. In Cairo I saw a smartly dressed officer, of military age and fitness, wearing an armlet inscribed MTO, an office hitherto unknown to me. These mystic letters stood, so a shop assistant informed me, for Military Traffic Officer, an appointment involving the soldierly duty of hanging across certain streets in Cairo the notice 'No Lorries This Way'. There were inspectors of cook houses, with rank and pay of staff captain second class, horse advisers with the rank of colonel, and of course the appropriate pay and allowances, claims officers, a civilian of military age as military governor with the rank of brigadier general, an inspector general of line of communications who congratulated me on my possession of a field kitchen while gazing at a delousing boiler called a Thresh Disinfector (we had an unauthorised field kitchen at that time whose chimney was actually protruding from the waters of the Galiko River in which we had sunk it to avoid awkward questions during the inspection).

It must not be supposed that my own experience of staff officers and other non-combatants in uniform was more than ordinarily unfortunate; quite the contrary, with two or three outstanding exceptions I was invariably treated with courtesy and consideration by these members of the military hierarchy. It was the base wallah spirit that was wrong, and it existed the whole way from Whitehall to the point just behind the war zone where a sentry stood beside the notice board which proclaimed 'forward from this point gas masks must be worn in the ready position.' From that point forward the atmosphere was different, and, as the scenery deteriorated from trees with green leaves to bleached and shell torn skeletons of tree trunks, so the human atmosphere improved suddenly to an order of friendliness irrespective of rank in place of patronage, helpfulness without regard to age or status in place of senseless fault finding, and sportsmanship and unselfishness in place of self-seeking and jealousy. Most of us fighting troops – or, as the professional officer termed us, regimental officers – breathed a sigh of relief on our return from an expedition behind the lines.

True, we had returned from areas of safety and comfort to dangerous surroundings where discomforts of every kind were the daily experience of all, but those things and the hideousness of modern war were less distasteful to every one of us than the base wallah attitude to the fighting soldier which seemed to infect the majority of good fellows as soon as the fatal words 'staff appointment' preceded their names in the *Gazette*.

Professional officers, with whom I have discussed this phenomenon, seem to take the view that such criticisms imply a want of loyalty to the higher authorities, with the excuse for the staff officers that all they lacked was training. As I am trying to draw a true to life picture of active service in the Great War, and, as in every battery or infantry mess of which I was a member or a guest, the standard topic of conversation was the utter inefficiency and offensiveness of the average staff officer, my picture would be a false one unless I included this subject.

It is not want of loyalty, but a sorrowful appreciation of what seems to me to be a weakness inherent in human nature. If you set a group of men apart from their fellows, give them special uniforms, special rates of pay, more comforts and greater safety, you create a class of men out of sympathy with the ordinary regimental officer because they are quite out of touch with his difficulties and needs, and are prone to forget that they are only there to serve and help the troops that live in danger and discomfort and do the actual fighting. For, in fact, the staff officer is not in any way a superior being, presented with a safe and comfortable job with extra pay and extra decorations for being ornamental. We amateur soldiers felt in our hearts that all but a few of the gilded staff failed us. That, instead of being pampered pets keeping office hours, their real job was to strive night and day to lighten the burden of the real soldiers, and not make difficulties more difficult by issuing complaints and demands for trifling returns on every impossible occasion. Of course many of these 'red tabs' were gallant and unselfish gentlemen who deserved, and won, our gratitude and admiration.

The following occurrence serves to show that criticism of the British staff was not uncalled for. There joined our brigade a Major 'B', a fine soldier commanding a most efficient 18-pounder battery. He was a professional soldier who had lately served on the General Staff at GHQ, British Salonica Force. Soon after joining our brigade he found reason to reprove the officers of our battery for their harsh criticism of staff officers. He said, 'You have no right to say such things. I have only just left the General Staff, and they are, one and all, hardworking and conscientious men devoted to their duties.' Until then he had seen staff work from above. After less than two months' experience of staff work as seen from below, his criticisms left ours pale by comparison, and, if we had chastised them verbally with whips, Major 'B', after first-hand experience of staff incompetence from the regimental officer's standpoint, strafed them with the most venomous verbal scorpions in his vocabulary, having first stated that he withdrew every word that he had said formerly regarding the criticisms he had heard us express.

The Spirit of the Firing Line

In every country participating in the Great War there was a large number of men of military age and fitness who evaded, in one way or another, all danger to life, limb, or pocket during the period of hostilities. These were, in army slang, said to belong to 'The First Royal Stand-backs', the only regiment to number among its members a plain clothes, as well as a uniformed, branch. The motto of the regiment, which of course they did not wear prominently displayed, was 'Let George do it.' (Note: 'George' would seem to be two separate individuals. In cases where the job to be done is unpleasant, un-remunerative, and dangerous, 'George' is my neighbour. For good jobs 'George' is myself.)

In the firing line there were no members of this regiment. An American general once stated that 'war is hell'. Like most generalisations this is only partly true because imbedded in the hideousness of war there is something utterly beautiful which I have called 'The Spirit of the Firing Line.'

In the period of permanent trench warfare in France there grew up in the trenches an atmosphere of brotherhood such as I have never met elsewhere, and shall certainly never meet again. There social distinctions, differences of age, rank, means and status had no significance. An officer of any rank or social position would accept a cigarette or a biscuit from a fellow soldier of the humblest possible order, and I have seen a brigadier general hand his tobacco pouch, quite as a matter of course, to a runner waiting to carry back a reply to some message, and naturally, as one soldier to another.

War is not altogether hell when it breeds a spirit of unselfishness and universal consideration for others. Friendships between officers of importance and privates of the least possible significance were quite common in the firing line, not a trace of condescension or patronage entered into them on the one side, and not an atom of servility or subservience on the other.

On my many journeys up and down the communication trenches when on my tour of duty as FOO I frequently saw some big hefty private heavily laden with trench stores overtake a poorly built soldier, probably a complete stranger, loaded like a pack mule and staggering along beneath his enormous burden. In almost every case the big man would hail the smaller with the words: 'You've got a bit more than you can manage in that lot, chum,' at the same time transferring part of the little man's load to his own broader shoulder, after which the two would trudge along the duckboards together as naturally as possible. Often my telephonist and I would be offered a mug of tea by some party of complete strangers who happened to be having theirs as we passed. The fact that I was an officer and they were probably company cooks didn't matter to either of us. An officer gets just as thirsty as a private on a scorching hot day in a deep communication trench and, if he has a full cigarette case to hand round in return, he hands it round in exactly the same spirit as the tea was offered.

THE BASE WALLAH AND THE SPIRIT OF THE FIRING LINE

Somehow in the face of the enemy and in the presence of a common danger the brotherhood of men of all ranks, and even colours, becomes a reality. There is no conscious striving after it, it just happens naturally. One experienced exactly the same feeling in the company of Lancashire miners, Gurkhas and Gharwalis, Scottish Highlanders, or Cockney privates, and anything anybody had was there to be shared, as a matter of course, with anyone who happened to be on the spot.

It is an incontestable fact that discipline was in no way impaired by this fraternisation. The moment an urgent call for action came, officer, NCO and man naturally resumed their military positions, and one could bark an order with the usual truculence at the very man who had handed back your cigarette case with a friendly smile the second before, without any feeling of awkwardness or incongruity.

The truth of the matter seems to be that in the firing line men had gone back to the primitive realities of existence. The paltry distinctions so necessary and important in a civilised community ceased to have any significance whatever, and I have no doubt that respect and confidence between soldiers of different status was considerably increased rather than impaired in the process. Certainly the all-important reliance on the part of the rank and file of the infantry upon the gunners, on whose support they counted in time of danger, was vastly greater where the infantry privates knew the gunner-officers, however slightly; and it was most pleasant for an artillery subaltern, who had put up a barrage at night to cover a sector from an enemy raid, to be greeted next morning with grinning faces and cheerful remarks such as: 'that was an A1 barrage you done for us last night, Sir.' You may be sure that after this handsome recognition, which was regularly passed on to the gun teams concerned, the FOOs next barrage would be, if possible, even a trifle more effective.

I will conclude this chapter by quoting a poem found on the body of an Australian who fell at Gallipoli, and published in *The Spectator*, April, 1916, first printed in *The Australian Intercollegian*:

Jesus, whose lot with us was cast,
Who saw it out from first to last;
Patient and fearless, tender, true.
Carpenter, vagabond, felon, Jew –

219

AMATEUR GUNNERS

Whose humorous eyes took in each phase
Of full rich life this world displays;
Yet evermore kept full in view
The far-off goal it leads us to;
Who, as your hour neared, did not fail –
The World's fate trembling in the scale
With your half-hearted band to dine,
And speak across the bread and wine;
Then went out firm to face the end,
Alone, without a single friend;
Who felt as your last words confessed
Wrung from a proud unflinching breast
By hours of dull, ignoble, pain,
Your whole life's fight was fought in vain;
Would I could win and keep and feel
That heart of love, that spirit of steel.
I would not to thy bosom fly
To shirk off till the storms go by;
If you are like the man you were
You'd turn in scorn from such a prayer,
Unless from some poor workhouse crone,
Too toilworn to do aught but moan.
Flog me and spur me, set me straight
At some vile job I fear and hate;
Some sickening round of long endeavour,
No light, no rest, no outlet ever;
All at a pace that must not slack
Tho' heart would burst and sinews crack;
Fog in one's eyes, the brain aswim,
A weight like lead in every limb
And a raw pit that hurts like hell
Where the light breath once rose and fell.
Do you but keep me, hope or none,
Cheery and staunch till all is done,
And at the last gasp quick to lend
One effort more to serve a friend,

And when, for so I sometimes dream,
I've swum the dark – the silent stream –
So cold it takes the breath away –
That parts the dead world from the day,
And see upon the further strand
The lazy, listless angels stand;
And, with their frank and fearless eyes
The comrades whom I most did prize;
Then clear, unburdened, careless, cool,
I'll saunter down from the grim pool
And join my friends. Then you'll come by
The Captain of our company,
Call me out, look me up and down
And pass me thro' without a frown
With half a smile, but never a word;
And so—I shall have met my Lord.

With this I turn the last page of this book of memories of war in grateful recognition of the patience and good humour of those who succeeded in turning an unwarlike cotton broker into an efficient artillery officer. With even more heartfelt gratitude I have to acknowledge the loyalty, devotion and brotherhood displayed towards me by the gunners, drivers and NCOs who bore the very heavy burdens I had to assign to them with such cheerful endurance and willingness – and last, but not by any means least – I tender the best thanks words can convey to those brother officers, battery commanders, colonels and generals in whom the 'Spirit of the Firing Line' shone out so brightly that now the memory of the good things that came my way will live long after recollections of mud and blood, fear of death and of mutilation, and the very smell of death and corruption have faded into the limbo of things forgotten.

If a book upon war should close on a solemn note, what better words could come from a fortunate survivor than those of Mr Laurence Housman: 'Dead man's aim is the best of all. The battle is won by the men that fall.'

Envoi

The Old Battery

My task is done.

If I have hit the target, readers of these memories will have already discovered why we were all so proud of our old battery.

As an Old Carthusian and an ex-schoolmaster, I can confidently assert that the spirit that inspired us was the spirit of the public school. That is the spirit of 'playing for the team instead of for personal distinction'. It is the spirit of the amateur as opposed to the code of the professional whose motive is naturally advancement in his chosen profession.

The officers – with the exception of 'LH', the youngest – were, from February, 1917, onwards, amateurs to a man, as were almost all the rank and file. Only the sergeant major and four of the nine sergeants who served with the battery were professional soldiers and, of these four regular sergeants, one was with us for only a few weeks.

The spur to extraordinary effort (and times without number endurance to the limit was asked of all hands and cheerfully given) was, I believe, not in any member of the battery the lure of pay, promotion and decorations, and consequently petty jealousies did not exist among us.

In the officers' mess we were a band of brothers', each ready to help the other at all times. Apart from a real knowledge of practical soldiering, won in the hard school of active service, we could muster expert engineering skill in the ingenious 'B', in 'K' horsemanship probably unmatched in the British Army (in civil life 'K' was manager of the finest estancia in the Argentine), Major 'M', our CO, had exceptional gifts of leadership and added to them proficiency in signalling and map reading of the highest order. 'H', the oldest of us, had an imperturbability that nothing could disturb. 'LH', a regular of war time vintage, the enthusiasm of youth.

My own contributions to the common stock were such assets as I could muster from my personal resources. I fancy the most valuable were a brain that works rapidly in emergencies, an innate love and understanding of the animals, a reliable sense of direction, a capacity for carrying on indefinitely with insufficient sleep, a memory of almost photographic accuracy and a gift for getting the best out of subordinates.

Without these assets the multifarious tasks of endless variety that fall to the lot of the captain of a battery of field artillery in action would tax the capacity of most men beyond endurance.

The senior and junior NCOs were entirely loyal to their battery; the men, with few exceptions, were keen and determined soldiers.

There was nothing amateurish about us as a unit. The shooting was very good, the laying accurate and quick, the driving was excellent, in military exercises such as 'alarm turn out' we broke, so I was told, all regular army records for speed. The discipline was admirable, as it could not fail to be with BSM 'G' to maintain it, the shoeing under Farrier-Sergeant 'Y' was beyond all praise.

In the Cromwellian phrase we were a 'lovely company', though perhaps not invariably from a strictly Puritan standpoint. Anyhow as a battery we did not disgrace The Royal Regiment.

And so, in spite of mud and blood and death and wounds, and physical discomforts of the most extreme descriptions, and the loss of valued friends, and all the hideous trappings of modern war, I can truthfully say that the happiest and most wholesome days of all my life were those spent in the company of the stout-hearted and devoted friends of all ranks and ages who together constituted the old battery.

Finis

Glossary

ASC	Army Service Corps
AVC	Army Veterinary Corps
BSM	Battery Sergeant Major
CO	Commanding Officer
CRA	Commander Royal Artillery
CSM	Company Sergeant Major
CTC	Camel Transport Company
FGO	Forward Ground Observation
FOO	Forward Observation Officer
GOC	General Officer Commanding
GS	General Service
HE	High explosive
MO	Medical Officer
NCO	Non-Commissioned Officer
OC	Officer Commanding
OP	Observation post
QMS	Quartermaster Sergeant
RTO	Railway Transport Officer
RSM	Regimental Sergeant Major
RA	Royal Artillery
RAMC	Royal Army Medical Corps
RE	Royal Engineers
RFA	Royal Field Artillery
RGA	Royal Garrison Artillery
RHA	Royal Horse Artillery

Acknowledgements and Further Reading

Without the foresight, agreement and support shown by the present day family of Alexander Douglas Thorburn, it would not have been possible to create this book, so thanks must go firstly to Andy and Derek Pemberton. Thanks also to publishers Pen & Sword for seeing the potential in Thorburn and his Amateur Gunners and for helping to bring this important work back into current publication. To Ned Malet de Carteret, thanks for his work transcribing Thorburn's letters and general support on the project. And to Brigadier Colin Tadier, CBE, sincere thanks for agreeing to provide a worthy preface from a modern-day gunner to one who served his country in the past.

For anyone interested in learning more about battles and campaigns in which Alexander Douglas Thorburn took part, there are a number of books to consider. The history of the 60th (2/2nd London) Division is written by Colonel P.H. Dalbiac while that of the 74th (Yeomanry) Division is set out by Major C.H. Dudley Ward. On the campaigns in France and Belgium, there is extensive work that will no doubt continue to be added to. When it comes to Salonica and Palestine, however, the choice is regrettably far less extensive. For the former, the 1965 *The Gardeners of Salonika, The Macedonian Campaign 1915–1918* by Alan Palmer is an excellent read, along with the more recently published *Under the Devil's Eye: Britain's Forgotten Army at Salonika 1915–1918* by Alan Wakefield. On the battles of the Egyptian Expeditionary Force, there are a number of useful books, including *The Last Crusade: The Palestine Campaign in the First World War* by Anthony Bruce and *The Battle for Palestine 1917* by John D. Grainger.

Index